Advanced Introduction to U.S. Criminal Procedure

Elgar Advanced Introductions are stimulating and thoughtful introductions to major fields in the social sciences and law, expertly written by the world's leading scholars. Designed to be accessible yet rigorous, they offer concise and lucid surveys of the substantive and policy issues associated with discrete subject areas.

The aims of the series are two-fold: to pinpoint essential principles of a particular field, and to offer insights that stimulate critical thinking. By distilling the vast and often technical corpus of information on the subject into a concise and meaningful form, the books serve as accessible introductions for undergraduate and graduate students coming to the subject for the first time. Importantly, they also develop well-informed, nuanced critiques of the field that will challenge and extend the understanding of advanced students, scholars and policy-makers.

Recent titles in the series include:

Law and Globalisation
Jaakko Husa

Regional Innovation Systems
Bjørn T. Asheim, Arne Isaksen and Michaela Trippl

International Political Economy
Second Edition
Benjamin J. Cohen

International Tax Law
Second Edition
Reuven S. Avi-Yonah

Social Innovation
Frank Moulaert and Diana MacCallum

The Creative City
Charles Landry

International Trade Law
Michael J. Trebilcock and Joel Trachtman

European Union Law
Jacques Ziller

Planning Theory
Robert A. Beauregard

Tourism Destination Management
Chris Ryan

International Investment Law
August Reinisch

Sustainable Tourism
David Weaver

Austrian School of Economics
Second Edition
Randall G. Holombe

U.S. Criminal Procedure
Christopher Slobogin

Advanced Introduction to

U.S. Criminal Procedure

CHRISTOPHER SLOBOGIN

Milton Underwood Professor of Law, Vanderbilt University Law School, USA

Elgar Advanced Introductions

Edward Elgar PUBLISHING

Cheltenham, UK • Northampton, MA, USA

Published by
Edward Elgar Publishing Limited
The Lypiatts
15 Lansdown Road
Cheltenham
Glos GL50 2JA
UK

Edward Elgar Publishing, Inc.
William Pratt House
9 Dewey Court
Northampton
Massachusetts 01060
USA

A catalogue record for this book
is available from the British Library

Library of Congress Control Number: 2020940516

Printed on elemental chlorine free (ECF)
recycled paper containing 30% Post-Consumer Waste

ISBN 978 1 83910 165 6 (cased)
ISBN 978 1 83910 167 0 (paperback)
ISBN 978 1 83910 166 3 (eBook)

Typeset by Servis Filmsetting Ltd, Stockport, Cheshire
Printed and bound in the USA

This book is dedicated to my grandsons, Willard and Jacob

Contents

1 An overview of American criminal procedure law

1.1 The criminal process in the United States

The American criminal process is often described as a funnel. Police investigate tens of millions of people and criminal incidents every year. Of these, perhaps 10 to 15 million result in arrest and prosecution, the vast majority of them for misdemeanors (i.e., crimes resulting in incarceration of a year or less) rather than felonies.[1] A significant percentage of crimes that are prosecuted end in dismissal of the charges, acquittals, or diversion out of the system, so that the number of people convicted of crime is much smaller than the number arrested. Of these, the number that go to prison rather than receive a suspended sentence and probation is much smaller still. Even with this winnowing process, today approximately 2 million Americans are serving time in prison, representing about 5 percent of the world's incarcerated population,[2] and another 5 to 7 million offenders are on some type of supervised release.[3] Roughly 35 percent of the current American population has an arrest record.[4] When victims and witnesses are included, the criminal process directly affects a huge proportion of the population.

The precise procedures governing this process vary substantially among the 50 states, the federal government, and the District of Columbia (the criminal laws of which come from Congress). But in broad overview the process is similar in all 52 American jurisdictions. An investigation begins with police observation of conduct they think warrants inquiry or with the report of a crime from a "confidential" informant, a victim, an eyewitness, or some other source. If they iden-

1 U.S. Dep't of Justice, Crime in the United States, 2019, accessed April 8, 2020, at https://ucr.fbi.gov/crime-in-the-u.s/2018/crime-in-the-u.s.-2018/topic-pages/persons-arrested.

2 E. Ann Carson and Elizabeth Anderson, Prisoners in 2015 (Bureau of Justice Statistics, 2016).

3 Alessandro Corder, Mariel Alper and Kevin R. Reitz, American Exceptionalism in Parole Supervision, Robina Institute of Criminal Law and Criminal Justice (Oxford University Press, New York 2016).

4 Elisha Jain, Arrests as Regulation, 67 Stan. L. Rev. 809, 817 (2015).

tify a potential suspect, police might conduct brief questioning, a more intensive "stop and frisk," a search for evidence, or an arrest. Under some circumstances—usually involving an arrest in, or search of, a home—police may seek a warrant from a judge, and in situations in which the government wants documentary information, it may resort to subpoenas issued through the grand jury process or by the prosecutor's office. Upon arrest, the suspect is booked and possibly subject to interrogation or an identification procedure such as a lineup. Relying on the information gleaned by the police and perhaps its own investigation, the prosecutor's office decides whether to sustain the police complaint and bring formal charges. Based either on this decision or on the police complaint, the individual is brought before a judge, usually within 48 hours of arrest. The judge's main job at this "first appearance" (sometimes called an arraignment) is to determine whether the person can be released pending further proceedings, or instead should be subject to bail conditions or detention designed to prevent flight or reoffending. Counsel is usually appointed at this stage as well.

Once charges are formalized, the prosecutor may be required to make a prima facie case against the defendant at a preliminary hearing, a grand jury proceeding, or both, depending on the jurisdiction and type of case. Meanwhile, the defense may seek "discovery" of information such as witness statements and the results of forensic tests held by the prosecution, which then usually has reciprocal discovery rights from the defense. In most jurisdictions, statutes require that trial take place within three months or so after arrest. However, these "speedy trial" statutes also recognize several exceptions to this rule.

More importantly, over 90 percent of criminal cases never go to trial.[5] Rather, they are resolved through a more informal process, sometimes involving unilateral action by the prosecutor, involving dismissal of charges or diversion, but usually after negotiations between the prosecution and the defense. During this plea bargaining process, which can take place any time after arrest, the prosecutor offers to reduce the charge or recommend a lighter sentence in exchange for a guilty plea, testimony against a co-defendant, or some other consideration. A guilty plea must be endorsed by a judge, who is supposed to ensure there is a factual basis for it and that the defendant understands the trial rights that a guilty plea waives. If the defense instead decides to

5 Stephanos Bibas, Regulating the Plea-Bargaining Market: From Caveat Emptor to Consumer Protection, 99 Calif. L. Rev. 1117, 1138 (2011).

go to trial and the potential sentence is more than six months, the defendant is entitled to have the case heard by a jury, selected through a process designed to ensure the people on it are representative of the community and impartial. The defendant is also entitled to have the trial take place in public, as well as to a face-to-face confrontation with the state's witnesses and a process for compelling evidence helpful to the defense. The prosecution must prove each element of the crime beyond a reasonable doubt and a jury verdict must be unanimous, whether the decision is for conviction or acquittal.

If conviction occurs the defendant is usually sentenced by a judge after a relatively informal hearing, except in capital cases, where a jury decides whether to impose the death penalty after a proceeding that resembles a trial. In some states, the judge has fairly broad discretion in choosing a sentence, while in others the judge is required to impose a sentence within a relatively narrow range unless good reasons can be given for departing from that range. The convicted offender is generally entitled to appeal both the conviction and the sentence, although a plea bargain often contains a waiver of the right to appeal, and a failure to raise an issue at trial sometimes forecloses raising it on appeal. Similarly, a defendant who loses on appeal can often bring a post-conviction or "collateral" action challenging the conviction or sentence, but may be foreclosed from doing so by failing to raise the issue in previous proceedings or by various other procedural rules. An individual convicted in state court may, after completing the state court post-conviction process, also challenge the conviction in federal court through the writ of habeas corpus, although there are several limitations to seeking this remedy as well. In contrast, the prosecution is barred by the prohibition on double jeopardy from appealing an acquittal, although under some circumstances it can appeal a sentence.

This book will provide more detail about each of these stages of the process. But before doing so, two preliminary matters must be addressed. First, no analysis of the criminal process can take place without understanding the goals that the process seeks to achieve. Second, the important role that the federal constitution and the courts play in regulating the criminal process in the United States needs to be outlined.

1.2 Goals of criminal procedure

A primary objective of any criminal process is to determine who has committed crime and to convict and punish those who have done so, in as efficient a manner as possible. But the American system also aims to achieve other goals, some of which may conflict with efficient truth-finding. These various goals can be placed in four categories: assuring outcomes that are consistent with the criminal law; limiting government power; maintaining a process that appears fair; and ensuring lay participation. To provide some perspective on how these goals might be achieved, the following discussion contrasts examples from American criminal procedure (which later chapters explain in more depth) with the quite different procedural regime that exists in many western European countries.

1.2.1 Assuring outcomes consistent with the criminal law

In the United States, crimes and defenses to crimes are defined primarily by statutes enacted by the state and federal legislatures, with the courts involved only to the extent the statutes require interpretation. A principal goal of the criminal process—the main reason that police, prosecutors, defense attorneys, judges, and juries exist—is to provide the government with the capacity to identify and convict those who have committed these crimes and to ensure that only those who have committed crime are convicted. That goal requires more than proving that an individual has engaged in a wrongful act. Assume, for instance, that the police can produce conclusive evidence that a criminal defendant has killed someone. In such a case, a criminal justice system that seeks to obtain a result consistent with the definition of homicide and other pertinent law must not only establish that the person was the proximate cause of the victim's death, but that the act was not accidental, carried out in self-defense, or committed while the person was insane. Furthermore, even in the absence of a complete defense to the crime, the precise type of homicide the person has committed must be determined. While first degree murder usually requires premeditation, an unjustified killing that is committed recklessly or negligently rather than after deliberation and planning may constitute only second degree murder or some form of manslaughter, which comes with a much lower sentence.

Several aspects of the American criminal process attempt to recognize and implement these types of legal nuances. Prosecutors are obligated to charge only the offense, or offenses, that most closely fits with the facts. Those charges may be subject to review by a judge or a grand jury before the case gets to trial, and defense counsel is appointed to subject them to further scrutiny, initially through discovery and preliminary hearings, but especially during trial, through cross-examination and presentation of rebuttal evidence. Judges ensure that guilty pleas have a factual basis, that juries are impartial, that evidentiary rules are followed at trial, and that juries are properly instructed about the law. Appellate courts correct errors of law, and may also overturn jury or judge findings of fact when they are irrational. These formal rules are not always followed; for instance, prosecutors seeking bargaining leverage may overcharge or fail to disclose exculpatory evidence. But the rules do increase the likelihood the ultimate verdict will accurately reflect the legislature's mandate.

In assessing whether these rules are the optimal means of doing so, the American criminal process is usefully compared to the most common criminal process on the European continent, which is usually dubbed inquisitorial, to distinguish it from the adversarial nature of American procedure. In both systems, the prosecution and the defense are "adversaries." However, whereas in the American system the adversaries are responsible for producing the relevant evidence, which is then assessed by the factfinder (the judge or the jury), in an inquisitorial regime a judge or a panel of judges is not only the ultimate decision-maker but also has considerable control over the witness list, including the selection of experts, and conducts much of the questioning of witnesses; lawyers play a much less prominent role at trial, and American-style juries composed solely of laypeople do not exist. Some have argued that leaving control of evidence production to the parties, as occurs in the American system, undermines the goal of implementing the criminal law, because it tempts the parties to seek a "win" rather than justice; prosecutors and defense attorneys in an adversarial system, it is said, are more likely to exaggerate their positions, hide information from the other side, and focus on matters that distract from ascertaining the truth.[6] At the same time, the inquisitorial system's minimization of the defense attorney's role and its judicially dominated confrontation of witnesses may curtail aggressive cross-examination and skew factfinding in the prosecution's favor.[7]

6 See Marvin E. Frankel, The Search for Truth: An Umpireal View, 12 U. Pa. L. Rev. 1031 (1975).

7 See Kweke Vandepuye, Traditions in Conflict: The Internationalization of Confrontation, 43 Cornell Int'l L.J. 513 (2010).

The two systems also differ in another way: whereas modern inquisitorial systems permit plea bargaining, they do not allow guilty pleas, at least in serious cases.[8] It is often stated that American criminal justice is a system of pleas, and that even if the number of cases that went to trial increased only marginally, the system would be overwhelmed. Inquisitorial systems, in contrast, can "afford" to have trials in these cases, because judicial factfinding is more efficient than factfinding by laypeople, which requires selection of juries, complicated instructions about the law, and elaborate rules of evidence that assume laypeople are unable to process certain types of information fairly (e.g., hearsay or criminal history). As a result, all serious cases in inquisitorial regimes are heard by a court even when there is a confession, in contrast to the American system, in which the outcome in most cases is determined by the parties through a plea bargain that is only perfunctorily monitored by a judge, and the bulk of remaining cases are resolved by a group of laypeople with no legal training. Some have claimed that, despite its historical association with torture, the inquisitorial system in its modern form is better at implementing the substantive criminal law than an adversary-driven system of pleas.[9]

Unfortunately, good empirical evidence for making such a comparison does not exist. Looking solely at the American system, it has been estimated that anywhere from 0.5 to 2 percent of all convictions are of people who did not commit the conduct charged[10] (analogous data from Europe is not readily available). The reasons wrongful convictions occur in the United States are numerous, and include: coerced or manipulated confessions; faulty eyewitness identifications; flawed forensic laboratory analysis; "tunnel vision" on the part of prosecutors who become convinced the defendant is guilty despite evidence to the contrary; poor lawyering by defense attorneys; biased judges; juries that do not understand their instructions or assume that anyone charged with crime is probably guilty of it; and overloaded appellate courts that fail to examine cases closely.[11] Even convictions secured through

---

8 Maximo Langer, From Legal Transplants to Legal Translations: The Globalization of Plea Bargaining and the Americanization Thesis in Criminal Procedure, 45 Harv. Int'l L.J. 1, 11 (2004).

9 See, e.g., Rudolf B. Schlesinger, Comparative Criminal Procedure: A Plea for Utilizing Foreign Experience, 26 Buff. L. Rev. 361 (1977).

10 D. Michael Risinger, Tragic Consequences of Deadly Dilemmas: A Response to Allen and Laudan, 40 Seton Hall L. Rev. 991, 996 (2010).

11 See Dan Simon, In Doubt: The Psychology of the Criminal Justice Process (Harvard University Press, Cambridge 2017); Brandon Garrett, Convicting the Innocent: Where Criminal Prosecutions Go Wrong (Harvard University Press, Cambridge 2012).

guilty pleas can be suspect, especially when defendants plead out of fear that going to trial will result in a significantly greater sentence, which in some jurisdictions can be many times more punitive than a bargained-for disposition.[12] "Inaccurate" acquittals are also likely; in fact, as discussed below, such acquittals are built into the system given the heavy burden of proof placed on the prosecution. Finally, even when a conviction is sound, the extent to which a sentence imposed by a judge reflects the legislature's intent is difficult to gauge, in part because the purposes of punishment—ranging from retribution and deterrence to incapacitation and rehabilitation—are often conflicting, and in part because the sentencing process is much more informal than trial, and thus may not provide judges with the necessary high-quality, relevant information.

1.2.2 Limiting government power

Reliability of outcome is an important goal of any criminal process, but in the United States it is clearly not the only one. One reason the American system remains wedded to the adversarial approach—independent of any ability it has to ascertain the truth—stems from concern about overreaching by government officials, a fear that harks back to colonial outrage at British tyranny. Rather than the government-led inquiry into the evidence that dominates the inquisitorial system, American adversarialism envisions the criminal process as a battle between the defendant and the government, characterizes the defense attorney as a "zealous advocate" for the defendant regardless of the strength of the prosecution's evidence, and views the lay jury as a necessary buffer between the government and the accused, regardless of how cumbersome or inexpert it might be.[13] In all of these ways, the American process reflects a greater distrust of state power.

That distrust is also reflected in the burden the American system places on the government to prove its case, which is decidedly heavier than the proof burden other types of litigants must face. In some ways, the adversarialism of the criminal process is mimicked in the typical civil case in the United States, one that might be brought after a car accident or in connection with a medical malpractice claim; in particular, just as in a criminal case, the opposing lawyers in such a lawsuit are in charge

12 See Josh Bowers, Punishing Innocence, 156 U. Pa. L. Rev. 1117 (2006).

13 Mirjan Damaska, Evidentiary Barriers to Conviction and Two Models of Criminal Procedure, 121 U. Pa. L. Rev. 507 (1972).

of presenting their evidence to an otherwise uninformed judge or jury. However, because a civil suit involves relatively equally situated private parties rather than the all-powerful government against a citizen, a civil plaintiff need only meet the preponderance of the evidence standard, usually associated with a more-likely-than-not showing. In criminal cases, in contrast, concern about government abuse, in combination with the facts that a criminal conviction can result in a significant deprivation of liberty and is much more stigmatizing than a loss in a civil case, has led to the rule that the prosecution must dispel all reasonable doubt about guilt.[14] This much more onerous burden is captured by the adage that it is better to let ten guilty people go free than convict one innocent person. Again, this proof requirement is in some tension with the first goal of accurately implementing the substantive criminal law.

In even more tension with that goal are the limitations placed on the type of evidence the government may use to make its case. If reliability of outcome were the only concern, one might countenance a system where all parties are required to reveal what they know—especially the accused, who if the allegations by the prosecution are correct, is probably the person who knows most about the crime. However, in the United States, not only does the government bear a heavy burden to prove its case, it must do so without any help from the defendant (unless the defendant voluntarily decides to provide such help), a practice that is sometimes called accusatorial. Whereas in an inquisitorial system the defendant is expected to testify at trial and is often the first witness,[15] in the United States defendants are entitled to remain silent, and juries are admonished not to draw an adverse inference from a defendant's decision to avoid taking the stand. Further, in an attempt to minimize police coercion, the right to silence extends backward through the pretrial process (a stance, it must be noted, that European countries are beginning to adopt as well[16]). The rationale for these rules is in large part the idea that, without a right to remain silent, government would routinely resort to coercing defendants into talking, which could harm innocent and guilty alike.

The desire to cabin government power has even led to adoption of procedural mechanisms that prevent U.S. prosecutors from relying on

14 In re Winship, 397 U.S. 358 (1970).

15 See Christopher Slobogin, Lessons from Inquisitorialism, 87 U.S.C. L. Rev. 699, 727 (2014).

16 Jacqueline Hodgson, Safeguarding Suspects' Rights in Europe: A Comparative Perspective, 14 New Crim. L. Rev. 611 (2011).

evidence known to be reliable. Most obvious in this regard is the judicial refusal to allow prosecution use of items found during an illegal search or seizure. Such evidence—illicit drugs, the weapon used in a robbery—is usually very probative proof of guilt. But if the government obtains it in a high-handed manner, for instance, by invading a person's home without a warrant or by frisking a person on a mere hunch, then the judicial response since the 1960s has been to exclude any evidence thereby found, which often means the government cannot prove its case. This "exclusionary rule" exists because American courts have concluded that the only effective way of deterring arbitrary police actions is through suppression of the evidence they produce. Confessions obtained in violation of Miranda v. Arizona,[17] which requires that an arrested individual be told of the right to remain silent, are also often excluded, even when they appear to be reliable. A few countries have begun to adopt exclusionary practices, particularly with respect to confessions,[18] but the United States, driven by concern about government excess, has clearly been the pioneer in this regard.

1.2.3 Appearance of fairness

Fairness is a very broad concept, and can encompass both the reliability and abuse-minimization goals already discussed. As defined here, however, the fairness goal is aimed at constructing a process that not only tries to be fair in these senses, but also appears to be fair, to both the defendant and the public at large. Procedural justice research suggests that litigants and outside observers are much more willing to accept the legitimacy of an outcome, and of the government that seeks it, if it stems from a process that allows the parties to express their views and that treats similarly situated litigants equally.[19] Thus, a procedure that appears fair might produce substantial benefits, independently of other goals.

For instance, even if the adversarial process is flawed as a means of ferreting out the truth, its contest-orientation may enhance the overall legitimacy of the system by emphasizing that the defendant has a voice

17 384 U.S. 436 (1966).

18 Christopher Slobogin, A Comparative Perspective on the Exclusionary Rule in Search and Seizure Cases, in Comparative Criminal Procedure 286–93 (Jacqueline E. Ross and Stephen C. Thaman eds., Edward Elgar Publishing, Cheltenham, U.K. and Northampton, Mass.,, U.S.A. 2016).

19 See generally, Tom R. Tyler, Why People Obey the Law (Yale University Press, New Haven, Conn. 2016).

in the process and is an "equal antagonist" to the government, which will have to abide by the decision of ordinary citizens like the defendant.[20] Of course, in a system where the responsibility of generating evidence for the defendant rests primarily on the defense rather than with the state, wealthier individuals are much better able to realize these benefits in practice (which has led some to assert that, while wealthier defendants are better off in the American system, poorer defendants may do better in an inquisitorial one). But the American system tries to rectify this imbalance by providing lawyers to indigent defendants, at least those charged with a jailable offense, and also provides such defendants with some investigative resources, albeit with significant limitations. More importantly, compared to the European inquiry model, the adversarial model more clearly positions the defense attorney as the defendant's champion who aims to ensure "equality of arms."

Ensuring the appearance of racial equality is also a very important aspect of fairness, especially in the United States, given its long history of slavery and Jim Crow laws. The possibility, amply supported by data from a number of American jurisdictions, that people of color are more likely than whites to be stopped, arrested, and prosecuted for certain types of crimes—especially lower level offenses and drug offenses—undermines this goal, with predictable harm to the legitimacy of the system.[21] Unfortunately, the courts have done little to redress these concerns about the pretrial process. They have been more attentive to the appearance of racial fairness at trial once prosecution begins, in particular by adopting guidelines that inhibit exclusion of people from the jury on racial grounds.

Many other aspects of American procedure can be seen as more general attempts to ensure fairness during the adjudication process, including rules that allow removal of biased judges or jurors, require public, speedy trials, and prohibit retrials for the same offense under certain circumstances. While such rules may also enhance reliability and curb government power, they most strongly resonate with the notion that, regardless of these other goals, the state should always operate in an impartial, transparent manner that minimizes unnecessary harm to the defendant. Over the past several decades, there has also been a strong movement toward fair treatment of victims, not only

20 Thurman Arnold, Symbols of Government 145 (Yale University Press, New Haven, Conn. 1935).

21 See Bennett Capers, Crime, Legitimacy, and Testilying, 83 Ind. L.J. 835 (2008).

for its own sake but because it improves victim cooperation with the authorities and the public's perception of the system. Many jurisdictions now have statutes that direct prosecutors and courts to ensure, inter alia, that the victim receives restitution, counseling services, protection against intimidation, and a concrete role in the charging or sentencing process.[22]

1.2.4 Encouraging lay participation

This fourth goal is most obviously achieved in the United States through the institution of the jury, which ranges in size from 6 to 12 people depending on the jurisdiction. But it is also furthered by the grand jury, a larger group of laypeople which in roughly a third of the states and in federal cases is involved in monitoring the prosecutor's charging decision. Although one or more laypeople are often found on decision-making panels in inquisitorial systems as well, they are dominated by the panel's judicial members (thus, the pejorative term of "head-nodders" sometimes assigned to them). Furthermore, these inquisitorial jurors usually sit for a several-month period and hear a large number of cases, which may dilute the point of having untutored laypeople as factfinders.

The American jury is thought to serve all three of the previous goals. There is some debate about whether juries are as accurate as judges in arriving at conclusions about guilt and innocence.[23] But even if juries sometimes have trouble understanding their instructions or intentionally disobey them (which occurs often enough that it has been dubbed jury nullification), they can inject lay insights into a process that might otherwise be too rigidly legalistic or prone to judicial cynicism or stereotyping. Recall the homicide example given earlier. In light of the many possible permutations of self-defense and insanity, and the difficulty of defining and distinguishing terms like premeditation, recklessness, and negligence, leaving the ultimate determination of how these concepts apply in a given case to the consensus opinion of laypeople may be the optimal method of capturing ultimately unknowable gradations of moral blameworthiness. The jury also lessens government dominance of the process and may enhance perceptions of fairness. In high profile cases in particular, a verdict from a jury chosen from the defendant's community might be perceived as more legitimate than

22 See Symposium, Emerging Issues in Crime Victims' Rights, 13 Ohio St. J. Crim. L. (2015).

23 See Duncan v. Louisiana, 391 U.S. 145, 188–89 (1968) (Harlan, J., dissenting).

a trial or plea-bargained verdict pronounced or approved by a single, government-appointed judge; at the least, when a jury makes the decision, the legal system avoids direct blame for a controversial verdict, because it is the jury, not the government, that delivers it.

The primary rationale for encouraging lay participation through the jury, however, is that it brings democracy into the courtroom. The jury's verdict is a form of voting that signals what the community thinks about crime. Further, the jury involves laypeople directly in the functioning of government in a way that few other institutions do, and thus gives citizens a stake in the democratic enterprise.

1.3 Sources of law

The various rules of criminal procedure alluded to in the foregoing discussion come from a number of sources. The federal system and each state system have their own codes of criminal procedure, usually drafted by judicially oriented bodies and then endorsed, with minor tweaks, by the relevant legislature. Police agencies, prosecutor offices, and public defender organizations also develop their own internal procedures. But to a remarkable extent, especially when compared to the substantive criminal law or the procedural rules of other countries, the American law of criminal procedure is based on judicial opinions, and more particularly, federal judicial opinions construing the United States Constitution, most of them from the United States Supreme Court. How this state of affairs came to be is important to understand before looking at the rules themselves.

1.3.1 Incorporation doctrine and its consequences

Most of the procedural rules discussed in this book are based on judicial interpretations of the United States Constitution, and more specifically, four of the ten amendments to the Constitution found in the Bill of Rights, all of which were ratified by the states by 1791. The Fourth Amendment protects against "unreasonable searches and seizures" by the government, and requires that warrants be based on "probable cause." The Fifth Amendment is the basis for the right to remain silent, indictment by grand jury, and the double jeopardy prohibition, and also stipulates that a person may not be deprived of life, liberty, and property without due process of law. The Sixth Amendment guarantees the criminal accused the rights to counsel, to notice of the charges, to a public and speedy jury trial, to confrontation of one's accusers, and to compulsory process (such as subpoenas). And the Eighth Amendment bars cruel and unusual punishment and excessive bail and fines.

As originally construed, these various restrictions on government affected only the federal government, a body that those who drafted the amendments worried might otherwise infringe citizens' rights just as Great Britain had.[24] With the ratification of the Fourteenth Amendment after the Civil War, however, language in that amendment meant primarily to ensure that ex-slaves were treated equally also provided an avenue for applying the Bill of Rights to the states. Specifically, in relevant part the Fourteenth Amendment provides that "[no] state shall make or enforce any law which shall abridge the privileges or immunities of citizens of the United States; nor shall any State deprive any person of life, liberty, or property, without due process of law." The latter phrase is identical to the due process of law language found in the Fifth Amendment, with one important exception: it clearly placed limits on state governments as well as on the federal government. The question then became whether the rights found in the Bill of Rights are "incorporated" by the Fourteenth Amendment as aspects of "due process of law" that state criminal justice systems must respect.

That question was eventually answered affirmatively by the United States Supreme Court, although it took over 100 years to fully settle the matter, through a series of decisions that became known as incorporation doctrine. When first confronted with the issue of whether a right found in the Bill of Rights applied to the states, in 1884, the Court concluded that only those provisions that are "essential to the preservation of public and private rights" are an aspect of due process; specifically, it held that the Fifth Amendment's requirement that defendants be charged through grand jury indictments was not essential (a holding that still stands, which explains why a number of states have not adopted or have eliminated the grand jury).[25] In 1908, the Court came to the same conclusion with respect to the privilege against self-incrimination, concluding that the right to remain silent was not one of the "immutable principles of justice which inhere in the very idea of free government which no member of the Union may

24 Barron v. City of Baltimore, 32 U.S. 243 (1833).

25 Hurtado v. California, 110 U.S. 516 (1884); see also Palko v. Connecticut, 302 U.S. 319 (1937).

disregard."[26] That holding was affirmed 40 years later because, in the words of Justice Felix Frankfurter, it was not one of "those canons of decency and fairness which express the notions of justice of English-speaking peoples."[27] For the same reason, in 1942 the Supreme Court refused to require the states to abide by the federal right to counsel in all felony cases,[28] and in 1949, in Wolf v. Colorado, it held that only "core" aspects of the Fourth Amendment need be followed by state and local police and that the exclusionary rule that applied in federal court need not be adopted by the states.[29]

With the appointment of Earl Warren as Chief Justice of the Supreme Court in 1954, however, the attitude of the Court toward incorporation doctrine shifted significantly, beginning with reversal of both aspects of Wolf. In 1961, the Court held in Mapp v. Ohio[30] that state courts, like federal courts, are required to exclude evidence obtained in violation of the Fourth Amendment, and two years later it made clear that all Fourth Amendment rules, not just those at its "core," are part of due process that must be followed by the states.[31] In 1963, in Gideon v. Wainwright,[32] the Court incorporated the right to counsel, and one year later it followed suit with respect to the privilege against self-incrimination, reversing its earlier decisions.[33] By 1969, it had incorporated all of the criminal procedure guarantees found in the Bill of Rights except the right to indictment by a grand jury and the Eighth Amendment's prohibition on excessive fines, and 50 years later it finally applied the latter provision to the states as well.[34]

The incorporation doctrine still has some teeth, however, as evidenced by the grand jury decisions, as well as by the Court's treatment of the right to trial by jury. While Duncan v. Louisiana[35] held that the right to jury trial is "fundamental" to "an Anglo-American regime of ordered liberty," the Court subsequently made clear that not every aspect of the federal jury trial right is such a fundamental aspect of due process that

26 Twining v. New Jersey, 211 U.S. 78 (1908).
27 Adamson v. California, 332 U.S. 46 (1947).
28 Betts v. Brady, 316 U.S. 455 (1942).
29 338 U.S. 25 (1949).
30 367 U.S. 643 (1961).
31 Ker v. California, 374 U.S. 23 (1963).
32 372 U.S. 335 (1963).
33 Malloy v. Hogan, 378 U.S. 1 (1964).
34 Timbs v. Indiana, 139 S.Ct. 682 (2019).
35 391 U.S. 145 (1968).

it need be adopted by the states. Specifically, while federal juries must be 12 in number, state juries can constitutionally be half that size.[36]

Nonetheless, there is no doubt that the Warren Court's approach to incorporation revolutionized American criminal procedure. This upheaval in the Court's take on the applicability of the Bill of Rights to the states was not due simply to changes in the Court's membership. During the period when the Warren Court was active, from the mid 1950s to the late 1960s, the country witnessed numerous blatantly racist actions by state and local police and their governments, especially in the South, and state courts often seemed to be complicit. Just as the Court's 1954 decision in Brown v. Board of Education[37] famously mandated desegregation of the schools, many of its criminal procedure opinions helped combat discriminatory police and judicial practices.[38] The state criminal cases heard by the Court also highlighted the lack of uniformity in criminal procedure rules across the country, particularly with respect to the police. Partly a legacy of the colonists' distaste of centralized power, there are thousands of separate police department and sheriff offices in the United States that—in contrast to law enforcement organizations in many other countries—are controlled by local municipalities and counties rather than federal or state governments; further, each state and many municipalities have their own court systems. The result can be a cacophony of police and adjudicatory practices, which the Warren Court helped redress through its constitutionalization of criminal procedure. Further evidence that the goals of racial equality and nationally applicable rules were a major driving force behind the Warren Court's criminal procedure decisions comes from that Court's efforts to expand the scope of habeas corpus, so that federal courts could more easily oversee state court decisions (see §12.4).

The incorporation decisions of the Warren Court have not been uncontroversial. The exclusionary rule's tendency to trigger dismissal of cases against clearly guilty people, Miranda's admonition to tell suspects not to talk, and many of the other rules announced by the Court have all been attacked on the grounds alluded to in §1.2, as well as on the separate ground that they are inconsistent with the "original

36 Williams v. Florida, 399 U.S. 78 (1970).

37 347 U.S. 483 (1954).

38 Archibald Cox, The Warren Court: Constitutional Decision as an Instrument of Reform (Harvard University Press, Cambridge, Mass. 1968).

intent" of the Framers. More generally, critics have decried the nationalization of criminal procedure rules as a violation of state prerogatives, and have also noted that it diminishes the benefits that would otherwise come from 50 state "laboratories" experimenting with different procedures.[39] Some have even voiced the concern that the Warren Court's procedural revolution backfired, in that it made obtaining admissible evidence and going to trial such expensive propositions that plea bargaining's rise became inevitable, with the result that the centerpiece of the revolution—the adversarial jury trial—rarely occurs.[40]

These and other criticisms may in part be responsible for the significant retrenchment on the Warren Court's classic decisions that has occurred since Earl Warren and many of the Warren Court's other members left the Court in the late 1960s and early 1970s. As this book documents, subsequent Court holdings have created numerous exceptions to the Fourth Amendment exclusionary rule and Miranda, whittled back some of the protections afforded by the rights to counsel, confrontation, and public jury trial, and seriously limited state offenders' access to the federal courts. In turn, however, this retrenchment has led to a resurgence of state constitutional law.

1.3.2 State constitutional law

Every state has a constitution that in most respects is very similar to the federal constitution. For instance, many state constitutions prohibit "unreasonable" searches and seizures and guarantee counsel and a right to confront accusers. Before the Warren Court revolution and the development of incorporation doctrine, these provisions and the state decisions interpreting them were the governing law in each state. Then, during the Warren Court era, this body of law in effect became moot, because it usually did not provide as much protection to defendants as the Supreme Court's decisions did. However, as the post-Warren Court carried out its retrenchment, some state courts took a new look at their constitutions and concluded that criminal defendants in their state are entitled to broader rights than are afforded federal defendants. For instance, in the first 15 years after the end of the Warren Court era (usually pegged at 1969, when Warren and Justice Abe Fortas left the Court), over 300 state decisions established state

39 Duncan v. Louisiana, 391 U.S. 145, 193 (1968) (Harlan, J., dissenting).

40 William J. Stuntz, The Collapse of American Criminal Justice 235–6 (Harvard University Press, Cambridge, Mass. 2011).

rules that went beyond the federal rights pronounced by the Supreme Court, on issues such as searches incident to arrest, the scope of the Fourth Amendment's exclusionary rule, interrogation, the right to jury trial, and the double jeopardy ban.[41]

The basis for this state judicial renaissance, dubbed the new federalism, is the Tenth Amendment, which states that "[t]he powers not delegated to the United States by the Constitution, nor prohibited by it to the States, are reserved to the states respectively, or to the people." The Supreme Court itself has explicitly recognized this authority. For instance, as the Court stated in Cooper v. California,[42] its own interpretation of the Fourth Amendment "does not affect the State's power to impose higher standards on searches and seizures than required by the Federal Constitution if it chooses to do so." Accordingly, rules dealing with the procedures referenced in the Bill of Rights may differ from state to state and between the states and the federal domain (although the federal rule supersedes any state rule that provides defendants with less protection).

This development too has come in for criticism. Some commentators contend that federal court interpretations of language in the federal constitution that is essentially identical to that found in state constitutions should be preferred, on the assumption that federal courts are generally more qualified or at least better resourced than state court judges; at bottom, it is argued, the new federalism is "result-oriented," not based on sound judicial reasoning.[43] It is also pointed out that, in states where courts have exercised their state constitutional muscle, two sets of rules apply, one for those officials implementing federal law and another for those investigating and prosecuting state crime, thus undermining the uniformity the Warren Court sought to achieve.[44] Even these critics concede, however, that where state constitutional language diverges from federal language or where state history or practice is demonstrably different than federal practice, differing standards are permissible, as long as federal constitutional law trumps state constitutional law when the latter provides less protection to criminal

---

41 Ronald Colins and Peter Galie, The New Federalism: The Methodology, Nat'l L.J., Sept. 29, 1986, at S-8.

42 386 U.S. 58 (1967).

43 Earl M. Maltz, The Dark Side of State Court Activism, 63 Tex. L. Rev. 995, 1005–6 (1985).

44 State v. Bolt, 698 P.2d 519 (Ariz. 1984).

defendants.[45] Some have also defended state court activism on the ground that the floor created by federal constitutional law is lower than it should be, because Supreme Court justices are inhibited by the knowledge that their constitutional pronouncements apply not only in the federal domain, but to every jurisdiction in the country.[46]

1.4 The judicial orientation of this book

The foregoing makes clear that the United States Supreme Court has been crucial in setting the baseline of American criminal procedure. This is in distinction to countries elsewhere in the world, including Europe, where rules governing the police and the courts are primarily the product of statute. Only recently, as international tribunals have begun pouring content into international treaties and conventions, has the judiciary had a similarly significant say in regulating European criminal procedure.[47]

In the United States, judicial opinions remain the dominant force in establishing the scope of criminal procedure rules. Thus, while this book will not ignore important statutes and regulations, it will consist primarily of descriptions of those opinions and, more specifically, Supreme Court opinions, because these are the only decisions that are clearly the law of the land. It begins with three chapters on the law of search and seizure, most of which derives from the Fourth Amendment. Next are two chapters on how the Fifth and Sixth Amendments regulate the three other prevalent police investigative techniques—interrogation and undercover activity in the first chapter, identification procedures in the second—followed by a chapter on the exclusionary rule and other remedies for police misconduct. Moving from the investigative phase to the adjudicative phase of the criminal process (especially as it applies to felony cases), the second half of the book begins with a chapter on the pretrial process—including bail and charging decisions, discovery, and preliminary and grand jury hearings—the structure of which is heavily influenced by all four

45 See Eugene L. Shapiro, State Constitutional Doctrine and the Criminal Process, 16 Seton Hall L. Rev. 630, 650–54 (1986).

46 Lawrence G. Sager, Fair Measure: The Legal Status of Underenforced Constitutional Norms, 91 Harv. L. Rev. 1212, 1242–63 (1978).

47 See Jacqueline E. Ross and Stephen C. Thaman, Introduction: Mapping Dialogue and Change in Comparative Criminal Procedure, in Comparative Criminal Procedure, supra note 18, at 3.

criminal procedure guarantees in the Bill of Rights. That chapter is followed by a chapter on adjudication by guilty plea, where the Due Process Clause plays a significant role, and a chapter on adjudication by public jury trial, which is guaranteed by the Sixth Amendment, but also influenced by the First Amendment's protection of the public's right to know. The book ends with a chapter on the adversarial rights found in the Sixth Amendment (the rights to be present, counsel, confront witnesses, and compel evidence), and a chapter on the post-adjudication process, specifically, sentencing procedures, appeal, habeas corpus, and the double jeopardy ban.

2 The threshold of the Fourth Amendment

2.1 Rationale of the Fourth Amendment

The Fourth Amendment to the U.S. Constitution reads in full:

> The right of the people to be secure in their persons, houses, papers and effects, against unreasonable searches and seizures, shall not be violated, and no Warrants shall issue, but upon probable cause, supported by Oath or affirmation, and particularly describing the place to be searched, and the persons or things to be seized.

While there is considerable debate over the meaning and intent of this language, all agree that the primary reason it was included in the Bill of Rights was the Framers' reaction to English abuse of the warrant process in the years preceding the Revolutionary War. Particularly galling to the colonists was the profligate use of "writs of assistance," which authorized constables to obtain "assistance" in seizing, at their discretion, any "prohibited or uncustomed" goods from houses, shops, and any "other Place." In contrast to the traditional common law warrant, which was issued by a justice of the peace when a citizen swore there was probable cause to believe stolen property could be found in a particular home, these "general warrants" gave British soldiers carte blanche to search any place they thought might contain contraband. The colonist James Otis called the writ of assistance "the worst instrument of arbitrary power, the most destructive of English liberty, and the fundamental principles of law, that ever was found in an English law book, [because it placed] the liberty of every man in the hands of every petty officer."[1]

The Fourth Amendment, then, was at a minimum meant to curb arbitrary government intrusions into houses, persons, papers, and effects by ensuring that warrants authorizing searches and seizures

1 Quoted in Boyd v. United States, 116 U.S. 616, 625 (1886).

are issued by a magistrate, are based on probable cause, and contain a particular description of the place to be searched and the person or items to be seized. The amendment voices an extremely important limitation on government power, especially so since the development of organized police forces in the middle of the nineteenth century. As Monrad Paulsen stated, "All the other freedoms, freedom of speech, of assembly, of religion, of political action, presuppose that arbitrary and capricious police action has been restrained."[2]

As construed by the courts, the Fourth Amendment could be said to raise three issues. The first involves when the amendment applies. Only a search or seizure, carried out by the government in the absence of consent, triggers the Fourth Amendment's protection. The second issue focuses on the requisites of the preeminent Fourth Amendment protection—the warrant, based on probable cause and describing with particularity the objects of the search or seizure. The third issue concerns when dispensing with these requirements is permissible.

This chapter discusses the first issue. Again, if the contested action is not carried out or directed by a government official, if it is not a "search" or "seizure," or if it occurs after proper consent has been obtained, then the Fourth Amendment is not applicable; it places no constraints on the police. While statutes might govern such situations, their limitations usually do not approach the requirements the Fourth Amendment would impose and, because they are not constitutionally based, can be repealed or amended at the legislature's will.

2.2 Definition of government conduct

The Fourth Amendment, like the rest of the Bill of Rights, only applies to government actors. Recall that the Fourteenth Amendment specifically provides that "no state" may deprive a person of life or liberty without due process of law (§1.3.1). Purely private actions, no matter how egregious, do not implicate the Constitution. Thus, in Burdeau v. McDowell,[3] the Supreme Court easily concluded that no Fourth Amendment violation occurred when private individuals burglarized the defendant's business office and seized papers, which later found

2 Monrad G. Paulsen, The Exclusionary Rule and Misconduct by the Police, in Police Power and Individual Freedom 87, 97 (Claude R. Sowle ed., Aldine Publishing Company, Chicago 1962).

3 256 U.S. 465 (1921).

their way into the government's possession and were used to prosecute him. For the same reason, private police and security guards, while subject to tort and false arrest suits, are not governed by the Fourth Amendment.[4]

However, the amendment does apply to the actions of all government officials, not just the police, but also inspectors,[5] government employers,[6] and public school officials.[7] Further, the amendment governs all "agents" of government officials, so that private individuals who are directed or strongly encouraged by the police to conduct a search must abide by the Fourth Amendment. For instance, the Supreme Court has held that the Fourth Amendment applies to private railway employers mandated by government regulations to carry out drug testing of railway workers involved in accidents and violations of safety rules.[8]

To trigger constitutional protection, the government conduct must be aimed at a person who is considered one of "the people" referenced in the Fourth Amendment. In United States v. Verdugo-Urquidez,[9] the Court held that this phrase "refers to a class of people who are part of a national community or who have otherwise developed sufficient connection with this country to be considered part of that community." A plurality of the court then decided that Verdugo-Urquidez did not have such a connection because his presence in the country was "involuntary," in that it resulted from his transport to the U.S. after his arrest in Mexico. A few courts have interpreted Verdugo-Urquidez to mean that previously deported aliens or aliens who are in the country illegally do not have Fourth Amendment rights.[10]

2.3 Definition of search

One might think that defining the word "search" is a fairly straightforward endeavor. But while a layperson would probably describe a search as an effort to look for or examine something, the courts have never defined

4 See David Sklansky, The Private Police, 46 UCLA L. Rev. 1165, 1184–7 (1999).

5 See, e.g., Camara v. Municipal Court, 387 U.S. 523 (1967).

6 O'Connor v. Ortega, 480 U.S. 709 (1987).

7 New Jersey v. T.L.O. 469 U.S. 325 (1985).

8 Skinner v. Railway Labor Executives' Ass'n, 489 U.S. 602 (1989).

9 494 U.S. 259 (1990).

10 D. Carolina Nunez, Inside the Border, Outside the Law: Undocumented Immigrants and the Fourth Amendment, 85 S. Cal. L. Rev. 85, 108–12 (2011).

the term that broadly. Rather they have framed their analysis of the concept with reference to the values they think the Fourth Amendment protects, principally having to do with property and privacy.

The first cases defining "search" focused on whether the police action involved a physical intrusion or trespass into one of the four "protected areas" mentioned in the Fourth Amendment: houses, persons, papers, and effects. Thus, inserting a spike mike underneath the baseboard of a wall was held to be a search,[11] but tapping a phone outside a suspect's premises and attaching a detectaphone on an outside wall were not.[12] In Katz v. United States,[13] however, the Warren Court rejected this property-orientation in favor of an inquiry that eventually came to be called the "reasonable expectation of privacy" test. The Katz test's focus on whether the government action infringed the target's reasonable expectations of privacy was meant to expand the scope of the Fourth Amendment. But the extent to which it did so remains unclear. The new focus on privacy enabled the Court to hold that electronic surveillance of the type considered immune under a property-based approach is in fact governed by the Fourth Amendment.[14] But in most other situations the post-Warren Court continued to track the pre-Katz, property-orientation of search doctrine, and in its earlier years even contracted the definition of search beyond what the logic of pre-Katz law would suggest. More recently, the government's increasing use of technology to investigate crime appears to have spurred the Court to rethink the Fourth Amendment's scope.

2.3.1 Knowing exposure doctrine

In Katz, the Court held that bugging a telephone booth being used by the defendant required a warrant even though the bugging did not involve a trespass and the booth was not a house, person, paper, or effect. In determining that trespass law should no longer be the primary framework for establishing the Fourth Amendment's scope, the Court asserted that "what [a person] seeks to preserve as private, even in an area accessible to the public, may be constitutionally protected." However, based on the same privacy rationale, Katz also stated that "What a person knowingly exposes to the public, even in his own home

11 Silverman v. United States, 365 U.S. 505 (1961).

12 Olmstead v. United States, 277 U.S. 438 (1928); Goldman v. United States, 316 U.S. 129 (1942).

13 389 U.S. 347 (1967).

14 See Berger v. New York, 388 U.S. 41 (1967).

or office, is not a subject of Fourth Amendment protection." This "knowing exposure doctrine" subsequently provided the rationale for a number of decisions holding that police actions that most laypeople would call searches are in fact outside the Fourth Amendment's scope.

Thus, the Court held that a Fourth Amendment search did not occur when police examined pornographic material meant for sale to the general public,[15] tracked a car on public roads for an hour,[16] trespassed on privately owned "open fields" outside the home's "curtilage" (i.e., the area immediately surrounding the home) to look for drugs,[17] and used an airplane to observe activities in a fenced-in backyard.[18] In all four of these situations, the Court said, the defendant knowingly exposed his activities to the public. The same reasoning supported decisions permitting warrantless examination of trash left at curbside,[19] of containers that "reveal the nature of their contents" (such as transparent vials and gun cases),[20] and of prisoner cells, in the latter case because an expectation of privacy "is fundamentally incompatible with the close and continual surveillance of inmates and their cells required to ensure institutional security and internal order."[21]

At the same time, the Court has been leery of pushing the knowing exposure doctrine too far, especially as technology has made government monitoring of public activities easier and more prevalent. In a 2012 decision, United States v. Jones,[22] the Court held that tracking a driver on public roads using a GPS device attached to the car was a search; although the majority emphasized that its holding was based on the fact that putting the device on the car worked a trespass, five members of the Court clearly believed that the Fourth Amendment is implicated by any long-term technological tracking of a car (in Jones, the tracking lasted for 28 days, in contrast to the case noted above in which it lasted only one hour). And in Grady v. North Carolina,[23] the Court held that using an ankle bracelet to monitor a released

15 Maryland v. Macon, 472 U.S. 463 (1985).

16 United States v. Knotts, 460 U.S. 276 (1983).

17 Oliver v. United States, 466 U.S. 170 (1984); United States v. Dunn, 480 U.S. 294 (1987).

18 California v. Ciraolo, 476 U.S. 207 (1986).

19 California v. Greenwood, 486 U.S. 35 (1988).

20 Noted in Arkansas v. Sanders, 442 U.S. 753 (1979). Compare Bond v. United Sates, 529 U.S. 334 (2000) (squeezing closed, opaque bag to determine its contents is a search).

21 Hudson v. Palmer, 468 U.S. 517 (1984).

22 565 U.S. 400 (2012).

23 575 U.S. 306 (2015).

prisoner was a search. It is likely that any long-term, technologically enhanced surveillance targeting a person in real time is now a Fourth Amendment search, even if the activities under surveillance can be said to be "knowingly" exposed to the public.

2.3.2 General public use doctrine

In Dow Chemical v. Environmental Protection Agency,[24] the government not only observed Dow Chemical's private business curtilage from the air—an action that, on its own, was probably justifiable under the knowing exposure doctrine—but used a $22,000 mapmaking camera to do so. Dow Chemical argued that citizens should be able to expect privacy from surveillance using such sophisticated technology. However, the Court concluded that no search occurred, based on the questionable assertion that such a camera is "generally available" to the public and thus people should not expect privacy from its use. Twenty years later, in Kyllo v. United States,[25] the Court reiterated this stance, albeit in "dictum" (i.e., language not necessary to the decision of the case). Specifically, the Court stated, technology that is in "general public use" may be used for investigative purposes without a warrant, even to look inside a home. At the same time, Kyllo held that the thermal imager used in that case to detect heat differentials inside Kyllo's home was not in general public use, despite the fact that a thermal imager is considerably cheaper than the mapmaking camera relied on in Dow Chemical. Nor did the Kyllo Court accept the government's argument that the heat emanating from Kyllo's house, which is what the imager detected, was abandoned or knowingly exposed.

The better explanation for the different results in Dow Chemical and Kyllo is probably found in the following language from the latter case: "obtaining by sense-enhancing technology any information regarding the interior of the home that could not otherwise have been obtained without physical intrusion into a constitutionally protected area constitutes a search." This statement appears to distinguish Kyllo from Dow Chemical on the ground that Dow Chemical involved business property viewable from the air, while Kyllo involved the inside of a home, which is associated with a much higher level of privacy. Any device, no matter how generally available, that enables police to view activities in the home they could not see with the naked eye without

24 476 U.S. 227 (1986).

25 533 U.S. 27 (2001).

trespassing implicates the Fourth Amendment. At the same time, it appears that even looking inside a home using technology that is not in general public use (say, a satellite camera) avoids regulation under the Fourth Amendment if the same activities could be viewed with the naked eye from a lawful vantage point (for instance, from the public sidewalk through an uncurtained window).

2.3.3 Contraband-specific doctrine

A third doctrine the Court has developed in defining the scope of the Fourth Amendment looks at the type of information discovered in the search. In United States v. Place,[26] the police used a drug-sniffing dog to determine whether the defendant's luggage contained illegal drugs. The Court held that a search did not occur because the dog alerted only to the presence of contraband, not to any legitimate private fact, and thus did not compromise a protected interest. Citing Place, the Court subsequently held that police search of a package that merely replicates a search by a private party does not implicate the Fourth Amendment if the police have a "virtual certainty" that their subsequent examination will discover nothing of significance but contraband.[27] The logic of Place suggests that, if the government is able to develop a device that is contraband-specific—that is, one that detects only the presence of an illegal drug or weapon—it use would not be limited by the Fourth Amendment.

However, in Florida v. Jardines,[28] decided 30 years later, the Court was confronted with a dog sniff of drug odors emanating from a home, after police had brought the dog through the defendant's front yard to the front door. Consistent with Kyllo but seemingly contrary to Place, the Court held that this action constituted a search. Although the Court conceded that normal use of the path to the house would not be considered a trespass, it explained that the police behavior in Jardines went beyond the typical implicit license granted visitors: "To find a visitor knocking on the door is routine (even if sometimes unwelcome); to spot that same visitor exploring the front path with a metal detector, or marching his bloodhound into the garden before saying hello and asking permission, would inspire most of us to—well, call the police." Once again the specter of privacy-invading technology

26 462 U.S. 696 (1983).

27 United States v. Jacobsen, 466 U.S. 109 (1984).

28 569 U.S. 1 (2013).

appeared to be the reason the Court did not follow the logic of its earlier doctrine to its conclusion.

2.3.4 Assumption of risk/third party doctrine

The most controversial aspect of the Supreme Court's approach to the scope of the Fourth Amendment is usually called the third party doctrine, which rests on the idea that one does not have a reasonable expectation of privacy in information one surrenders to a third party, even if there is no intent to reveal it to the general public, because one assumes the risk the third party will disclose it to others. The Warren Court adopted this view in several cases involving informants.[29] The post-Warren Court took the concept much further when it held, in United States v. Miller,[30] that a bank depositor

> takes the risk, in revealing his affairs to another, that the information will be conveyed by that person to the government . . . even if the information is revealed on the assumption that it will be used only for a limited purpose and the confidence placed in the third party will not be betrayed.

Three years later, in Smith v. Maryland,[31] the Court similarly held that people lack a reasonable expectation of privacy in the phone numbers they dial because they know or should know that the numbers are recorded on a routine basis.

These decisions mean that the police can obtain bank and phone company information without any restrictions as far as the Fourth Amendment is concerned. The extension of the Warren Court's informant cases to institutions like banks and phone companies, which have a formal fiduciary duty to their patrons and which are essential to modern life, has been vigorously criticized.[32] Although Congress later enacted statutes requiring a subpoena before the government can obtain bank, phone, and various other types of records,[33] a subpoena is much more easily obtained than a warrant (see §§8.4.1; 8.7.4) and, as a result of Miller and Smith, not even a subpoena is constitutionally required.

---

29 Lewis v. United States, 385 U.S. 206 (1966); Hoffa v. United States, 385 U.S. 293 (1966).

30 425 U.S. 435 (1976).

31 442 U.S. 735 (1979).

32 See, e.g., Erin Murphy, The Case against the Case for the Third Party Doctrine: A Reply to Epstein and Kerr, 24 Berk. Tech. L.J. 1239 (2009).

33 Right to Financial Privacy Act, 12 U.S.C. §3401 (1978); Electronic Communications Privacy Act, 18 U.S.C. §§2703; 3121 (1986).

Cracks in the third party doctrine first appeared at the Supreme Court level in a case involving medical records,[34] but it took 40 years for the Court to seriously question Miller and Smith, once again in a case involving police use of technology. In Carpenter v. United States,[35] the Court held that a warrant is required to obtain cell-site location information from the defendant's common carrier, at least when, as in Carpenter, multiple locations on multiple days are involved. The government relied on Miller and especially Smith in arguing that the location data constituted a "business record" of the carrier that contained information knowingly surrendered by the defendant when he carried his cellphone. But the Court distinguished those cases on two grounds. First, the Court stated, there is "a world of difference" between the few bits of communication and financial data that the police obtained in *Smith* and *Miller* and "the exhaustive chronicle of location information casually collected by wireless carriers today." Second, "[c]ell phone location information is not truly 'shared' as one normally understands the term [because] cell phones and the services they provide are . . . indispensable to participation in modern society" and because "there is no way to avoid leaving behind a trail of location data." Accordingly, the five-member majority concluded, "in no meaningful sense does the user voluntarily 'assume[ ] the risk' of turning over a comprehensive dossier of his physical movements."

Whether Carpenter is the death knell for the third party doctrine remains to be seen. The Court emphasized that its holding did not necessarily apply to other surveillance techniques or business records. But the dissenting justices pointed out that the majority's statements about cell phone location information could also apply to the "indispensable" bank or phone records that, at present, Miller and Smith allow the government to obtain in any quantity without worrying about the Fourth Amendment.

2.4 Definition of seizure

The definition of seizure for Fourth Amendment purposes comes closer to the lay definition of that term than the Court's cases defining "search," but still differs in significant respects. Seizure of an item occurs when there is "some meaningful interference with an indi-

34 Ferguson v. City of Charleston, 532 U.S. 67 (2001).

35 138 S.Ct. 2206 (2018).

vidual's possessory interest,"[36] which can occur not only when police take the item, but when they destroy it (as in a drug test[37]) or change its nature (as by putting a GPS device on a car bumper, as occurred in Jones). In contrast, a seizure does not occur when the property the police confiscate is abandoned (as in cases involving examination of trash) or is obtained with the defendant's consent, even if the consent is obtained through fraud (as might occur in a situation involving an informant posing as a drug buyer).

A seizure of a person occurs when "a reasonable innocent person" would not feel free to "terminate the encounter."[38] Many people might feel that, once accosted by an officer, they are not free to leave. But, at least in the pedestrian context,[39] the Court has not adopted that position, on the ground that police should be able to conduct preliminary inquiries without triggering the Fourth Amendment.

Thus, in United States v. Mendenhall,[40] the opinion that attracted the most justices pronounced "extremely close" the question whether a seizure occurred when two plainclothes officers asked an airport passenger for her identification and ticket and queried her about her travel. And, according to the Supreme Court, a seizure definitely does not occur when police board a bus and ask people if they could search their luggage,[41] or when immigration authorities enter a factory and prevent workers from leaving without answering their questions,[42] in part, the Court explained, because the people police confronted in these cases would have wanted to stay where they were in any event. Nor did a seizure occur when the defendant "agreed" to accompany an officer to where his colleagues were being questioned by another officer.[43] Finally, the Court has held that no seizure occurs until some type of police-citizen confrontation has taken place, meaning that the Fourth Amendment is not implicated when police follow or chase the defendant.[44]

36 United States v. Jacobsen, 466 U.S. 109 (1984).

37 Id.

38 Florida v. Bostick, 501 U.S. 429 (1991).

39 An intentional stop of a car is always a seizure. Brendlin v. California, 551 U.S. 249 (2007).

40 446 U.S. 544 (1980).

41 Florida v. Bostick, 501 U.S. 429 (1991); United States v. Drayton, 536 U.S. 194 (2002).

42 I.N.S. v. Delgado, 466 U.S. 210 (1984).

43 Florida v. Rodriguez, 469 U.S. 1 (1984).

44 Michigan v. Chesternut, 486 U.S. 567 (1988); California v. Hodari D., 499 U.S. 621 (1991).

2.5 Requirements for a valid consent

Even a search or seizure carried out by a government agent is not governed by the Fourth Amendment if the defendant has voluntarily consented to the police action. As with seizures of the person, one might argue that people rarely feel free to refuse consent when an officer asks for it. To minimize such coercion, it has been argued that individuals should be told of their right to refuse consent, analogous to the requirement that suspects be told of their right to remain silent. But in Schneckloth v. Bustamonte,[45] the Supreme Court held that such a warning need not be given. Rather, the voluntariness of a consent to search is to be determined by evaluating the "totality of the circumstances," including the conduct of the police and the behavior of the defendant.

Early cases made clear that, if the police simply announce they are going to search or say they have authority to do so, any subsequent "consent" is involuntary.[46] More recent cases have involved more nuanced facts. In the Mendenhall case mentioned above, the defendant, a 22 year-old African-American woman, began shaking and mumbling incoherently after the agents identified themselves. However, because she followed them to a private room in the airport and said "Go ahead" when a policewoman there asked if she would consent to a search, the Court held the consent was voluntary, emphasizing that the defendant had twice been told she could decline. In Ohio v. Robinette,[47] the officer issued the defendant a traffic ticket and then stated: "One question before you get gone: are you carrying any illegal contraband in your car? Any weapons of any kind, drugs, anything like that?" When Robinette said no, the officer asked to search the car and Robinette consented. Although there was evidence that police had been trained to engage in this type of conduct as a way of increasing driver acquiescence to such requests, the Court found the consent to be voluntary and, following Schneckloth, rejected the lower court's holding that Robinette should have been told of his right to refuse.

In theory, the defendant can control the scope of a consent search. Thus, for instance, Robinette could have allowed the officer to search

45 412 U.S. 218 (1973).

46 Amos v. United States, 255 U.S. 313 (1921); Johnson v. United States, 333 U.S. 10 (1948); Bumper v. North Carolina, 391 U.S. 543 (1968).

47 519 U.S. 33 (1996).

the interior of the car but not the trunk. This type of scenario arose in Florida v. Jimeno,[48] where the defendant consented to search of his car and the officer found drugs in a folded, brown paper bag on the floorboard of the passenger side. Although the defendant objected that he had not consented to examination of closed containers within the car, the Court upheld the search; at the same time, it suggested that the result might have been different had the search instead been of a locked briefcase inside the car's trunk. Presumably, if an individual does refuse consent, or consents with restrictions on a search's scope, the police cannot use the refusal or restriction as a justification for further search.[49] Otherwise, the right to refuse consent would be useless.

2.6 Third party consent

Unlike most other criminal procedure rights such as the right to counsel or the right to remain silent, the right to privacy protected by the Fourth Amendment can be "waived" by a third party's voluntary consent. According to the Supreme Court's decision in United States v. Matlock,[50] anyone with "common authority" over an area may consent to its search. Common authority exists when "it is reasonable to recognize that any of the co-inhabitants has the right to permit the inspection in his own right and that the others have assumed the risk that one of their number might permit the common area to be searched." This language resonates with the third party search doctrine and the definition of search generally, because all of these bodies of law focus on when a person has a reasonable expectation of privacy in the area searched. It should be noted, however, that after Carpenter, discussed in §2.3.4, there is an open question whether an institution such as a common carrier, as distinguished from a person, can give a valid third party consent.

To date, all of the Supreme Court's third party consent cases have involved consent by a natural person. In Matlock, the defendant's girlfriend consented to search of the bedroom they shared, and the evidence found there was held to be admissible. That result can be justified on the ground that the girlfriend had as much right as Matlock to determine how mutually occupied premises are used. The same

48 500 U.S. 248 (1991).

49 Cf. State v. Zelinske, 779 P.2d 971 (N.M. 1989).

50 415 U.S. 164 (1974).

reasoning also supports the Court's earlier decisions holding that a landlord and a hotel clerk do not have authority to consent, respectively, to a tenant's apartment and a hotel patron's room.[51] In these cases the third party did not have mutual control over the premises searched.

More questionable are the results of two other Court decisions involving third party consent. In Illinois v. Rodriguez,[52] the defendant's ex-girlfriend consented to search of an apartment in which she no longer lived (although she still had a key to the apartment and kept some clothes there). The Court held that even if the ex-girlfriend did not have actual common authority over the apartment, her consent was valid if the officers "reasonably believed" she did; thus, the Court endorsed what is now called the apparent authority approach to third party consent. In contrast, in Georgia v. Randolph,[53] the defendant's estranged wife did have actual authority over the searched bedroom, but the Court held that her consent was trumped by the refusal of the defendant who, unlike Matlock and Rodriguez, was present at the time of the police request.

Although they arrive at opposing results, both cases seem antithetical to the privacy value that is at the core of Fourth Amendment protection. In Rodriguez, the Court held that a person who in fact has no privacy interest in a place may nonetheless consent to its search; in Randolph, it held that a person who does have a privacy interest in premises and wants to waive it may be ignored. At least in the latter situation, the Court subsequently backtracked. In Fernandez v. California,[54] the Court held that a refusal by a defendant to allow a search of an apartment for evidence of domestic abuse can be overridden by the consent of the alleged victim, if given after the defendant has been arrested and taken to the stationhouse.

The third party consent cases, like all of the cases delineating the Fourth Amendment's threshold, are an attempt to balance individual interests in privacy, autonomy, and dignity against the state's interest in detecting and solving crime. This analysis is sometimes cast as zero-sum: either a police action is governed by the Fourth Amendment and

51 Chapman v. United States, 365 U.S. 610 (1961); Stoner v. California, 376 U.S. 483 (1964).

52 497 U.S. 177 (1990).

53 547 U.S. 103 (2006).

54 571 U.S. 292 (2014).

requires a warrant based on probable cause, or it is not governed by the Fourth Amendment and is entirely unregulated by the Constitution. Yet an intermediate ground can exist. While the next chapter describes the benefits of the warrant and probable cause requirements, Chapter 4 will illustrate that the Fourth Amendment's reasonableness mandate can be implemented in many other ways.

3 The warrant and probable cause requirements

3.1 Why warrants are important

If government agents conduct a nonconsensual search or seizure, as described in the previous chapter, the Fourth Amendment is implicated and the conduct must be "reasonable." A search or seizure authorized by a valid warrant based on probable cause is almost always reasonable. Of course, as the next chapter details, the absence of a valid warrant does not necessarily make the police conduct unreasonable; in fact, the "vast majority" of searches and seizures are not authorized by a warrant.[1] However, when a police search or seizure is particularly intrusive, as with an arrest in or search of a home, a warrant tends to be required, because these are situations in which the Fourth Amendment's reasonableness standard should be most demanding.

The warrant is seen as the preeminent protection afforded by the amendment because, as Justice Robert Jackson put it, the warrant process ensures that the inferences that justify the search or seizure are "drawn by a neutral and detached magistrate" rather than "the officer engaged in the often competitive enterprise of ferreting out crime."[2] To obtain a warrant, an officer must prepare an application, a supporting affidavit, and often a draft of the warrant itself, and then submit the paperwork to a judge; although officers can find this process "burdensome, time-consuming, intimidating, frustrating, and confusing,"[3] they often seek help from prosecutors and, in most jurisdictions, can file the warrant telephonically, which reduces the effort and time required.[4] While a study of warrant practice in seven cities found that many

1 Richard Van Duizend, L. Paul Sutton and Charlotte A. Carter, The Search Warrant Process: Preconceptions, Perceptions and Practices 17 (National Center for State Courts, Williamsburg, Va. 1985).

2 Johnson v. United States, 333 U.S. 10 (1948).

3 Van Duizend et al., supra note 1, at 149.

4 See, e.g., Fed. R. Crim. P. 41(c)(2).

magistrates virtually rubberstamp police applications for warrants, it also found that police knowledge that judges will review their application heightens their "standard of care."[5] Additionally, requiring the police to justify their decision to a judge before they know what they will find, rather than after discovery of evidence of crime, reduces their ability to shape the account of why a search is justified, and ensures that the judge's decision will not be tainted by hindsight bias that might arise from knowledge that a search was successful.[6] Finally, the warrant reduces the potential for misunderstanding or abuse during its execution by informing the target of the search or seizure "of the lawful authority of the executing officer, his need to search, and the limits of his power to search."[7]

Accordingly, once one determines that the Fourth Amendment is triggered, the next obvious step is to determine whether a valid warrant has been obtained; if so, the Fourth Amendment inquiry is usually at an end. Recall that the Fourth Amendment states in part that "no Warrants shall issue, but upon probable cause, supported by Oath or affirmation, and particularly describing the place to be searched, and the person or things to be seized." Given the rationale and language of the Fourth Amendment, a warrant-based search must meet four requirements: (1) it must be issued by a neutral and detached magistrate; (2) it must be based on a probable cause belief, derived from facts provided under oath, that the person to be arrested or the place to be searched and the items to be seized are associated with wrongdoing; (3) it must state with particularity the place to be searched and the person or things to be seized; and (4) it must be executed in a reasonable manner. Except in the few situations noted at the end of this chapter, if police meet these requirements, the search or seizure will be constitutional. Note also that many of the issues discussed here—in particular, the definition of probable cause, the use of excessive force, and pretextual police actions—are also very relevant to the next chapter's discussion of searches conducted without a warrant.

5 Van Duizend et al., supra note 1, at 148–9.

6 William J. Stuntz, Warrants and Fourth Amendment Remedies, 77 Val. L. Rev. 881, 910–18 (1991).

7 United States v. Chadwick, 433 U.S. 1, 9 (1977).

3.2 Neutral and detached magistrate

Since the point of the warrant process is to ensure the warrant is based on findings by a judicial officer who is not directly engaged in the "often competitive enterprise of ferreting out crime," the Supreme Court has taken pains to ensure issuing magistrates are independent of law enforcement. For instance, warrants authorized by prosecutors and other executive branch officials, including the Attorney General of the United States, are invalid on their face[8] (in contrast to subpoenas and other lesser authorizations that can sometimes be issued by prosecutors, administrative officers, and law enforcement agents). In some cases, even judicial officers may not be sufficiently independent to issue warrants. For instance, the Court has found invalid warrants issued by a magistrate who accompanied the police to the search location to determine which items could be seized,[9] as well as warrants issued under a statute that provided unsalaried justices of the peace five dollars if they approved a warrant application but no compensation if they declined it.[10]

At the same time, if the issuing officer is sufficiently removed from law enforcement endeavors, legal training is not always necessary. In Shadwick v. City of Tampa,[11] the Court held that clerks of the Tampa municipal court could issue arrest warrants for violations of city ordinances, because they were appointed from a classified civil service list and operated under the supervision of the municipal court judge, not the executive branch. This holding means that non-lawyers, such as justices of the peace, may issue warrants, at least for certain types of crimes, a result that is consistent with the Court's flexible approach to the definition of probable cause.

3.3 Probable cause

Probable cause is the core justification for searches and seizures. It exists, according to the Supreme Court's decision in Brinegar v. United

8 Coolidge v. New Hampshire, 403 U.S. 443 (1971); United States v. U.S. Dist. Court for E. Dist. of Mich., S. Div., 407 U.S. 297 (1972).

9 Lo-Ji Sales, Inc. v. New York, 442 U.S. 319 (1979).

10 Connally v. Georgia, 429 U.S. 245 (1977).

11 407 U.S. 345 (1972).

States,[12] when there are "sufficient . . . reasonable trustworthy" facts and circumstances to lead a "prudent" person to believe an individual has committed a crime or that evidence of crime will be found in a particular location; the probable cause standard requires more than a "bare suspicion" but "less than evidence that would justify condemnation." On several other occasions, the Court has emphasized that the definition of probable cause is not meant to be "hypertechnical" but rather should be based on "commonsense."[13]

Probable cause is fruitfully distinguished from other justification standards recognized in the law. As Brinegar makes clear, probable cause contemplates something less than proof beyond a reasonable doubt—the proof that is required for "condemnation"—but is a more demanding standard than "bare suspicion," which is probably all that is needed to obtain a subpoena (an authorization that the Supreme Court once stated could be issued on "nothing more than official curiosity"[14]). Probable cause is also more demanding than another type of justification found in many Fourth Amendment cases: "reasonable suspicion." As described in §4.5, the latter formulation also requires something more than a "bare suspicion" or hunch but is insufficient to justify, as probable cause does, an arrest or search of a home; rather it authorizes only lesser actions such as investigative stops and frisks or patdowns. One way of thinking about Fourth Amendment requirements comes from a survey of 166 federal judges finding that, on average, they quantified probable cause at near a 45 percent level of certainty and reasonable suspicion at close to a 30 percent level of certainty.[15] However, these quantifications are only a heuristic; it would probably be a mistake to conclude from this type of study that the Constitution would have nothing to say about a policing regime in which, as a routine matter, half the people arrested and two-thirds of the people stopped turned out to be innocent of wrongdoing.

A few cases can provide the flavor of the Supreme Court's view on probable cause. While observing the defendant walk back and forth in front of a store looking in the window several times was an insufficient

12 338 U.S. 160 (1949).

13 United States v. Ventresca, 380 U.S. 102 (1965); Illinois v. Gates, 462 U.S. 213 (1983).

14 United States v. Morton Salt, 338 U.S. 632 (1950).

15 C.M.A. McCauliff, Burdens of Proof: Degrees of Belief, Quanta of Evidence, or Constitutional Guarantees?, 35 Vand. L. Rev. 1293, 1325 (1982).

basis for arrest and at most constituted reasonable suspicion,[16] seeing two strangers tiptoeing furtively down an apartment building hallway at 1:00 p.m. and then take flight when they heard a door slam clearly provided probable cause; according to the Court's decision in the latter case, "it is difficult to conceive of stronger grounds for an arrest, short of actual eyewitness observation of criminal activity."[17] While mere proximity to a person whom the police have probable cause to believe has engaged in crime is insufficient for an arrest,[18] probable cause exists when police come upon three people in a car containing cocaine and each person denies ownership of it, because "a reasonable officer could conclude" that each had committed the crime of cocaine possession either solely or jointly.[19] Finally, consider Florida v. Royer,[20] where the police detained the defendant in a small airport room because he fit the following elements of a "drug courier profile": he was carrying American Tourister luggage which appeared to be heavy; was young and casually dressed; appeared nervous and evasive; paid for his ticket with cash; did not write his full name and address on his luggage identification tags; and was departing from Miami, a major drug center, and destined for New York, a major drug distribution center; further the police determined that the name on the ticket was not Royer's. While ignoring the assertion that Royer fit a "profile," the Court agreed that these facts provided reasonable suspicion. But the majority refused to say that these facts amounted to probable cause: "We cannot . . . agree that every nervous young man paying cash for a ticket to New York City under an assumed name and carrying two heavy American Tourister bags may be arrested and held to answer for a serious felony charge."

Most of the caselaw defining probable cause has focused not on the quantity of suspicion associated with it, but on the quality or accuracy of the information that underlies the suspicion. For instance, in Aguilar v. Texas,[21] the affidavit swore that two police officers had received "reliable information from a credible person and do believe" that illegal narcotics were stored in Aguilar's house. If believed, this assertion clearly established probable cause; the question in Aguilar was whether the "credible person" to which the affidavit referred was in fact credible. Because

16 Terry v. Ohio, 392 U.S. 1 (1968).
17 Peters v. New York, 392 U.S. 40 (1968).
18 United States v. Di Re, 332 U.S. 581 (1948); Ybarra v. Illinois, 444 U.S. 85 (1979).
19 Maryland v. Pringle, 540 U.S. 366 (2003).
20 460 U.S. 491 (1983).
21 378 U.S. 108 (1964).

the affidavit was devoid of information about who the person was or how he or she obtained the information, the Supreme Court easily found the warrant invalid. More difficult was the decision in Spinelli v. United States,[22] where the affidavit stated: (1) that FBI agents had been informed by a "confidential reliable informant" that Spinelli was operating a gambling operation using two specific phone numbers; (2) that officers had tracked Spinelli to an apartment address associated with both numbers; and (3) that Spinelli had a reputation as a bookmaker and an associate of gamblers. In invalidating the warrant, the Court noted that the phone numbers "could easily have been obtained from an offhand remark heard at a neighborhood bar," that no facts backed up the allegations about the informant's reliability or Spinelli's reputation, and that the informant provided no detail about how he knew about the gambling operation. The Court contrasted this situation with the facts of Draper v. United States,[23] where the Court had held that probable cause existed to arrest Draper for possession of heroin when police corroborated a named informant's prediction of when the suspect would arrive in the Denver train station from Chicago, as well as the informant's description of the clothing the suspect would be wearing, which the informant had described with "minute particularity."

These Warren Court decisions established what became known as the two-pronged Aguilar-Spinelli test. That test required that warrant affidavits or applications establish: (1) sufficient underlying circumstances to permit the magistrate to determine how informants obtained their information; and (2) sufficient underlying circumstances establishing informant veracity. Both of these queries are usually easily answered when the warrant is based on observations by the affiant police, who are under oath, or on reports from other police or an identified, ordinary citizen.[24] They are more likely to raise an issue when the police are relying either on anonymous sources or on confidential informants whom they want to protect (and whose credibility is often suspect because of their involvement in crime, drug usage, or desire to trade information for immunity from arrest or conviction);[25]

22 393 U.S. 410 (1969).

23 358 U.S. 307 (1959).

24 See United States v. Ventresca, 380 U.S. 102 (1965) (police affiant); Whiteley v. Warden, 401 U.S. 560 (1971) (police bulletin); Jaben v. United States, 381 U.S. 214 (1965) (suspect's business associates).

25 See, e.g., Albright v. Oliver, 510 U.S. 266, 271 n. 3 (1994) (recounting one informant, addicted to cocaine, who "falsely implicated over 50 individuals in criminal activity, resulting each time in a dismissed prosecution").

combined, the latter two sources provide the basis for warrants in almost 90 percent of the cases in some jurisdictions, yet they are much less likely to be reliable.[26]

Nonetheless, in Illinois v. Gates,[27] a post-Warren Court decision, the Court decided to abandon the Aguilar-Spinelli rule and "reaffirm the totality of the circumstances analysis that traditionally has informed probable cause determinations." While Gates held that the inquiries raised by the two prongs of the Aguilar-Spinelli test are still relevant, "a deficiency in one may be compensated for, in determining the overall reliability of a tip, by a strong showing as to the other, or by some other indicia of reliability." Thus, in Gates, where the informant was anonymous, the fact that the veracity of the informant could not be directly ascertained was counterbalanced by the amount of detail the tip provided and the fact that police were able to corroborate much of what was in it. Other factors that are relevant in determining informant veracity include whether: the informant predicts activities that are later corroborated (suggesting, as in Draper, intimate knowledge of the suspect); the informant has provided reliable reports in the past; the informant's declarations subject the informant to criminal liability; and the police can substantiate that the suspect has a criminal reputation.[28]

The Court has emphasized on several occasions that the probable cause determination is an objective one, based on what a reasonable officer could have believed at the time of the search or seizure. Thus, an arrest of a different person than the one identified in the warrant,[29] an arrest for a non-existent crime when the facts also support an actual crime,[30] and the discovery that the basis for an executed warrant turned out to be false,[31] are not violations of the Fourth Amendment if the police beliefs were reasonable at the time of the search or seizure. The Court has even held that an arrest for actions that do not constitute any crime is permissible under the Fourth Amendment if the officer is reasonable in believing a crime occurred, over a dissent arguing that mistakes about the law can never be reasonable.[32]

---

26 Laurence A. Benner and Charles T. Samarkos, Searching for Narcotics in San Diego: Preliminary Findings from the San Diego Search Warrant Project, 36 Calif. West. L. Rev. 221 (2000).

27 462 U.S. 213 (1983).

28 See Draper, 358 U.S. 307 (1959); United States v. Harris, 403 U.S. 573 (1971).

29 Hill v. California, 401 U.S. 797 (1971).

30 Devenpeck v. Alford, 543 U.S. 146 (2004).

31 Franks v. Delaware, 438 U.S. 154 (1978).

32 Heien v. North Carolina, 574 U.S. 54 (2015).

3.4 Particularity

The Fourth Amendment requires not only probable cause to believe the requested search will discover evidence, but also probable cause with respect to both the nature of the evidence sought and where it will be found. As the Supreme Court stated in Maryland v. Garrison,[33]

> [b]y limiting the authorization to search to the specific area and things for which there is probable cause to search, the [particularity] requirement ensures that the search will be carefully tailored to its justifications, and will not take on the character of the wide-ranging exploratory searches the Framers intended to prohibit.

Further, this tailoring of the search's scope must appear on the face of the warrant. In Groh v. Ramirez,[34] the Court held invalid a warrant that did not list the items to be seized, even though the affidavit submitted by the police did list the items; without at least a cross-reference to the affidavit, the Court said, "we . . . cannot know whether the Magistrate was aware of the scope of the search he was authorizing." Such a warrant also fails to inform the target about the need for and the limits on the search.

The warrant's description of the place and object of the search must be accurate if officer discretion is to be limited. But the Court, again emphasizing that the Fourth Amendment only requires reasonableness, has concluded that an erroneous description does not violate the Fourth Amendment unless the requesting officers knew or should have known of the error.[35] Furthermore, the Court has upheld warrants containing fairly vague, open-ended descriptions of the object of the search. For instance, in Andresen v. Maryland,[36] a warrant authorizing search of the office of an attorney suspected of fraud listed a large number of specific items, but then ended with a reference to "books, records, documents, papers, memoranda and correspondence, showing or tending to show a fraudulent intent and/or knowledge as elements of the crime of false pretenses, in violation of [Maryland's false pretenses statute], *together with other fruits, instrumentalities and evidence of crime at this [time] unknown*" (emphasis added). In

33 480 U.S. 79 (1987).

34 540 U.S. 551 (2004).

35 Maryland v. Garrison, 480 U.S. 79 (1987).

36 427 U.S. 463 (1976).

Messerschmidt v. Millender,[37] the warrant authorized search of the Millenders' house for "all" weapons as well as "articles of evidence showing gang membership or affiliation" of the Millenders' foster child. Although the Andresen warrant gave the searching officers a considerable amount of discretion to look through virtually any files in Andresen's office, and the Millender warrant did not specify what a "weapon" is and authorized search of items (gang affiliation) that are not evidence of crime at all, the Court upheld both warrants.

In some jurisdictions, warrants routinely include language referring to "rent receipts, personal correspondence and effects, keys and other items that demonstrate dominion or control of the premises," even though ownership or control of the premises is not in dispute and not an element of the suspected crime.[38] The worry about such warrants is that they authorize, seemingly disingenuously, searches of places that police could not search based on their probable cause showing; for instance, such warrants might permit searches of file folders for evidence of "dominion or control of the premises" even when the primary focus of the search is a murder weapon. In short, as the next section explains, permitting such clauses in warrants encourages pretextual searches.

3.5 Execution rules

Securing a valid warrant does not end the matter. The warrant must also be executed in a valid manner. Numerous issues can arise in connection with the execution of a warrant, which are addressed here under the categories of procedural requirements, use of force rules, and plain view/pretext doctrine.

3.5.1 Procedural requirements

Either the Constitution or local rules require that police follow a number of procedures in carrying out searches or arrests pursuant to a warrant. To ensure that the probable cause on which the warrant is based does not go stale, courts have required that the search or arrest usually occur within a relatively short period of time after issuance.[39]

37 565 U.S. 535 (2012).

38 Benner and Samarkos, supra note 26.

39 See Sgro v. United States, 287 U.S. 206 (1932) (holding a delay of three weeks rendered search invalid).

Unless a special finding of extenuating circumstances is made, warrants must generally be executed during daylight hours or the evening, in an effort to minimize the insult to dignity and the fear and potential harm that might result from rousting a person out of bed in the middle of the night.[40] For the same types of reasons, and to prevent needless property damage, police should generally knock and announce their presence before entering,[41] although the Supreme Court has held that the police may enter immediately when they have a reasonable suspicion that evidence will be destroyed if they knock.[42]

During the search itself, police are required to keep an inventory of the items seized, which generally should be completed in the presence of the owner of the items or another occupant of the premises if the owner is not present.[43] Some countries *require* the presence of the resident or other non-governmental third parties to monitor the search.[44] Nothing akin to that is mandated in the United States; further, the Court has held, over a First Amendment challenge, that Fourth Amendment privacy is violated when police allow the media to accompany them on searches, unless the media is somehow directly involved in helping to execute the warrant.[45]

3.5.2 Excessive force

The Fourth Amendment protects both property and persons from unreasonable police force during searches and seizures. In dictum, the Supreme Court has stated that the amendment is violated both by "excessive force or restraints that cause unnecessary pain or are imposed for a prolonged and unnecessary period of time"[46] and by "unnecessary destruction of property ... even though the entry itself is lawful."[47] At the same time, some courts have given police considerable leeway in determining when use of force is reasonable. One lower court characterized as "frivolous" the claim that responding to an intruder call by slamming the (innocent) occupant of the house to

40 See Fed. R. Crim. P. 41(h).

41 Wilson v. Arkansas, 514 U.S. 927 (1995).

42 Richards v. Wisconsin, 520 U.S. 385 (1997).

43 Fed. R. Crim. P. 41(d).

44 Richard Frase, Comparative Criminal Justice as a Guide to American Law Reform: How Do the French Do It, How Can We Find Out, and Why Should We Care?, 78 Cal. L. Rev. 539, 580 (1990).

45 Wilson v. Layne, 526 U.S. 603 (1999).

46 City of Los Angeles, Calif. v. Rettele, 550 U.S. 609 (2007).

47 United States v. Ramirez, 523 U.S. 65 (1998).

the ground and handcuffing her for an hour was unreasonable.[48] The Supreme Court itself has found reasonable the use of a battering ram to break down the door of a person suspected of being a drug dealer, 15 to 20 seconds after police knocked and announced their presence.[49] More generally, it has emphasized that judgements about reasonableness "must embody allowance for the fact that police officers are often forced to make split-second judgments—in circumstances that are tense, uncertain, and rapidly evolving—about the amount of force that is necessary in a particular situation."[50]

The use of deadly force has been a particular focus of litigation for obvious reasons. In Tennessee v. Garner,[51] the Court held such force may not be used to seize a person unless it is necessary to prevent escape and the officer has probable cause to believe the suspect poses a significant threat of death or serious physical injury to the officer or others. In Garner itself the Court held the Fourth Amendment was violated by an officer who, in responding to a burglary call, shot the suspect in the back of the head as he was trying to jump a fence, even though the officer was "reasonably sure" the individual was unarmed. However, attentive to the difficult demands of law enforcement, the Court has refused to find officers liable under the Fourth Amendment in a number of cases involving deadly force, including where an officer shot a man in the back as he tried to drive away from her,[52] where officers engaging in a high speed chase rammed the suspect's rear bumper and caused the suspect to crash,[53] and where officers shot a person they knew was mentally ill who had threatened them with a knife.[54] In each of these cases, the Court held that the officers acted reasonably, in light of law established at the time (which, as described in more detail in §7.7, is the inquiry the Court pursues in determining whether officers have qualified immunity in constitutional damages actions).

3.5.3 Plain view doctrine and pretext

Assume, as in the Messerschmidt case described in §3.4, that the police have a valid warrant authorizing a search of a home for gang parapher-

48 Frunz v. City of Tacoma, 476 F.3d 661 (9th Cir. 2006).

49 United States v. Banks, 540 U.S. 31 (2003).

50 Graham v. Connor, 490 U.S. 386 (1989).

51 471 U.S. 1 (1985).

52 Brosseau v. Haugen, 543 U.S. 194 (2004).

53 Scott v. Harris, 550 U.S. 372 (2007).

54 City & Cty. of San Francisco, Calif. v. Sheehan, 135 S.Ct. 1765 (2015).

nalia and, while executing it, see a plastic sandwich bag full of a green leafy substance sitting on the living room coffee table. Or suppose that the police executing the warrant in Andresen come across a vial containing white powder while going through the lawyer's files. May police seize these items?

The Supreme Court's plain view doctrine seeks to answer that question. As originally formulated, in Coolidge v. New Hampshire,[55] the doctrine held that items not listed in a warrant may nonetheless be seized if: (1) they are found in an area the police have validly entered; (2) the criminal nature of the item is "immediately apparent"; and (3) discovery of the item is "inadvertent," meaning that the police did not suspect they would find the item at the time they applied for the warrant. The Court reasoned that a warrantless seizure under these circumstances should be allowed because

> [a]s against the minor peril to Fourth Amendment protections, there is a major gain in effective law enforcement. . . . [I]t would be a needless inconvenience, and sometimes dangerous—to the evidence or to the police themselves—to require them to ignore it until they have obtained a warrant particularly describing it.

Since Coolidge, the Court has significantly broadened the plain view doctrine. With respect to the first criterion, the Court has made clear that not only a warrant but any exception to the warrant requirement, as well as a valid consent, can provide the basis for the initial police intrusion.[56] With respect to the second criterion, the Court has stated that Coolidge's "immediately apparent" language "was very likely an unhappy choice of words" to the extent it required anything more than probable cause.[57] And the Court has eliminated the third criterion, on the ground that "scrupulous adherence to [the first two] requirements serves the interest in limiting the area and duration of the search [and] no additional Fourth Amendment interest is furthered by requiring that the discovery of evidence be inadvertent."[58] Thus, returning to the two examples based on Messerschmidt and Andresen, if the police have probable cause to believe that what they have discovered is illegal contraband, they may seize it, even if it is not

55 403 U.S. 443 (1973).

56 See, e.g., Texas v. Brown, 460 U.S. 730 (1983) (plain view seizure during roadblock stop).

57 Id.

58 Horton v. California, 496 U.S. 128 (1990).

described in the warrant and they in fact suspected or had a hunch it would be there.

The elimination of Coolidge's third criterion has been controversial. While it is true that the first two requirements ensure that the plain view doctrine does not expand the area subject to search or permit arbitrary seizures of items found there, they do not prevent the police from using a warrant or some other valid ground as a pretext for a fishing expedition concerning an entirely different crime. This concern is particularly salient in the context of traffic law enforcement. There are literally dozens of traffic laws—governing matters such as speeding, stopping, signaling, and turning; passing and lane violations; use of seatbelts and phones; and faulty brake lights and other equipment—that many people violate on a routine basis. Police do not, and in fact could not, issue citations for all such violations. But they can use them as pretexts to stop cars, ask questions, request consent, and see what they can find in plain view. Some commentators, noting the ubiquity of traffic laws and the power they give the police to confront citizens, have analogized traffic stops to the writs of assistance and general warrants that triggered the drafting of the Fourth Amendment.[59] Others claim, with significant supporting data, that race is often the precipitant of these stops.[60]

Nonetheless, in Whren v. United States,[61] the Court unanimously upheld the post-Coolidge version of the plain view doctrine, in a case involving discovery of drugs found in the possession of two African-American men whose car was stopped for failing to signal and for driving at a speed the police considered "unreasonable" (although within the speed limit). The Court's reasons for doing so were essentially pragmatic. To the general-warrant argument against pretextual traffic stops, the Court responded, "[w]e are aware of no principle that would allow us to decide at what point a code of law becomes so expansive and so commonly violated that infraction itself can no longer be the ordinary measure of lawfulness of enforcement." Furthermore, the Court stated, attempting to determine when an officer's discovery is

59 See, e.g., Barbara C. Salken, The General Warrant of the Twentieth Century? A Fourth Amendment Solution to Unchecked Discretion to Arrest for Traffic Offenses, 62 Temp. L.Q. 221 (1989).

60 David Harris, "Driving while Black" and All Other Traffic Offenses: The Supreme Court and Pretextual Traffic Stops, 87 J. Crim. L. & Criminol. 544 (1997).

61 517 U.S. 806 (1996).

based on a pretext rather than inadvertent would usually be a futile enterprise. The defendants in Whren disputed the latter point, at least on the facts of their case; they pointed out that the police who stopped them were plainclothes vice-squad officers who, under local regulations, were only permitted to enforce traffic laws in life-threatening situations, facts that strongly suggested they were after drugs, not traffic violations. But the Court iterated that "subjective intentions play no role in ordinary, probable cause Fourth Amendment analysis."

The Whren Court did intimate that, despite their subjective nature, pretext arguments might be heard if the defendant could show the police conduct was motivated by race, or if the pretextual search or seizure, while legitimate, involved a particularly intrusive act (such as use of deadly force or entry into a home without a warrant) or was not based on individualized suspicion (such as a random stop at a checkpoint). However, the Court's decisions addressing racial claims make evident that without strong proof of intentional discrimination the first type of claim is unlikely to prevail.[62] And while the Court has yet to address a case in which the other two claims have been made, pre-Whren cases suggest they likewise will be difficult to sustain. For instance, despite very strong evidence of bad faith, in Scott v. United States,[63] the Court found no Fourth Amendment violation when federal agents executing a surveillance warrant listened to the phone conversations of people they knew were not listed in the warrant and were not likely to make incriminating statements (which might be considered a particularly intrusive act). And in United States v. Villamonte-Marquez[64] the Court found no violation when customs agents, along with an ordinary police officer who apparently was acting on rumors of illegal smuggling, boarded a boat in international waters (conduct which, by statute, does not require individualized suspicion).

While pretext arguments will generally be to no avail, the plain view doctrine still has significant bite. In Ybarra v. Illinois,[65] the Court held that, although they were acting pursuant to a valid warrant authorizing search of a tavern and the tavern's bartender, the police violated the Fourth Amendment when they frisked Ybarra, a patron in the bar;

62 See generally, David Rudovsky, Litigating Civil Rights Cases to Reform Racially Biased Criminal Justice Practices, 39 Colum. Hum. Rts. L. Rev. 97 (2007).

63 436 U.S. 128 (1978).

64 462 U.S. 579 (1983).

65 444 U.S. 85 (1979).

applying the plain view doctrine's first criterion, the Court rejected the government's argument that the warrant authorized search of anyone found in the tavern. In Arizona v. Hicks,[66] police who had validly entered an apartment from which a shot had been fired examined the serial numbers of two sets of stereo equipment they found there; assuming the police lacked probable cause to believe the stereo sets were stolen, the Court found the second plain view criterion was not met and refused to water it down. Plain view doctrine has also played a role in searches of computers. For instance, a lower court found that a warrant authorizing search of a computer's files for "names, telephone numbers, ledger receipts, addresses and other documents pertaining to the sale and distribution of controlled substances" did not authorize opening files with a .jpg suffix (usually indicating a picture file) or with titles such as "teen" and "young," despite the fact that these files turned out to contain pornography.[67]

3.6 When a warrant is insufficient

A warrant issued by a neutral and detached magistrate, based on probable cause, describing the objects of the search or seizure with particularity and executed properly will usually ensure immunity from a Fourth Amendment claim. However, there are at least three situations in which more than a traditional warrant may be or is required. These involve search and seizure of very private papers, significant intrusions into the body, and most forms of electronic surveillance.

3.6.1 Private papers and mere evidence

Drawing heavily on eighteenth century English cases, the Supreme Court's 1886 decision in Boyd v. United States[68] essentially prohibited the seizure of private papers from the owner's home. The constitutional basis of its ruling, the Court stated, was twofold: a police search for papers, or a seizure of them through a court order, compelled a person to be "a witness against himself" in violation of the Fifth Amendment, which also made the government action unreasonable under the Fourth Amendment. But the real rationale for the decision appeared to be property-based. As the Court put it,

66 480 U.S. 321 (1987).

67 United States v. Carey, 172 F.3d 1268 (10th Cir. 1999).

68 116 U.S. 616 (1886).

> [t]he search for and seizure of stolen or forfeited goods, or goods liable to duties and concealed to avoid the payment thereof, are totally different things from a search for and seizure of a man's private books and papers for the purpose of obtaining information therein contained, [because in] the one case, the government is entitled to the possession of the property; in the other it is not.

Out of this language was born the distinction between, on the one hand, "fruits" of crime (e.g., stolen goods), "instrumentalities" of crime (e.g., the murder weapon or getaway car), and contraband (e.g., uncustomed goods, drugs) and, on the other hand, "mere evidence." According to Boyd, fruits, instrumentalities, and contraband could be seized with a valid warrant because the government could claim a legitimate property interest in them. But mere evidence, and in particular private papers, could never be seized; as the Court noted, even "the obnoxious writs of assistance . . . did not go so far as this." The exemption of mere evidence from even warrant-based seizure was affirmed 35 years later in Gouled v. United States,[69] which excluded contracts and attorney's bills seized by the government because they were items of only "evidential value," in which neither the government nor any other private citizen beside the defendant could assert a legal or possessory interest.

However, the Court slowly whittled away at this absolute prohibition, in a number of ways. Even before Gouled, it had held that, if authorized by valid process, the government could seize corporate papers, because of their quasi-public aspect and because corporations, unlike persons, do not have a right to remain silent;[70] as a practical matter, the Court was also undoubtedly influenced by the fact that a contrary holding would make regulation of corporations all but impossible. After Gouled it extended that ruling to virtually any records that are "regulatory in nature."[71] And in Warden v. Hayden,[72] it did away almost entirely with the mere evidence rule. It began by noting that, to avoid Gouled's prohibition, courts had contorted the definition of instrumentality beyond recognition (to include in Hayden, for instance, clothing worn by the defendant). But principally the Court relied on the conclusion that the language of the Fourth Amendment does not make distinctions

69 255 U.S. 298 (1921).

70 Hale v. Henkel, 201 U.S. 43 (1906).

71 Shapiro v. United States, 335 U.S. 1 (1948).

72 387 U.S. 294 (1967).

between types of property. At the same time, the Court reiterated the Fifth Amendment basis for prohibiting some seizures, by emphasizing that it did not mean to revoke protection of evidence that was "testimonial" in nature, given the Fifth Amendment's prohibition on compelling a person to be a self-incriminating "witness." Private papers, the Court implied, were testimony that were still exempt from search even when authorized by a warrant.

As recounted in more detail in §8.7.1, however, the Court eventually eliminated Fifth Amendment protection of the content of private papers as well, except under very narrow circumstances amounting to compelled fishing expeditions. The possibility that the First Amendment's protection of speech and thought poses an obstacle to searches of private papers also appears slim, given the Court's statement in New York v. P.J. Video, Inc.[73] that "an application for a warrant authorizing the seizure of material presumptively protected by the First Amendment should be evaluated under the same standard of probable cause used to review warrant applications generally."[74] Thus today, probably no type of evidence, regardless of how private it may be, is categorically exempt from government seizure. However, akin to rules governing bodily intrusions and electronic surveillance (discussed below), government efforts to obtain diaries and other items that express one's innermost thoughts may still require authorization beyond a traditional warrant.

3.6.2 Bodily intrusions

In 1957, three members of the Warren Court stated that "due process means at least that law-enforcement officers in their efforts to obtain evidence from persons suspected of crime must stop short of bruising the body, breaking skin, puncturing tissue or extracting body fluids, whether they contemplate doing it by force or by stealth."[75] That prohibition has never been adopted by the full Court. Indeed, the Warren Court itself later held, in Schmerber v. California,[76] that drawing blood from a driver to determine his alcohol content, if carried out reason-

73 475 U.S. 868 (1986).

74 See also, Zurcher v. Stanford Daily, 436 U.S. 547 (1978) (upholding search of newspaper offices for photos of a third party's criminal activity).

75 See Breithaupt v. Abram, 352 U.S. 432 (1957) (dissent by Chief Justice Warren, joined by Justices Black and Douglas).

76 384 U.S. 757 (1966).

ably and with probable cause, does not violate the Fourth Amendment even when conducted without a warrant.

However, the Court has also held that where the bodily intrusion is particularly significant, additional process beyond that required for an ordinary search and seizure may be required. In Winston v. Lee,[77] police wanted to compel Lee to undergo surgery to recover a bullet thought to be lodged in his collarbone. The Court unanimously prohibited the proposed surgery, and held that medical procedures of this type, especially when they require anesthesia, should take place only after a court has considered the extent to which the procedure threatens the health or safety of the individual and impinges upon the person's "dignitary interest in personal privacy and bodily integrity"; further, surgery may take place only if the sought-after evidence is necessary to "fairly and accurately" determine guilt. The strong suggestion in Lee that such surgery may take place only after an adversarial hearing—one in which the defense attorney is permitted to inquire into the medical procedures the state plans to use and whether the item sought is crucial to the government's case—obviously distinguishes this situation from the typical ex parte warrant process that does not require consideration of less intrusive alternatives.

3.6.3 Electronic surveillance

In Olmstead v. United States,[78] one of the cases recounted in §2.3 holding that tapping telephone lines outside the defendant's home was not a search, Justice Louis Brandeis wrote a dissenting opinion that not only disagreed with this conclusion, but argued that electronic surveillance should be banned entirely. To him, covertly listening to a person's phone conversations undermined "the right to be let alone—the most comprehensive of rights and the right most valued by civilized man." While the Court never adopted Brandeis' ultimate position, it did eventually partially endorse his concerns when it reversed Olmstead in Katz v. United States[79] and then signaled in Berger v. New York[80] that it would impose the full warrant process in such cases. Moreover, soon after Katz and Berger, Congress enacted Title III of the Omnibus

77 470 U.S. 753 (1985).

78 277 U.S. 438 (1928).

79 389 U.S. 347 (1967).

80 388 U.S. 41 (1967).

Crime Control and Safe Streets Act,[81] which has established that, at least as a statutory matter, electronic surveillance requires more than an ordinary warrant.

More specifically, with respect to each aspect of the warrant process—judicial involvement, the probable cause determination, the particularity requirement, and execution of the warrant—Title III, as it is usually called, created special rules that in effect invent a "super-warrant" meant to protect the privacy of communications. First, Title III warrants may only be issued by a judge with felony jurisdiction (which excludes justices of the peace) and only for specified offenses (all of them felonies). Second, the government must not only show probable cause to believe the surveillance will discover evidence of the offense, but also that "normal investigative procedures have been tried and failed or reasonably appear to be unlikely to succeed if tried or to be too dangerous." Third, the warrant must identify the target, the location of the intercept, and the type of communications to be intercepted. And fourth, the order "shall be executed as soon as practicable," state the period of time during which interception is authorized (which can be no longer than 30 days), and command that the interception "be conducted in such a way as to minimize the interception of communications not otherwise subject to interception." The government must also submit periodic reports to the judge. These are all more onerous requirements than those imposed on the typical warrant process. At the same time, they have not been particularly successful at limiting the number of people intercepted. During execution of the typical federal surveillance warrant, for instance, over 3000 interceptions occur, during which the conversations of well over 100 people are overheard, only about 20 percent of which disclose incriminating information.[82]

The original Title III enacted in 1968 only covered wire and oral communications. In 1986 Congress added the Electronic Communications Privacy Act (ECPA),[83] which applies the same requirements to interception of electronic mail, texts, and conversations on cellular phones. The key difference between the two laws is that, while Title III provides for exclusion even in some situations where the Fourth Amendment would not (e.g., failure to provide an inventory within ten days of trial

81 18 U.S.C. §§2510–20 (1968).

82 Administrative Office of the United States Courts, Wiretap Reports, accessed April 10, 2020 at https://www.uscourts.gov/statistics-reports/analysis-reports/wiretap-reports.

83 18 U.S.C. §2511(2)(a)(ii) (1986).

or failure to disclose to a judge communications not related to the offense being investigated), the ECPA relies solely on civil and criminal penalties in these situations. The ECPA also provides that the government need only obtain a lesser court order, akin to a subpoena, to obtain communications stored on a server for more than 180 days, "envelope" information about phone calls, texts, and emails, and various other types of non-content information.[84]

The foregoing discussion illustrates that certain types of government intrusions can be subject to special restrictions beyond those afforded by the warrant. Nonetheless, the notion that citizens are entitled to a sacrosanct zone of privacy or property immune from government intrusion—endorsed by the nineteenth century decision in Boyd and by several individual justices since then—appears to be dead, at least for all but minor infractions.[85] In his Olmstead dissent, Justice Brandeis worried that if the Court did not draw the line at electronic surveillance, government would eventually take advantage of "[a]dvances in the psychic and related sciences" that could "bring means of exploring unexpressed beliefs, thoughts and emotions." With the advent of functional magnetic resonance imaging (fMRIs) and other means of "reading" people's minds, such advances may soon come to fruition. If so, it will be wise to once again visit the question of whether an absolute zone of privacy should exist.

84 18 U.S.C. §2701 et seq.

85 See Welsh v. Wisconsin, 466 U.S. 740 (1984), discussed in §4.2.

4 Exceptions to the warrant and probable cause requirements

4.1 Overview

In Katz v. United States,[1] the Supreme Court stated that a warrant is required before every search or seizure, "subject only to a few specifically established and well-delineated exceptions." Since Katz, however, it has become clear that exceptions to the warrant and probable cause requirements are neither few nor well-delineated. The post-Warren Court has tended to focus on whether a search or seizure was reasonable, rather than on whether a warrant could or should have been obtained, and thus has tended to produce rulings that are case-specific rather than rule-oriented, with the result that neither a warrant nor probable cause is required in a large number of situations.

The oldest and most common reason given for forgoing a warrant is "exigency"—the concern that police or others will be harmed or that evidence will be destroyed if the police take the time to obtain a warrant. The most common reason given for permitting a search or seizure on less than probable cause is the perception that the action in question is relatively unintrusive. The modern tendency has been to define exigency broadly and intrusiveness narrowly. Other rationales for justifying particular exceptions to the warrant and probable cause standards include the minimal consequence of finding evidence of wrongdoing, the benign motives or lack of expertise of the enforcing government officials, the existence of other constraints that are thought to provide a sufficient substitute for a warrant, and, as the next section makes clear, tradition.

1 389 U.S. 347 (1967).

4.2 Arrests

Of all of the routine police actions that implicate the Fourth Amendment, a custodial arrest—an arrest that results in the police taking the individual into custody for booking—is the most significant. But while such an arrest must be based on probable cause to believe the person arrested has committed a crime, it need not be authorized by a warrant if it occurs outside the home. This was the long-standing common law rule developed in England before the Constitution was drafted, and the Supreme Court affirmed it as a matter of Fourth Amendment law in 1976, principally on historical grounds.[2] As a result, no specific exigency is needed to justify a warrantless arrest in public, although most states still follow the common law rule that limits warrantless misdemeanor arrests to cases where police directly observe the wrongdoing.

The common law rule with respect to arrests in the home is much less clear, with some authorities stating that, even here, traditionally a warrant was not necessary. But in Payton v. New York,[3] the Court held that, in the absence of exigent circumstances, a warrant is required for arrests in the arrestee's residence, because in no other place "is the zone of privacy more clearly defined than when bounded by the unambiguous physical dimensions of an individual's home," language that summarizes a common refrain in the Court's opinions. One year later the Court added that, if the arrest takes place in the home of a third party, not only is an arrest warrant required, but so is a search warrant authorizing entry into that residence, again assuming exigent circumstances are not present.[4]

The definition of exigency thus becomes crucial. As a general matter, the Court has said that a warrantless intrusion into the home, to make an arrest or otherwise, may be justified by "hot pursuit of a fleeing felon, or imminent destruction of evidence, . . . or the need to prevent a suspect's escape, or the risk of danger to the police or to other persons inside or outside the dwelling." Warden v. Hayden,[5] which upheld a warrantless arrest of Hayden in his home five minutes after police were told by reliable informants that he had committed armed robbery, is

2 United States v. Watson, 423 U.S. 411 (1976).

3 445 U.S. 573 (1980).

4 Steagald v. United States, 451 U.S. 204 (1981).

5 387 U.S. 294 (1967).

a good illustration of the hot pursuit scenario; the Court stressed that the officers had probable cause to believe both that Hayden had committed a crime and that he was in the home, and could also justly term their pursuit "hot." While an oft-cited 1970 lower court case, Dorman v. United States,[6] allowed warrantless entry four hours after the crime was discovered, that amount of delay may no longer be justifiable with the development of the telephonic warrant process; in other cases, the Supreme Court has signaled that, given the existence of that process, a delay of even 25 minutes may be overlong.[7]

One reason Dorman gave for its holding otherwise was that a serious crime was involved (armed robbery). While that fact might be relevant to whether police or others are in imminent danger, the relationship between the nature of the crime, by itself, and the ability to obtain a warrant is attenuated, something the Supreme Court seemed to recognize in Mincey v. Arizona,[8] where it rejected a stand-alone "homicide exception" to the warrant requirement in the absence of exigency. At the same time, the Court has held that, when minor, the nature of the crime can sometimes *prohibit* a warrantless search, even when there is exigency. In Welsh v. Wisconsin,[9] the police learned from a witness that Welsh, apparently inebriated, had abandoned his car. Fearing his blood alcohol would dissipate, they ascertained Welsh's address from the car registration and immediately went to his home, where they arrested him, less than an hour after he left the accident scene. The Court conceded that exigent circumstances may have existed but, consistent with the above-mentioned common law rule regarding misdemeanor arrests, held that warrantless entry into the home is simply not permitted when the police are investigating a "minor" crime; because driving while drunk was a civil infraction in Wisconsin at the time, police needed a warrant to pursue Welsh into his house. Although Welsh raises some difficult questions about when wrongdoing is "minor" (for instance, in most states, including Wisconsin today, drunk driving is, at the least, a serious misdemeanor), it sends the message that the zone of privacy in the home may still sometimes prevent the state from obtaining evidence in the absence of a warrant even when it can demonstrate both probable cause and exigency.

6 435 F.2d 385 (D.C. Cir. 1970).

7 Missouri v. McNeely, 569 U.S. 141 (2013).

8 437 U.S. 385 (1978).

9 466 U.S. 740 (1984).

In some cases, the police can be said to "create" the exigency, perhaps in an intentional effort to avoid the warrant requirement. But that possibility appears to be irrelevant to Fourth Amendment analysis. For instance, in United States v. Santana,[10] the police probably could have obtained a warrant after an undercover agent confirmed that Santana was selling drugs, but instead immediately went to her home and found her standing in the doorway; after they shouted "Police," she retreated into the house, where they arrested her. Although the exigencies of evidence destruction and escape were clearly present at the time of arrest, they would not have existed had the police instead gone to a magistrate. Similarly, in Kentucky v. King,[11] the police, instead of seeking a warrant after smelling the odor of marijuana emanating from King's apartment, shouted "Police," heard rustling noises behind King's door consistent with drug destruction, and made a warrantless entry. In both cases, the Court held that the police acted reasonably. Consistent with its pretext doctrine (see §3.5.3), the Court declared that if the police action, viewed in isolation and objectively, is lawful, the fact that there might be a hidden agenda is irrelevant.

4.3 Searches associated with arrest

Three types of warrantless searches can occur in connection with arrests. The first is defined by the aforementioned hot pursuit doctrine. In Warden v. Hayden,[12] the Supreme Court held that if police are legitimately inside a home in pursuit of a suspect, they may look not only anywhere the suspect might be but also may search for and seize any weapons the suspect might use. Further, if in the course of these searches they come across other evidence of crime, they can seize it under the plain view doctrine (see §3.5.3). Thus, in Hayden, the Court held admissible clothing found in a washing machine while officers were searching the house for Hayden.

Once the suspect is found, of course, the pursuit is over and the hot pursuit basis for a warrantless search disappears. However, at this point search incident to arrest doctrine kicks in. To protect the police and to ensure evidence is not destroyed, the common law long permitted warrantless search of the arrestee at the time of arrest, and the

10 427 U.S. 38 (1976).

11 563 U.S. 452 (2011).

12 387 U.S. 294 (1967).

Supreme Court has upheld this rule as reasonable under the Fourth Amendment. Specifically, the Court's caselaw authorizes police who have made a valid custodial arrest to search the clothing and the area within the "armspan" of the arrestee for weapons and evidence,[13] as well as the "immediately adjoining area" for possible confederates.[14]

Several aspects of search incident doctrine limit its reach. The arrest must be based on probable cause and, when required (as with non-exigent arrests in the home), a warrant. Further, probable cause must precede the search; for obvious reasons, the search cannot provide the basis for the arrest.[15] Additionally, the arrest must be custodial;[16] the protective rationale undergirding search incident doctrine does not apply if the officer is comfortable issuing a citation and allowing the individual to go on his or her way.

However, a number of other rules expand the reach of search incident doctrine. First, the Court has made clear that the determination of when police may take an arrestee into custody is purely a matter of local law and officer discretion; thus, in Atwater v. Lago Vista,[17] the Court upheld the custodial arrest of a woman for violating the jurisdiction's seat belt law despite the apparent lack of justification for such a serious intervention. The Court reasoned that a rule forbidding custodial arrest in minor cases, such as those involving traffic infractions, "would come at the price of a systemic disincentive to arrest in situation where . . . arresting would serve an important societal interest," such as assuring that an out-of-state driver will pay a fine or that drugs discovered can be weighed to determine if jail time is warranted. Further, while an arrest must be based on pre-existing probable cause, the search incident to it need not be; under the Court's rules, police may conduct an immediate post-arrest search regardless of whether they think evidence or confederates will be found in adjoining areas. Finally, given the above-described rules about the scope of a search incident, police can examine areas of the home (or car) that otherwise would ordinarily be off-limits without a search warrant, especially if the terms "armspan" and "immediately adjoining" are interpreted generously.

13 Chimel v. California, 395 U.S. 752 (1969).

14 Maryland v. Buie, 494 U.S. 325 (1990).

15 Although the Court has also held that the search can precede the formal arrest, as long as probable cause to arrest exists at the time of arrest. Cupp v. Murphy, 412 U.S. 291 (1973).

16 Knowles v. Iowa, 525 U.S. 113 (1998).

17 532 U.S. 318 (2001).

With the aim of reducing search incident authority, some jurists have suggested that, once the arrested person has been handcuffed, automatic protective searches should not be permitted.[18] Some state courts also have rejected broad application of these rules as a matter of state constitutional law, on the ground that arrests for certain minor crimes, such as traffic offenses, usually do not raise concerns about either danger or evidence destruction once arrest has taken place.[19] These types of rules might also deter pretextual use of arrests for minor crimes, now that Atwater has authorized custodial arrests for such crimes. But the Supreme Court has opted for a bright-line rule giving the police maximum discretion, noting that "[a] police officer's determination as to how and where to search the person of a suspect whom he has arrested is necessarily a quick ad hoc judgment which the Fourth Amendment does not require to be broken down in each instance into an analysis of each step of the search."[20]

Nonetheless, perhaps cognizant of the considerations just mentioned, the Court has limited the scope of a search incident to arrest in two specific instances. Most importantly, in Riley v. California,[21] a unanimous Court held that a warrant is needed to search the cellphone of an arrested person, absent real exigency (such as when, for instance, information on the phone is necessary to catch a fleeing co-felon, or there is a strong likelihood that unpreventable remote wiping of the phone contents will occur). The Court refused to equate search of a phone with other searches of an arrestee's personal belongings: "That is like saying a ride on horseback is materially indistinguishable from a flight to the moon. . . . Modern cell phones, as a category, implicate privacy concerns far beyond those implicated by the search of a cigarette pack, a wallet, or a purse." In a similar vein, in Birchfield v. North Dakota,[22] the Court held that a warrantless blood test after arrest on driving-while-intoxicated charges violated the Fourth Amendment (although it also permitted warrantless breathalyzer testing, on the ground it was less intrusive than a blood test).

Outside of these two circumstances, police need not have any level of suspicion beyond the cause needed to arrest before they carry out

18 United States v. Perdoma, 631 F.3d 745, 757 (8th Cir. 2010) (Bye, J., dissenting).

19 See, e.g., Zehrung v. States, 569 P.2d 189 (Alaska 1977); People v. Clyne, 541 P.2d 71 (Colo. 1975).

20 United States v. Robinson, 414 U.S. 218 (1973).

21 573 U.S. 373 (2014).

22 136 S.Ct. 2160 (2016).

warrantless searches of the arrested person and adjoining area. Further, if police do have some degree of suspicion, warrantless searches of even greater scope are permitted. Various decisions from the Court suggest that if officers making an arrest in or near the home have probable cause to believe evidence is in the house and that it might disappear during the time it would take to obtain a warrant, they may conduct a warrantless search;[23] at the least, they may secure the premises pending arrival of a warrant.[24] Additionally, in Maryland v. Buie,[25] the Court held that mere reasonable suspicion that confederates are in the home authorizes a protective sweep of the entire house, not just the area adjoining the arrestee. Finally if, after arresting a car's occupants, police have "reason to believe" evidence of the offense of arrest will be discovered in the car, they may search it, per Arizona v. Gant.[26] Whether the Court thinks that "reason to believe" is the same as probable cause, equivalent to reasonable suspicion, or something in-between is not yet clear. In any event, all of these decisions broaden the scope of warrantless searches incident to arrest.

The third type of warrantless search associated with arrests, after hot pursuit and search incident searches, is governed by inventory search doctrine. Inventory searches of personal belongings are conducted by jail personnel after an arrestee has been taken to the stationhouse and booked and a decision has been made to detain the person. These searches are not based on individualized suspicion, but rather are conducted pursuant to policies that apply to every arrestee. Thus these searches, and the related post-arrest practices of inventories of impounded cars, buccal swabs for DNA, and strip searches for contraband and weapons, are discussed in §4.8.4, which focuses on suspicionless searches and seizures.

4.4 Vehicle searches not associated with arrest

If search of a car takes place after an arrest, then search incident or inventory doctrine likely applies. However, sometimes police search a vehicle that has no occupants. Or they may want to search to see if the

---

23 See, e.g., Segura v. United States, 468 U.S. 796 (1984); Richards v. Wisconsin, 520 U.S. 385 (1997); Washington v. Chrisman, 455 U.S. 1 (1982). But see Vale v. Louisiana, 399 U.S. 30 (1970).

24 Illinois v. McArthur, 531 U.S. 326 (2001).

25 494 U.S. 325 (1990).

26 556 U.S. 332 (2009).

car contains evidence that would justify an arrest or impoundment. In these situations, for reasons explained above, search incident doctrine does not authorize a warrantless search.

In Carroll v. United States[27] the Supreme Court held that a warrantless search of a vehicle is permitted independently of any grounds for arrest, if the vehicle is mobile and the police have probable cause to believe evidence will be found in it. Later cases explained that the rationale for this holding is not only the vehicle's mobility, which arguably creates exigency obviating a warrant, but also the lesser expectation of privacy associated with cars, which are subject to more significant regulation and are more exposed to public view than homes.[28] Both of these rationales can be questioned. Cars can be seized pending a warrant rather than subject to immediate search, and of course, trunks, glove compartments, and various other parts of the car are not in plain view.

However, primarily because it has concluded that cars are not entitled to as much protection as houses, the Court has not only given the police the option of conducting a warrantless search of the car in the field when the criteria of Carroll are met, but has also allowed them to seize the car and conduct a warrantless search at the station, even when there is time to get a warrant.[29] This search allows examination of any part of the car for which there is probable cause (as illustrated by Carroll itself, where the police tore up the car's upholstery). The Court has also permitted warrantless searches of mobile homes and boats,[30] even when they are functioning as a home, on the continued assumption that they are mobile and associated with a lesser expectation of privacy than stationary houses. Finally, it has allowed warrantless search of luggage and any other items in the vehicle for which probable cause to search exists, despite the fact they too can be seized and held pending a warrant.[31]

Cars and their contents are not entirely unprotected by the warrant requirement, however. If the vehicle is on the curtilage of the owner's home then, the Court held in Collins v. Virginia,[32] police need a warrant

27 267 U.S. 132 (1925).

28 See, e.g., United States v. Chadwick, 433 U.S. 1 (1977).

29 Chambers v. Maroney, 399 U.S. 42 (1970).

30 California v. Carney, 471 U.S. 386 (1985) (mobile home); United States v. Lee, 274 U.S. 559 (1927) (boat).

31 United States v. Ross, 456 U.S. 798 (1982).

32 138 S.Ct. 1663 (2018).

in the absence of actual exigency. In other words, if the car is part of the house, it is treated like one. For a similar reason, given Riley, a cellphone found in a car might be treated differently than other items.

4.5 Stop and frisk and other seizures short of arrest

Every doctrine discussed to this point—involving arrest, hot pursuit, search incident and vehicle searches—requires probable cause, at least as a threshold matter. For many years, the Supreme Court refused to recognize any lesser justification under the Fourth Amendment. As the Court stated in Henry v. United States,[33]

> as the early American decisions both before and immediately after [the Fourth Amendment's] adoption show, common rumor or report, suspicion, or even "strong reason to suspect" was not adequate to support a warrant for arrest . . . The infringement on personal liberty of any "seizure" of a person can only be "reasonable" under the Fourth Amendment if we require the police to possess "probable cause" before they seize him. . . .

Yet in Terry v. Ohio,[34] the Court held that a seizure necessary to conduct inquiries and a patdown of the seized person's outer clothing—colloquially known as a "stop and frisk"—can be based on "reasonable suspicion," which previous discussion has made clear is a less demanding standard than probable cause. Reasonable suspicion requires that the police officer "be able to point to specific and articulable facts which, taken together with rational inferences from those facts, reasonably warrant [the] intrusion." While this language is difficult to distinguish from the definition of probable cause, on the facts of Terry it permitted the officer to stop and frisk two individuals whose actions—which amounted to repeatedly walking back and forth in front of a store, looking in its windows, and conferring with a third individual—would not have justified an arrest. Rather than treating probable cause as the monolithic Fourth Amendment standard, the Court opined that the justification necessary for a search or seizure should depend on "balancing the need to search [or seize] against the invasion which the search [or seizure] entails." Since the "invasion" occasioned by a stop and frisk is not as significant as the intrusion associated with an arrest and full search of the person, it need not be based on probable cause

33 361 U.S. 98 (1959).

34 392 U.S. 1 (1968).

but rather can take place if the less demanding standard of reasonable suspicion is met.

The holding in Terry surprised many because it came from the Warren Court, whose decisions tended to expand criminal procedure rights and limit police discretion. Perhaps the Court felt that requiring probable cause for all seizures would generate too much pressure to declare that police conduct of the type involved in Terry is not a seizure at all, leaving it unregulated by the Fourth Amendment. The Court might also have wanted to avoid creating incentives for legislatures to enact low-level crimes, such as vagrancy and loitering laws, for which probable cause is easily established and which would vastly increase police discretion to arrest and conduct searches incident thereto. Furthermore, one can make the argument that when prevention of harm is the goal, as is often the case with a stop and frisk, less justification for action is necessary than when the harm has already occurred, a rationale that underlies the automatic searches allowed after an arrest, for instance.

Nonetheless, Terry's balancing test has been subject to intense criticism. The Court could have retained the probable cause standard and held that the officer in Terry did have probable cause—not to arrest but to question Terry and his colleagues. And it has had no difficulty finding vagrancy laws unconstitutional on vagueness grounds, precisely because they give police too much discretion to stop people who are dawdling, sauntering, or simply conferring with others.[35] Most importantly, it is argued, Terry's balancing analysis makes it too easy for courts faced with arguments about the need for public protection to abandon probable cause and opt for reasonable suspicion or some other lesser standard as the compromise, a dynamic that, as detailed throughout the rest of this chapter, appears to be at work in many of the Court's later decisions.[36]

More specific to Terry, the argument is made that the reasonable suspicion standard gives police too much discretion on the street, thereby increasing the potential for arbitrary and racially discriminatory conduct that, as Terry itself recognized, can exacerbate community-police tensions and decrease willingness to cooperate with the authorities.

---

35 See, e.g., Chicago v. Morales, 527 U.S. 41 (1999); Kolender v. Lawson, 461 U.S. 352 (1983).

36 See Scott Sundby, A Return to Fourth Amendment Basics: Undoing the Mischief of Camara and Terry, 72 Minn. L. Rev. 383 (1988).

Data suggests that, at least in some cities, less than 5 percent of stops result in the discovery of weapons or contraband (a number that can be compared to the 30 percent level of certainty judges assign to reasonable suspicion) and that people of color are significantly more likely to be stopped even when other relevant factors are taken into account.[37]

The first question that must be addressed in applying the Terry balancing test is whether the police action is a seizure or a search and, if so, whether the police action amounts to an arrest or the type of full search that requires probable cause. As previous discussion has made clear, if the investigative action is not a "seizure," then the Fourth Amendment does not apply, whereas if the action is an arrest or full search, then the balancing test is inapposite and probable cause is required. The Supreme Court has confronted a number of situations which it concluded fit in neither category, and thus trigger Terry's balancing analysis. The following discussion examines these in-between cases, starting with a more detailed look at stop and frisk doctrine.

4.5.1 Stop and frisk

As §2.4 indicated, a brief detention for the purpose of asking questions is not a seizure. But a brief detention accompanied by a frisk certainly is, as is a nonconsensual restraint of freedom that lasts more than a few minutes, as is any intentional stop of a car.[38] If the detention is focused on a particular person or car (as opposed, for instance, to a detention at a roadblock where multiple people are stopped, as discussed in §4.8.2), it must be justified by at least reasonable suspicion.

While the reasonable suspicion standard is lower than probable cause, it requires more than a hunch. Thus, according to the Supreme Court, a stop of a car in the absence of any traffic or equipment violation or any other suspicious behavior violates the Fourth Amendment.[39] Further, reasonable suspicion does not arise from the "mere act of talking to a number of known addicts,"[40] or from the sole fact that a car near the border is occupied by persons of Mexican ancestry.[41] Nor does

37 See Floyd v. City of New York, 861 F.Supp.2d 274 (S.D.N.Y. 2012) (recounting data and its impact).

38 Brendlin v. California, 551 U.S. 249 (2007).

39 Delaware v. Prouse, 440 U.S. 648 (1979).

40 Sibron v. New York, 392 U.S. 40 (1968).

41 United States v. Brignoni-Ponce, 422 U.S. 873 (1975).

it exist when a person walks quickly away from another individual as the police come upon the scene, even in a "high drug problem area,"[42] or when a person gets off a plane from Ft. Lauderdale (a supposed drug source) with no luggage other than shoulder bag, appears to make efforts to conceal he is traveling with someone else, and occasionally looks back at that person.[43] In contrast, reasonable suspicion is present when a person runs from police in a "high crime" area,[44] and when a person purchases two 48-hour roundtrip tickets from Honolulu to Miami with cash from a large roll of bills and gives the ticket agent a false phone number.[45] It also exists when the driver of a van on a dirt road near the border, one that is often used for smuggling, slows at the sight of an agent but fails to acknowledge his presence, and the children in the van wave "oddly" and sit with their knees raised as if resting on something.[46] On the one hand, the Court has been cautious about finding reasonable suspicion in circumstances that "describe a very large category of presumably innocent [people],"[47] and has also been very leery of formal "profiles." On the other hand, it has been willing to consider "the modes or patterns of operation of certain kinds of lawbreakers," as interpreted by "those versed in the field of law enforcement" as opposed to "library analysis by scholars."[48]

As with probable cause, the quality as well as the quantity of information considered by the police is intrinsic to the analysis of reasonable suspicion. The Court has held that police did not have reasonable suspicion based simply on an anonymous phone call stating that a young black male standing at a particular bus stop and wearing a plaid shirt was carrying a gun.[49] But it did exist when information that a person was carrying a gun in his waistband came from an informant who had informed in the past (even when he did not provide the basis for his information),[50] when an anonymous informant correctly identified the car and route of a person he said was carrying drugs (but incorrectly stated the person would be carrying the drugs in a brief case),[51] and

42 Brown v. Texas, 443 U.S. 47 (1979).
43 Reid v. Georgia, 448 U.S. 438 (1980).
44 Illinois v. Wardlow, 528 U.S. 119 (2000).
45 United States v. Sokolow, 490 U.S 1 (1989). See also §3.3 (defining probable cause).
46 United States v. Arvizu, 534 U.S. 266 (2002).
47 Reid v. Georgia, 448 U.S. 438 (1980).
48 United States v. Arvizu, 534 U.S. 266 (2002).
49 Florida v. J.L., 529 U.S. 266 (2000).
50 Adams v. Williams, 407 U.S. 143 (1972).
51 Alabama v. White, 496 U.S. 325 (1990).

when an anonymous 911 caller stated that the defendant had run her off the road (even though police responding to the call observed no erratic driving by the defendant for the five minutes they followed him).[52] These latter cases signal that even the relatively low level of informant reliability required for probable cause may not be required for reasonable suspicion.

In at least one circumstance, reasonable suspicion can authorize not just a stop but an arrest. In Hiibel v. Nevada Dist. Ct.,[53] Hiibel was arrested under a statute that criminalized failing to identify oneself when police have reasonable suspicion to believe a crime is being or has been committed. The Court earlier had held that the Fifth Amendment's guarantee of the right to remain silent prevents states from criminally penalizing a failure to identify oneself, standing alone.[54] But when a failure to identify is combined with reasonable suspicion of wrongdoing (in Hiibel, an alleged domestic dispute), arrest is permissible, at least where "the officer's request [for identity is] a commonsense inquiry, not an effort to obtain an arrest for failure to identify after a Terry stop yielded insufficient evidence," and where the person's name does not provide police with "a link in the chain of evidence needed to convict the individual of a separate offense."

Terry also held that, once legitimately stopped, a person may be subject to a frisk if, after inquiries, reasonable suspicion develops that the person is armed and dangerous. In Sibron v. New York,[55] the Court hinted that conducting a frisk merely to obtain drugs, rather than a weapon, is impermissible, because there is no danger to the police and there is not yet grounds for arrest. However, in Minnesota v. Dickerson,[56] the Court permitted a frisk simply on the ground that the person walked away from the police after coming out of a crack house that had previously been associated with drug crimes. Most lower courts hold that, for all but minor crimes, if police have grounds for a stop on suspicion of a felony, they almost always have grounds for a frisk, on the not unreasonable ground that some risk to the police is usually present in such confrontations.[57]

52 Navarette v. California, 572 U.S. 393 (2014).
53 542 U.S. 177 (2004).
54 Brown v. Texas, 443 U.S. 47 (1979).
55 392 U.S. 40 (1968).
56 508 U.S. 366 (1993).
57 David Harris, Frisking Every Suspect: The Withering of Terry, 28 U.C. Davis L. Rev. 1 (1994).

In practice, a police frisk can be quite intrusive, involving moving hands over the entire body, including up and down the legs; further, in the context of car stops, the Court has permitted a search well beyond a patdown, to include anyplace within a (very generous) armspan of the suspect.[58] But going through items inside the clothing is technically prohibited unless a weapon or contraband is detected. In Dickerson, the Court held that, although the frisk was permissible, "manipulating" the contents of Dickerson's pocket in the absence of probable cause was impermissible. In effect, analogous to the "plain view" doctrine, the Court established a "plain feel" doctrine that prohibits intrusion beyond a patdown unless the patdown, by itself, gives the police probable cause to believe the item felt is a seizable item.

4.5.2 Seizures that exceed a stop

Many Supreme Court cases involve seizures that clearly exceed a stop, but still do not amount to a formal arrest. In some of these cases, the Court has held that the police conduct was the functional equivalent of arrest and required probable cause. In United States v. Place,[59] for instance, a 90-minute detention of Place's luggage and concomitant "disruption of his travel plans" for that period of time was found unconstitutional because the police only had reasonable suspicion, not probable cause. In Dunaway v. New York,[60] the police asked Dunaway to come to the station and did not put him in handcuffs, but the Court nonetheless held that interrogating him for an hour after giving him Miranda warnings required probable cause. Similarly in Florida v. Royer,[61] the functional equivalent of arrest occurred when Royer was taken from an airport concourse to a small room some 40 feet away and asked if his bags could be searched, despite the fact that the encounter lasted only 15 minutes.

Royer is profitably compared to United States v. Sharpe,[62] where a police officer and a Drug Enforcement Administration (DEA) agent, in separate cars, attempted to pull over two cars suspected of carrying drugs; the DEA agent was able to stop one car almost immediately, but the second car, driven evasively, could not be pulled over by the

---

58 Michigan v. Long, 463 U.S. 1032 (1983).

59 462 U.S. 696 (1983).

60 442 U.S. 200 (1979).

61 460 U.S. 491 (1983).

62 470 U.S. 675 (1985).

other officer until a half-mile down the road. The Court held that detaining the second suspect for 20 minutes while waiting for the more experienced DEA agent was not an arrest, but only a stop requiring reasonable suspicion. The Court also stressed, however, that the officers "acted diligently" and that the "suspect's actions contribute[d] to the added delay," suggesting that if these two factors had not been in play, a 20-minute detention solely on reasonable suspicion would violate the Fourth Amendment; the fact that the detention took place in public rather than in a closed room may also distinguish the case from Royer.

Other cases where the Court has approved prolonged seizures on less than probable cause involved multiple-hour detentions of occupants of homes being searched pursuant to search warrants,[63] and a two-hour detention of a defendant in a home in which he had been staying while police, who already had an arrest warrant for another occupant of the house, went to get a search warrant;[64] in these cases, the Court reasoned that, given the warrants, the police had something more than reasonable suspicion and thus could conduct a seizure that was more invasive than a stop but not as invasive as a custodial arrest. More dramatically, the Court has held that mere reasonable suspicion can justify a 16-hour detention of a person trying to enter the country[65] (a case discussed further in §4.9 in connection with the special circumstances of border searches), and has suggested that reasonable suspicion is sufficient to hold a person as a "material witness" for 16 days[66] (a case described further in §8.3.3, on material witness statutes). In all of these decisions, the Court applied Terry's test "balancing the need to seize against the invasion which the seizure entails."

4.5.3 Seizures that do not amount to a stop

At the other end of the spectrum are police seizures that do not require even reasonable suspicion, because their invasiveness is perceived to be minimal. Thus, the seizure effected by ordering the driver of a stopped vehicle out of the car, even in the absence of

63 Michigan v. Summers, 452 U.S. 692 (1981); Muehler v. Mena, 544 U.S. 93 (2005). Compare Rawlings v. Kentucky, 448 U.S. 98 (1980) (where detention occurred during execution of an arrest warrant for someone else).

64 Illinois v. McArthur, 531 U.S. 326 (2001).

65 United States v. Montoya de Hernandez, 473 U.S. 531 (1985).

66 Ashcroft v. al-Kidd, 563 U.S. 731 (2011).

individualized suspicion of danger, is permissible because it is de minimis,[67] as is ordering a passenger out of the car.[68] And the Court has also permitted the police to conduct inquiries beyond those related to a traffic stop in the absence of reasonable suspicion of any other wrongdoing, as long as the inquiries do not "measurably extend the duration of the stop."[69] These cases can be compared to Rodriguez v. United States,[70] where the Court held that, after the police completed "duties incident to a traffic stop" (which the Court indicated included checking for outstanding warrants), continued detention lasting seven to eight minutes while waiting for a drug dog was not justified. Checkpoints and roadblocks can also involve seizures of car occupants on less than reasonable suspicion, but they are more usefully described in connection with seizures and searches of groups (see §4.8.2).

4.6 Caretaker searches

Police often carry out functions that have nothing to do with capturing criminals or discovering evidence of crime, but rather are aimed at helping members of the community, responding to emergencies, or carrying out other statutory duties. As the Supreme Court stated in Cady v. Dombrowski,[71] police "frequently . . . engage in what, for want of a better term, may be described as community caretaking functions, totally divorced from the detection, investigation, or acquisition of evidence relating to violation of a criminal statute." For instance, they investigate car accidents, respond to 911 calls or complaints about loud music, and serve subpoenas and child protective orders. In the course of doing so they may see evidence of crime in plain view.

Generally, the courts have found this evidence admissible, so long as the caretaking function the police were undertaking at the time was lawful. In Cady, police looking in a car for the revolver of another officer who had been involved in a car accident came upon evidence eventually connected with a murder. The Court held that the evidence was admissible because the officers had reasonably been carrying out

67 Pennsylvania v. Mimms, 434 U.S. 106 (1977).

68 Maryland v. Wilson, 519 U.S. 408 (1997).

69 Ohio v. Robinette, 519 U.S. 33 (1996); Arizona v. Johnson, 555 U.S. 323 (2009).

70 575 U.S. 348 (2015).

71 413 U.S. 433 (1973).

the caretaking function of dealing with a disabled vehicle involved in an accident. In Brigham City v. Stuart,[72] police responding to a call about a loud party at 3:00 a.m. observed an altercation through a screen door, announced their presence, and entered to quell it. Again, the Court refused to suppress evidence found as a result of this warrantless entry. Stuart argued that the altercation was a "minor" crime (citing Welsh), that the officers should have knocked in addition to announcing their presence, and that their plan all along had been to arrest, not help. But the Court concluded that, regardless of their subjective motives, the police had an "objectively reasonable basis" to believe that injured individuals needed assistance and that, unlike in Welsh, the violence was just beginning. As in most other situations, the Court has been unwilling to entertain pretext arguments in caretaker cases when the police can point to an objectively legitimate basis for the intrusion that leads to discovery of evidence in plain view.

4.7 Searches and seizures of special populations

Somewhat similar to caretaker searches are searches that are undertaken by officials other than the police who are charged with monitoring "special" populations such as schoolchildren or public employees; while these officials are explicitly looking for evidence of wrongdoing (unlike in the caretaker scenario), the wrongdoing is often not criminal in nature or is subject only to minor criminal sanctions, and the motivation behind the search is often, or at least often perceived to be, facilitative rather than punitive. In these cases, the courts have once again abandoned both the warrant and probable cause requirements, and instead used Terry balancing analysis. For instance, in Wyman v. James,[73] the Supreme Court held that a warrantless search of a woman's home by welfare authorities to determine whether she had physically harmed or neglected her children was reasonable despite the absence of a warrant or probable cause. Similarly, fire inspectors entering burned premises to ascertain the cause of the fire need only notify owners that they are doing so, unless the inquiry develops into a criminal investigation, in which case a warrant is required.[74]

72 547 U.S. 398 (2006).

73 400 U.S. 309 (1971).

74 Michigan v. Clifford, 464 U.S. 287 (1984).

The leading example of this type of case, however, is New Jersey v. T.L.O.,[75] involving a search in a public school by a school official.[76] There, a vice principal searching T.L.O.'s purse for cigarettes came across smoking papers, and then marijuana and other evidence of drug use. Assuming the vice principal did not have probable cause, the Court nonetheless upheld the search. Applying Terry balancing analysis, the Court concluded that youth attending school have a diminished privacy interest, at the same time imposition of the warrant and probable cause requirements "would unduly interfere with the maintenance of the swift and informal disciplinary procedures needed in the school" and mandate that school officials acquaint themselves with "the niceties of probable cause" (over a dissent that pointed out that the Court's decisions defining probable cause have emphasized its non-technical, "commonsense" nature).

As Justice Harry Blackmun's concurring opinion famously summarized the Court's approach in T.L.O., school searches involve "exceptional circumstances in which special needs, beyond the normal need for law enforcement, make the warrant and probable-cause requirements impracticable." These quotes from the majority and concurring opinions suggest that the result in T.L.O. might have been different had the search been conducted by police looking for evidence of drug possession rather than by school officials suspicious of a disciplinary infraction. But Justice Blackmun's special needs framework has since become a familiar one in a large variety of cases. Some of these cases involve searches and seizures of groups, discussed in §4.8. Others, discussed here, involve targeted searches or seizures, as in T.L.O.

For instance, relying on special needs reasoning, the Court has twice held that public employers need only meet the reasonableness test when carrying out "noninvestigatory work-related intrusions or an investigatory search for evidence of suspected work-related employee malfeasance."[77] And in a series of decisions, the Court has held that, despite their closer connection to law enforcement, even probation and parole officers need not abide by the warrant and probable cause requirements when conducting searches to determine whether

75 469 U.S. 325 (1985).

76 Recall that the Fourth Amendment governs searches and seizures of all government officials (but identical searches carried out by officials at private schools would not be). See §2.2.

77 O'Connor v. Ortega, 480 U.S. 709 (1987); City of Ontario v. Quon, 560 U.S. 746 (2010).

court-imposed conditions have been violated.[78] Indeed, perhaps realizing that the special needs rubric is a poor fit with these types of law enforcement actions, in its latest decision on the issue, Samson v. California,[79] the Court explicitly abandoned special needs analysis and simply reverted to straightforward Terry balancing. Further, it stated that because probationers and parolees have "severely diminished privacy expectations" (especially where, as in many states, they agree to random searches as a condition of release), and because they require "intensive supervision," even reasonable suspicion might not be required in such situations, so long as the search is not "arbitrary, capricious or harassing."

If a search in a special needs setting is particularly intrusive, the balancing might come out differently. In Safford Unified School District v. Redding,[80] the Court held that a school official's strip search of a student aimed at finding drugs was unreasonable because "there was no reason to suspect that the drugs presented a danger or were in her underwear." Even here, however, the Court did not state that either a warrant or probable cause was required.

4.8 Searches and seizures of groups in the absence of individualized suspicion

To this point, the searches and seizures canvassed in this chapter have involved government officials targeting a particular person based on some indicia of suspicion. Government agencies also carry out search and seizure programs aimed at large groups of people or entities, such as inspection programs, drug testing programs, and various types of checkpoints, all of which occur in the absence of any suspicion that the particular individuals or entities affected have engaged in wrongdoing. Despite the "suspicionless" nature of these programmatic searches and seizures, the Supreme Court has found many of them to be reasonable exercises of government power under the Fourth Amendment. Here too the Court has often used special needs language or its close cousin, Terry balancing analysis, in determining the extent to which the Fourth Amendment applies. Generally, the Court's cases indicate that when the "primary purpose" of the search or seizure "is distinguishable from

78 United States v. Knights, 534 U.S. 112 (2001); Griffin v. Wisconsin, 483 U.S. 868 (1987).

79 547 U.S. 843 (2006).

80 557 U.S. 364 (2009).

the general interest in crime control" it need not be based on probable cause and perhaps may even be carried out in the complete absence of individualized suspicion.

Yet, as the following discussion makes clear, in many of the cases in which the Court has relied on special needs analysis to justify abandoning the warrant and probable cause requirements, the police were looking for evidence of "ordinary" crime. The discussion in this section suggests that, where group searches and seizures are concerned, neither the traditional warrant/probable cause requirement nor the special needs/Terry balancing frameworks, both of which developed in cases where government is targeting specific individuals, is optimal. Rather, the Court would probably be better served reinvigorating the entirely different mode of analysis hinted at in some of its earliest programmatic search cases, one that focuses on whether a statute or written policy sets out criteria limiting the scope of the search or seizure program and whether it is applied in an even-handed fashion that minimizes the extent to which arbitrary government action is possible.[81]

4.8.1 Inspections

Governments run a number of inspection programs designed to ensure compliance with statutes, regulations, or ordinances enacted to protect the health and safety of consumers, employees, and the public at large. Because these programs can only be effective if all who come under their aegis submit, the relevant law usually penalizes refusals to participate or allow entry. In 1959, for instance, the Supreme Court upheld the constitutionality of a statute punishing property holders for refusing to cooperate with a health and safety inspection of residential buildings, even though inspectors were not required to have either a warrant or probable cause.[82]

Less than ten years later, however, in Camara v. Municipal Court,[83] the Court partially reversed itself, holding that a nonconsensual home inspection must be authorized by a warrant, given its "significant intrusion upon the interests protected by the Fourth Amendment" and the need to provide official confirmation of the official's authority. At

81 See Christopher Slobogin, Policing as Administration, 165 U. Pa. L. Rev. 91 (2017).

82 Frank v. Maryland, 359 U.S. 360 (1959).

83 387 U.S. 523 (1967).

the same time, recognizing the importance of such inspections, the difficulty of detecting problems such as faulty wiring or unsafe ventilation without them, and the limited, focused invasion involved, the Court held that the warrant need not be based on probable cause to believe a particular house has violated the relevant code. Rather, an order overriding a resident's objection can be issued if it is consistent with a plan permitting inspections based on neutral criteria such as "the passage of time, the nature of the building (e.g., a multi-family apartment house), or the condition of the entire area." While the Court's decision in Camara relied on balancing analysis in arriving at the conclusion that a traditional warrant is not required in these situations (using the famous language that was endorsed in Terry v. Ohio the following Term), the regulatory regime it adopted in its place was not based on reduced individualized suspicion, as in Terry. Rather Camara focused on whether the search and seizure was conducted pursuant to a neutral plan that applies across the board.

The Court has followed this basic prescription in a number of instances. For example, in a case involving inspections carried out by the Occupational Health and Safety Administration, the Court stated that, to protect business owners from the "unbridled discretion [of] executive and administrative officers," the judiciary must ensure that there are "reasonable legislative or administrative standards for conducting [an inspection]," and that nonconsensual inspections are authorized by a Camara-type warrant that ensures those standards are being followed.[84] In other inspection cases, beginning with cases involving liquor and guns stores, the Court has been willing to dispense with the warrant requirement entirely, because the industry at issue is so "pervasively regulated" that those involved in it could not reasonably expect significant privacy protection.[85] But even here it has required "a constitutionally adequate substitute for a warrant" in the form of specified criteria. For instance, in Donovan v. Dewey,[86] a case allowing warrantless inspections of coalmines, the Court emphasized that the governing statute "requires inspection of all mines and specifically defines the frequency of inspection" and, "[r]ather than leaving the frequency and purpose of inspection to the unchecked discretion of government officers, . . . establishes a predictable and guided federal

84 Marshall v. Barlow's, Inc., 436 U.S. 307 (1978).

85 United States v. Biswell, 406 U.S. 311 (1972) (guns); Colonnade Catering Corp. v. United States, 397 U.S. 72 (1970) (liquor).

86 452 U.S. 594 (1981).

regulatory presence." The Court seemed to be saying that requiring government officials to subject to inspection every business governed by the statute, according to the same pre-existing criteria, can provide protection against harassing, biased, or pretextual actions analogous to the warrant requirement.

Unfortunately, the Court has not always adhered to this approach. For instance, in Burger v. New York,[87] the Court relied on the "pervasively regulated industry" notion in upholding a statute that allowed warrantless, surprise inspections of junkyards and vehicle dismantlers for the purpose of checking whether, inter alia, they were licensed as required by the statute, their records were in order, and any vehicles or parts on the premises were stolen. In contrast to Dewey, not only were the inspections carried out by the police, who were searching for evidence of serious crime (stolen cars), their frequency was limited solely by the statute's provision that they take place during "business hours," meaning that searches could take place at any time of day, multiple times a day or week, at police discretion.

In City of Los Angeles v. Patel,[88] the Court confused matters further by using the special needs rubric in discussing these types of cases. In Patel, the Court considered a city ordinance permitting police officers to inspect hotel registries for the purpose of determining whether hotels were being used for prostitution, drug trafficking and other purposes clearly related to criminal activity. Here the Court did not accept the government's argument that, due to the licensure, tax, sanitation, and other laws they must follow, hotels are "pervasively" regulated; the Court noted that it had assigned that designation to only four industries (liquor, firearms, mining, and junkyards) and that "[i]f such general regulations were sufficient to invoke the closely regulated industry exception, it would be hard to imagine a type of business that would not qualify." But the Court also held, contrary to appearances, that the ordinance was not aimed at "furthering the general interest in crime control" and that therefore it should be analyzed as a special needs situation (a label it retroactively applied to all of the foregoing inspection cases, going back to Camara). Thus, while the Court did require, akin to the "warrant" created by Camara, an administrative subpoena that is based on a determination that the search fits statutory criteria before a nonconsensual inspection may take place, it did not address

87 482 U.S. 691 (1987).

88 576 U.S. 409 (2015).

whether, in fact, the statute was being neutrally applied. The Court suggested that its subpoena requirement would deter use of inspections "as a pretext to harass hotel operators and their guests." Yet protection against such actions can only be assured if the relevant statute is specific about the allowable frequency and scope of the searches.

Rather than reliance on vague and inconsistently applied concepts such as "pervasive regulation," "special needs," and "crime control" and a judicial-order regime more easily applicable to targeted rather than group searches and seizures, some have argued that the better approach in these cases is the neutral plan analysis suggested in Camara and most directly adopted in Dewey.[89] This approach would require that the inspection statute not only specify the scope of inspections, but also limit their frequency (e.g., once a month), and at the same time mandate that every covered entity be subject to such inspections. The latter requirement would increase the likelihood that the frequency and scope of inspections authorized by the law would be measured, because all members of the covered group, including those with the political power to object to oppressive inspection regimes, would be subject to them to the same extent.

4.8.2 Checkpoints

The Supreme Court's approach to checkpoints comes closer to this neutral plan model. In the Court's first case involving this type of police action, the Court made clear that stopping cars at checkpoints is a Fourth Amendment seizure, but that such seizures need not be based on individualized suspicion because the intrusion they occasion is "minimal"; citing Camara, the Court concluded that "the Fourth Amendment imposes no irreducible requirement of suspicion" in such a situation, assuming the checkpoint serves an "important government interest."[90] However, gesturing toward the neutral plan model, the Court emphasized that the location of the checkpoint was "not chosen by officers in the field, but by officials responsible for making overall decisions as to the most effective allocation of limited enforcement resources." And three years later, the Court added that this limitation is not enough; to eliminate discretion, the police must stop every car,

89 Barry Friedman and Maria Ponomarenko, Democratic Policing, 90 N.Y.U. L. Rev. 1827 (2015); Slobogin, supra note 81.

90 United States v. Martinez-Fuerte, 428 U.S. 543 (1976). This case is discussed further in §4.8.2.

or stop cars on a pre-specified basis (e.g., every third car).[91] Under these or similar conditions, the Court has permitted checkpoints aimed at uncovering illegal immigrants,[92] drunken drivers,[93] license and registration violations,[94] and potential eyewitnesses to a hit-and-run accident.[95]

However, even when these conditions are met, the Court has concluded that roadblocks that have as their "primary purpose" uncovering "evidence of ordinary criminal wrongdoing" violate the Fourth Amendment. This language, which comes from the Court's special needs jurisprudence, was first cited in a roadblock case in Indianapolis v. Edmond,[96] which held unconstitutional a roadblock set up to detect narcotics using drug-sniffing dogs. As with its application of this language in its inspection cases, the Court struggled to explain why roadblocks to detect illegal immigrants and drunk drivers—both of which can result in arrests for criminal behavior—are special needs situations while a narcotics roadblock is not. More importantly, it is not clear why, if it is established by upper level officers who have the wherewithal to pick checkpoint locations that make the most sense, the latter type of roadblock should be any less permissible. One possible reason is that, whereas immigrant and drunk driving checkpoints might be said to be crucial to enforcing the relevant laws, there are other, more effective ways, of detecting drug couriers. But determining whether this is so is a daunting task for a court (which does not have at its disposal the empirical resources that the other two branches do). In any event, in Michigan Dept. of State Police v. Sitz,[97] the sobriety checkpoint case, the Court essentially eliminated that line of reasoning; when confronted by evidence indicating that drunk drivers can be more effectively detected by watching for cars that are weaving or otherwise moving erratically than through checkpoints, the Court responded that "the choice among . . . reasonable alternatives remains with the governmental officials who have a unique understanding of, and a responsibility for, limited public resources, including a finite number of police officers."

91 Delaware v. Prouse, 440 U.S. 648 (1979).

92 United States v. Martinez-Fuerte, 428 U.S. 543 (1976).

93 Michigan Dept. of State Police v. Sitz, 496 U.S. 444 (1990).

94 Delaware v. Prouse, 440 U.S. 648 (1979) (dictum).

95 Illinois v. Lidster, 540 U.S. 419 (2004).

96 531 U.S. 32 (2000).

97 496 U.S. 444 (1990).

A further difficulty with the special needs framework in this and other contexts is determining what the "primary" purpose of a program is. In Illinois v. Caballes,[98] the police stopped the defendant for speeding and, while issuing a citation, arranged for a drug-sniffing dog to examine the car. Consistent with previously discussed cases (see §4.5.3), the Court upheld this action because the dog sniff did not extend the stop beyond the time necessary to issue the ticket and to conduct associated inquiries. While Caballes did not involve a roadblock, it suggests that, if a narcotics dog happened to be present at a duly authorized license checkpoint, narcotics detection could be considered only a "secondary" purpose of the stop, as several lower courts have held.[99] One might argue that such a checkpoint is pretextual, especially since the avowed reason for the seizure is not individualized suspicion. But, as discussed in §3.5.3, pretext arguments are difficult to win.

4.8.3 Drug testing

Another situation in which the government inconveniences large groups of people on little or no suspicion involves drug testing. The Supreme Court has held that such testing—whether using a needle, urinalysis, or a breathalyzer—implicates the Fourth Amendment.[100] But it has applied special needs/balancing analysis to permit most of the drug testing programs it has confronted, on the ground that the tests are minimally intrusive, take place in an environment where less privacy is expected, serve an important government interest, and are of a "standardized nature" that vests "minimal discretion . . . in those charged with administering the program."

This latter, neutral plan, language comes from Skinner v. Railway Labor Executives' Association,[101] where the Court approved a program that permitted testing of any railway employee involved in an accident or suspected of having violated certain safety rules. In the companion case of National Treasury Employees Union v. Von Raab,[102] the Court upheld regulations providing for drug testing of anyone applying for, or serving in, a customs agent job that involved drug interdic-

98 543 U.S. 405 (2005).

99 Brooks Holland, The Road 'round Edmond: Steering through Primary Purpose and Crime Control Agendas, 111 Penn. St. L. Rev. 293 (2006).

100 Skinner v. Railway Labor Executives' Association, 489 U.S. 602 (1989).

101 Id.

102 489 U.S. 656 (1989).

tion, carrying a firearm, or dealing with classified documents. And in two other decisions, the Court upheld drug testing programs aimed at high school student athletes and at high school students engaged in extracurricular activities.[103] The only drug testing program the Court has struck down on special needs grounds involved a Georgia statute requiring every person seeking nomination or election to state office to undergo a test for illegal drugs 30 days after notification of the test. In Chandler v. Miller,[104] the Court concluded that, given the low likelihood such testing would detect illegal drug use, the ease with which impairment of politicians can be detected through normal everyday scrutiny, and the lack of data showing drug abuse among politicians, "the need revealed [by the statute] is symbolic, not 'special,' as that term draws meaning from our case law."

The Court has also invalidated a drug testing program on the ground that it did not involve a special needs situation at all. In line with its roadblock jurisprudence, the Court made clear in Ferguson v. City of Charleston[105] that when the drug test results are obtained as part of a criminal law enforcement program, then a warrant is required. Ferguson involved a drug testing program for pregnant women suspected of drug use; while the women believed the testing was solely for diagnostic purposes, the results were also given to police as a means of cajoling patients into treatment. The Court conceded that the ultimate goal of the program might have been "benign." But when a program is conducted "for the specific purpose of incriminating patients," the Court held, citing Edmond, that the Fourth Amendment is violated unless the patient consents to the test after being informed about how the results will be used.

4.8.4 Searches of arrestees in custody

In every jurisdiction, arrested people who are to be detained in jail are subject to inventory of their personal belongings, regardless of any particularized suspicion of whether evidence or weapons will be found. The Supreme Court has held that these inventories are reasonable means of ensuring jail security and that they need not be authorized

---

103 Vernonia School District 47J v. Acton, 515 U.S. 646 (1995) (athletes); Pottawatomie County School District v. Earls, 536 U.S. 822 (2002) (extracurricular students).

104 520 U.S. 305 (1997).

105 532 U.S. 67 (2001).

by a warrant.[106] At the same time, in an effort to reduce discretion and ensure even-handed application, the Court has insisted that such inventories be carried out pursuant to a written policy that delineates the officer's authority,[107] an approach consistent with neutral plan analysis.

The Court has also held that when a car has been impounded because the occupants have been arrested, or for any other lawful reason (such as a parking violation), police may inventory and remove its contents for the purpose of protecting the property and the police, and to discourage false claims of theft against the police.[108] Here, in addition to requiring a written inventory policy, the Court has stated that the search may not be "pretextual," probably because, in contrast to the situations where the Court has held that pretext arguments are unavailing, the alleged basis of the search is not individualized suspicion (see §3.5.3). At the same time, in the one case in which the Court had an opportunity to apply this aspect of inventory doctrine, it ignored clear evidence that the police used an inventory as an excuse to look through a backpack in a van they impounded after the driver was arrested for drunk driving; the police not only insisted on impounding the car rather than allowing the driver to leave it parked or make other arrangements, they also inventoried it in the field rather than at the station, failed to put on the inventory list most of the valuable items found, left the van in disarray, and kept the driver's keys for two days.[109]

Arrestees can also be subjected to other types of suspicionless searches. In Maryland v. King,[110] the Supreme Court upheld a Maryland statute requiring every person charged with a crime of violence or burglary to submit to a buccal swab for the purpose of obtaining a DNA sample, regardless of whether the DNA might help solve the crime of arrest and despite the fact that the state already collected the DNA of those who are convicted. The Court could not rely directly on its search incident or inventory doctrines, even though they both permit suspicionless searches after arrest, because DNA is usually not evidence of the crime of arrest, is not in danger of destruction or disappearance,

---

106 Illinois v. Lafayette, 462 U.S. 640 (1983).

107 Florida v. Wells, 495 U.S. 1 (1990).

108 South Dakota v. Opperman, 428 U.S. 364 (1976).

109 Colorado v. Bertine, 479 U.S. 367 (1987).

110 569 U.S. 435 (2013).

and does not threaten jail security. Nor could it rely on its special needs jurisprudence because, despite the majority's attempt to suggest that DNA is obtained primarily to corroborate identification (a claim the dissent stated "taxes the credulity of the credulous"), in fact, the main purpose of such programs is to aid investigation of ordinary crime. But the Court had no problem applying Terry balancing analysis; the Court found that the state's interest in acquiring arrestee DNA justified the "minimal" intrusion associated with a buccal swab in the absence of suspicion.

The straightforward balancing of interests in King was also apparent in Florence v. County of Burlington,[111] which upheld a regulation authorizing strip and body cavity searches of all arrestees taken to jail, even arrestees like Florence, who was arrested for failing to appear at a hearing to enforce a fine. The Court held that this procedure was a reasonable seizure under the Fourth Amendment, given concerns about infectious diseases, gang violence, and drug-connected transactions in jail. A "minor offense" exception to this practice was not warranted, the Court concluded, since the seriousness of the offense of arrest "is a poor predictor of who has contraband," minor offenders can be coerced into sneaking weapons into prison, and jail personnel do not have access to criminal history. While that reasoning might justify treating all arrestees the same, the undignified treatment itself—which involved disrobing, lifting genitals, and coughing while squatting—seems grossly disproportionate to the anticipated harms, as suggested by the dissent's data showing that unsuspected contraband was discovered in only 1 out of 23,000 New York inmates subjected to the procedure and the fact that several professional correctional organizations and ten states reject the practice.

These cases and some of the Court's other cases permitting suspicionless searches and seizures suggest that, even if reliance on neutral plan analysis usually makes the most sense, balancing analysis may still be important as an initial matter. In some situations, most clearly represented by Chandler, but arguably represented as well by Florence (if the dissent's statistics are correct) and by King (depending on whether the DNA of arrestees who are not convicted is any more useful than the DNA of the general population), a suspicionless program might be invalidated simply because it is irrational, in light of the weak government interests and strong individual interests at

111 566 U.S. 318 (2012).

stake. Only if there is a rational basis for the program would courts then inquire into whether it meets the specificity and even-handedness tenets stated in Dewey.

4.9 Border and national security exceptions

It is sometimes said that there is "border exception" to the warrant and probable cause requirements. That is true with respect to searches and seizures *at* the border. In line with special needs and Terry balancing analysis, but well before the Court had invented either, the Court stated that "national self-protection" permits the government, acting in the absence of any suspicion, to require "one entering the country to identify himself as entitled to come in, and his belongings as effects which may be lawfully brought in."[112] More recently in United States v. Montoya de Hernandez,[113] the Court repeated that "[r]outine searches of the person and effects of entrants [at the border] are not subject to any requirement of reasonable suspicion, probable cause, or warrant," both because one's expectation of privacy is reduced at the border and because the government has such a strong interest in protecting its borders. Ideally, as with other group search situations, this authority would be limited by the stipulation that everyone coming through the border is subject to the same routine inquiries. However, the Court ignored that stipulation in United States v. Flores-Montano,[114] which held that a person crossing the border and his car could be detained for at least two hours to remove and inspect the car's gas tank without any demonstration of suspicion and in the absence of any neutral plan.

Montoya de Hernandez also made clear that, if the government does have some degree of individualized suspicion, much more intrusive searches at the border are permitted. There, it held that a 16-hour airport detention of a person trying to enter the country, based on mere reasonable suspicion that she had ingested drug-filled balloons, is not a violation of the Fourth Amendment, at least when the person refuses less intrusive alternatives such as returning to the country of origin or submitting to an X-ray examination. Even mail crossing the border may be inspected as long as officials have "reasonable cause

112 Carroll v. United States, 267 U.S. 132 (1925).

113 473 U.S. 531 (1985).

114 541 U.S. 149 (2004).

to suspect" that the mail contains illegally imported merchandize; no warrant is required.[115]

While searches and seizures at the border are subject to little regulation, government actions that take place near the border, even if in aid of immigration policies, are governed by normal Fourth Amendment standards. For instance, the Court has made clear that stops and searches of individual cars near the border must abide by the Carroll and Terry doctrines that apply everywhere else in the country.[116] And in United States v. Martinez-Fuerte,[117] where the Court upheld suspicionless seizures at a roadblock aimed at catching illegal immigrants on a road leading from the border, it did so not because of a "border exception" but based on the same analysis—eventually labeled special needs—that permits suspicionless seizures at other types of checkpoints (see §4.8.2).

The only aspect of Martinez-Fuerte that differed from the typical checkpoint—and one that is much more problematic—was that cars suspected of containing illegal immigrants at the initial checkpoint were referred to a secondary, document-examination checkpoint based in large part on the ancestry of the occupants. At this point, the seizure no longer was justified by a neutral plan (which might have involved asking all of those stopped for their papers), but rather was based on suspicion. The Court upheld this second detention as well; its only explanation for doing so was a cite to United States v. Brignoni-Ponce,[118] a Court decision that had noted that reasonable suspicion for a Terry stop on illegal immigration grounds could be based in part on the "characteristic appearance of persons who live in Mexico, relying on such factors as the mode of dress and haircut." However, Martinez-Fuerte allows one's "characteristic appearance" to form the sole basis for detention, a conclusion that comes perilously close to permitting stops based on race, which other Court decisions make categorically impermissible.[119]

Similar concerns arise in connection with searches and seizures carried out in the name of national security, since they are often aimed at

115 United States v. Ramsey, 431 U.S. 606 (1977).

116 Almeida-Sanchez v. United States, 413 U.S. 266 (1973); United States v. Ortiz, 422 U.S. 891 (1975); United States v. Brignoni-Ponce, 422 U.S. 873 (1975).

117 428 U.S. 543 (1976).

118 422 U.S. 873 (1975).

119 Buck v. Davis, 137 S.Ct. 759 (2017) ("it is inappropriate to allow race to be considered as a factor in our criminal justice system").

people from foreign countries. United States v. United States District Court[120] is the only Supreme Court case that has focused squarely on Fourth Amendment concerns in the national security context. There, the Court held that, even where national security is at stake, the Fourth Amendment applies to electronic surveillance of domestic communications between American citizens (as opposed to between foreign nationals overseas or foreign agents). However, it also indicated that Congress need not apply full Title III protections of the type discussed in §3.6.3 in this situation. In response, in 1978 Congress passed the Foreign Intelligence Surveillance Act (FISA), which established a special foreign intelligence court and authorized a secret FISA process that permits issuance of a surveillance warrant when the government can show that foreign intelligence gathering is the "primary" purpose of the surveillance and that the information sought cannot be obtained through "normal investigative techniques."[121] The Patriot Act, passed in 2001, relaxed these restrictions by allowing FISA warrants to issue whenever such intelligence gathering is a "significant" purpose of the surveillance. But the Act still requires such a warrant whenever any participant in the communication is "reasonably believed" to be a "U.S. person," even if all other persons involved in the communication are "non-U.S. persons."

Section 215 of the Patriot Act also permits the FBI to obtain a court order authorizing seizure of "any tangible things (including books, records, papers, documents and other items" if it can show "there are reasonable grounds to believe that the tangible things sought are relevant to an authorized [national security] investigation" and that procedures are in place to "minimize" dissemination of the information thereby acquired.[122] This authority was for some time construed by the FISA court to permit bulk collection of various communications records, including the metadata of phone calls and texts, of virtually everyone in the United States, apparently on the rationale that collecting such information would facilitate finding terrorists. While the Second Circuit Court of Appeals eventually strictly construed Section 215 to require warrants that specify the particular target being investigated,[123] and the bulk collection program was supposedly ended by the USA Freedom Act of 2015, the metadata of anyone within "two hops" of the target may still be accessed, which can allow the govern-

120 407 U.S. 297 (1972).

121 50 U.S.C. §1801 et seq.

122 50 U.S.C. §1861.

123 ACLU v. Clapper, 785 F.3d 787 (2d Cir. 2015).

ment to collect the records of thousands of individuals.[124] Furthermore, the Patriot Act still allows an FBI special agent to obtain a "National Security Letter" authorizing access to communication billing records, financial records, and credit records, upon a showing that the information sought is "relevant" to an investigation designed to protect against international terrorism or clandestine intelligence activities.[125]

One justification for the wide-ranging authorizations contemplated by Section 215 orders and National Security Letters—in addition to national security concerns—is that they do not involve searches, given the third party doctrine. But, as §2.3.4 explained, that doctrine is under attack, and, given the breadth of the information collected, unspecified claims about national security needs may no longer provide sufficient justification for searches and seizures based on a mere showing of relevance to an investigation.

4.10 Seizures of property

A final exception to the warrant and probable requirements concerns not searches or seizures of the person, but rather seizures of property in situations that do not involve a search. In Soldal v. Cook County,[126] the Supreme Court held that repossession of a mobile home implicates the Fourth Amendment even when no entry of the home is involved, because "the Amendment protects property as well as privacy." At the same time, a warrant is seldom required in stand-alone property-seizure situations. Warrantless seizures of cars,[127] luggage,[128] and even houses[129] have all been upheld as long as there is probable cause, unless the seizure causes "actual interference" with the owner's possessory interest[130] (as occurred in the aforementioned case of United States v. Place,[131] where an individual who was not under arrest was unable to access his luggage for 90 minutes).

---

124 Sharon B. Franklin, Fulfilling the Promise of the USA Freedom Act: Time to Truly End Bulk Collection of Americans' Calling Records, March 28, 2019, accessed April 12, 2020 at https://www.justsecurity.org/63399/.

125 12 U.S.C. §3414(a)(5); 31 U.S.C. §5312.

126 506 U.S. 56 (1992).

127 Chambers v. Maroney, 399 U.S. 42 (1970).

128 United States v. Chadwick, 433 U.S. 1 (1977).

129 Illinois v. McArthur, 531 U.S. 326 (2001).

130 Segura v. United States, 468 U.S. 796 (1984); United States v. Johns, 469 U.S. 478 (1985).

131 462 U.S. 696 (1983).

The most important issues connected with seizures of property arise in connection with federal and state forfeiture statutes that allow law enforcement to seize property connected to the commission of crime. At their most expansive, these statutes provide for forfeiture of any property, including real property, that "was used or attempted to be used as an instrumentality in the commission of, or in aiding or abetting the commission of, any felony," and the proceeds of these seizures often go in law enforcement coffers.[132] These statutes have been controversial, largely because they provide a financial incentive for police to seize property simply for its value "with no interest in ever actually pursuing convictions."[133]

Forfeiture laws have also been controversial because of the procedures for implementing them. These statutes usually provide for post-seizure hearings in which a forfeiture may be challenged, including on the ground (albeit one that is not constitutionally required[134]) that the owner was ignorant the property was being used in the commission of crime. However, the statutes usually do not require a pre-seizure hearing analogous to the warrant process. In Calero-Toledo v. Pearson Yacht Leasing Co.,[135] the Supreme Court held that such a hearing is not mandated by the Due Process Clause. In Florida v. White,[136] the Court affirmed that, under the Fourth Amendment as well, police do not need a warrant to seize items that they have probable cause to believe are forfeitable contraband, if the items are located in a public place. Congress has since enacted a statute allowing seizure of property that police have probable cause to believe is forfeitable and is seized "pursuant to a lawful arrest or search or another exception to the Fourth Amendment warrant requirement."[137]

132 Fla. Stat. Ann. §932.701.

133 Nkechi Taifa, Civil Forfeiture vs. Civil Liberties, 39 N.Y.L.S. L. Rev. 95, 106 (1995).

134 Bennis v. Michigan, 517 U.S. 1163 (1996).

135 416 U.S. 663 (1974).

136 526 U.S. 559 (1999).

137 18 U.S.C. §981(b)(2)(Bo) (2016).

5 Interrogation and entrapment

5.1 History and rationale of interrogation regulation

Virtually every serious criminal case involves a seizure of a person, and most involve searches. In contrast, confessions resulting from interrogation—police questioning of suspects—are probably crucial in no more than 20 percent of criminal cases.[1] Nonetheless, in a significant minority of investigations, confessions are very important, either because they help solve the confessor's case or because they help clear other cases.

The principal constitutional provision governing interrogation is the Fifth Amendment, which states in pertinent part that "[n]o person shall be compelled in any criminal case to be a witness against himself." That clause forms the basis for the Supreme Court's famous decision in Miranda v. Arizona,[2] requiring warnings about the right to silence and the right to counsel during interrogation of people who have been arrested. Interrogations are also regulated by the Sixth Amendment, which provides that "[i]n all criminal prosecutions, the accused shall enjoy the right to . . . have the Assistance of Counsel for his defense." This language has been construed to provide a basis for legal assistance separate from the Fifth Amendment, but one that is triggered only after formal criminal proceedings have begun, which is usually not until a day or two after arrest. Finally, the Due Process Clause in the Fifth and Fourteenth amendments also places some limitations on interrogation, in particular when it is directed at someone who is not in custody or subject to criminal prosecution.

1 Paul G. Cassell and Bret S. Hayman, Police Interrogations in the 1990s: An Empirical Study of the Effects of Miranda, 43 UCLA L. Rev. 839, 906 (1996); Michael Wald, Richard Ayres, David W. Hess, Mark Schantz, and Charles H. Whitebread II, Interrogations in New Haven: The Impact of Miranda, 76 Yale L.J. 1519, 1585, 1593–6 (1967); Richard H. Seeburger and R. Stanton Wettick, Miranda in Pittsburgh: A Statistical Study, 29 Pitt L. Rev. 1, 23 (1967).

2 384 U.S. 436 (1966).

By far the dominant source of law regulating interrogation, however, is the Fifth Amendment. The privilege against self-incrimination found there developed in England as a defense to the practice in heresy and treason trials of forcing individuals to take an oath "ex officio," which required them to swear to answer truthfully—upon pain of a perjury or contempt charge—all questions put to them, without being told why they were being questioned; the privilege allowed the individual to refuse to answer questions in such cases, without penalty.[3] By the time the Constitution was drafted, a number of colonies had expanded the privilege to any type of criminal case, which is the language reflected in the Fifth Amendment.

Despite that provision, the privilege had virtually no impact on police interrogation for over 100 years, even in the federal cases to which the Bill of Rights applied, in part because no organized police forces existed in this country until the mid-nineteenth century. Moreover, the courts were already regulating interrogation through rules of evidence that focused on whether confessions were reliable. For instance, in Hopt v. Utah,[4] the Supreme Court made no reference to the Fifth Amendment, but simply stated that, while improper inducements might produce an "untrue statement," a confession that is "freely and voluntarily made is evidence of the most satisfactory character," and then concluded that Hopt's incriminating statement to a policeman was "voluntary and uninfluenced by hopes of reward or fear of punishment." It was not until Bram v. United States,[5] decided in 1897, that the Court applied the Fifth Amendment to law enforcement interrogation, and then only to federal cases. There the Court held inadmissible a confession of murder obtained by a detective who had stripped Bram of his clothing, told Bram he had a statement from another person accusing Bram of the crime, and urged him to disclose his accomplice to avoid "the blame of this horrible crime on your own shoulders." The Court held this confession to be involuntary because "it must necessarily have been the result of either hope or fear, or both, operating on the mind."

In state cases, the Fifth Amendment did not apply until the 1960s (see §1.3.1). But beginning in the 1930s, the Court began excluding confessions made by state defendants that it considered "involuntary," on authority of the Fourteenth Amendment's prohibition of deprivations

3 Leonard W. Levy, Origins of the Fifth Amendment (Oxford University Press, Oxford 1968).

4 110 U.S. 574 (1884).

5 168 U.S. 532 (1897).

of liberty without due process of law, which expressly applies to the states. Most famously, in Brown v. Mississippi,[6] the Court excluded confessions from several African-American men who had been hung from a tree, whipped, and threatened in other ways. In subsequent cases applying the Due Process Clause, it ruled inadmissible confessions obtained after the suspect: was questioned continuously for 36 hours without rest or sleep;[7] was told he could not phone his wife or anyone else unless he gave the police a statement;[8] was informed that welfare for her children would be cut off and her children taken away from her if she failed to "cooperate";[9] and was hospitalized for a gunshot wound, suffering from extreme pain, and under the influence of morphine.[10] While many of the Court's early due process cases, like Hopt's evidentiary analysis, appeared to equate the involuntariness inquiry with an assessment of reliability, by the time of Rogers v. Richmond[11] the Court was prepared to say that involuntary confessions are excluded

> not because such confessions are unlikely to be true but because the methods used to extract them offend an underlying principle in the enforcement of our criminal law: that ours is an accusatorial and not an inquisitorial system—a system in which the State must establish guilt by evidence independently and freely secured and may not by coercion prove its charge against an accused out of his own mouth.

As the Court's due process cases illustrate, voluntariness analysis—whether aimed at determining reliability or offensiveness—requires close examination of the facts of each case, including not just the conduct of the police but the vulnerabilities of the suspect. Wanting a clearer rule, in 1964—the year after the Sixth Amendment was applied to the states—the Court held that defendants who have been formally charged are entitled to an attorney during interrogation.[12] That rule had little impact, however, since most interrogations take place between arrest and formal charging. Perhaps realizing this, in 1966, two years after the Fifth Amendment was applied to the states, the Court held in Miranda that, as a means of dealing with the "inherent

6 297 U.S. 278 (1936).

7 Ashcraft v. Tennessee, 322 U.S. 143 (1944).

8 Haynes v. Washington, 373 U.S. 503 (1963).

9 Lynumn v. Illinois, 372 U.S. 528 (1963).

10 Beecher v. Alabama, 408 U.S. 234 (1972).

11 365 U.S. 534 (1961).

12 Massiah v. United States, 377 U.S. 201 (1964).

coercion" of custodial interrogation, the amendment requires that confessions from arrested individuals be excluded unless they are first told they have a right to remain silent and a Fifth Amendment right to counsel, and then voluntarily waive those rights. More specifically, Miranda held that persons subject to custodial interrogation must be told they have a right to remain silent, that anything they say can and will be used against them, that they have the right to consult with a lawyer and to have a lawyer present during interrogation, and that if they cannot afford a lawyer one will be appointed for that purpose. Further, once these "warnings" are given, any indication of a desire to remain silent or consult an attorney must halt the interrogation. Finally, any statement obtained is admissible only if the government can show the individual "voluntarily, knowingly and intelligently" waived these rights.

Critics of Miranda claimed it would spell the end of effective interrogation. That has not come to pass. About 80 percent of those subjected to custodial interrogation and given the warnings talk, without counsel present, and between 50 and 60 percent confess, a rate which is not substantially lower than the pre-Miranda rate.[13] One reason for the minimal impact of Miranda on confession rates is that many people do not understand the warnings, either because they are incapable of doing so (the warnings described by the Court require reading skill at somewhere between sixth and tenth grade level[14]) or are confused by them. Thus, suspects might believe that "off the record" comments are inadmissible, that once counsel is requested police may continue questioning, that their silence may be used as evidence, that a waiver must be signed to be valid, or that statements may be retracted.[15] This confusion is sometimes exacerbated by police, who downplay the importance of the warnings by treating them as bureaucratic "boilerplate" or, as discussed in more detail below, by failing to clarify apparent misunderstandings about the rights, engaging in ruses that lead suspects to forget about them, or suggesting that waiving the rights

13 Richard A. Leo, Inside the Interrogation Room, 86 J. Crim. L. & Criminol. 266, 300–301 (1996); Paul Cassell, Miranda's Social Costs: An Empirical Reassessment, 90 Nw. U. L. Rev. 387, 495 (1996); George C. Thomas, III, Plain Talk about the Miranda Empirical Debate: A "Steady-State" Theory of Confessions, 43 UCLA L. Rev. 933 (1996).

14 Richard Rogers, Kimberly S. Harrison, Daniel W. Shuman, Kenneth W. Sewell, and Lisa L. Hazelwood, An Analysis of Miranda Warnings and Waivers: Comprehension and Coverage, 31 L. & Hum. Beh. 177 (2007).

15 Jill E. Rogstad and Nathan D. Gillard, "Everyone Knows Their Miranda Rights": Implicit Assumptions and Countervailing Evidence, 16 Psychol., Pub. Policy & L. 300, 307–11 (2010).

will be beneficial. Because post-Warren Court decisions have permitted some of these tactics, still another reason the confession rate has remained relatively stable is that post-Miranda decisions have significantly altered the regime that case established.

A separate criticism of Miranda is that, regardless of its impact on confession rates, it is likely to benefit only the guilty, who can remain silent about their crimes. But as Dean Wigmore explained, the right to remain silent protects the innocent as well:

> The exercise of the power to extract answers begets a forgetfulness of the just limitations of that power . . . If there is a right to an answer, there soon seems to be a right to the expected answer—that is, to a confession of guilt. Thus, the legitimate use grows into the unjust abuse; ultimately, the innocent are jeopardized by the encroachments of a bad system.[16]

The warnings also protect the innocent by reminding police that questioning can stop at any time, and thus that interrogators should be careful not to overstep. Providing counsel to those who want one reinforces those goals, and also ensures that everyone subjected to interrogation is afforded legal advice that otherwise only wealthier individuals enjoy. These abstract points about the theoretical benefits of taking the right to remain silent seriously are bolstered by DNA exonerations demonstrating that a significant number of people, when subjected to the right pressures, have confessed to crimes they did not commit.[17]

A final criticism of Miranda is that it overenforces the Fifth Amendment. As Justice Byron White pointed out in his dissent in Miranda, the decision has the effect of declaring that any unwarned statement made during custodial interrogation, even if it occurs after only one question, is "compelled"; Justice White found this result a "patently unsound" interpretation of the Fifth Amendment's language. But the majority backed up its assertion that custodial interrogation is "inherently coercive" by drawing from police manuals to describe in detail the typical interrogation process, which involves isolating the suspect in an interrogation room, positing the suspect's guilt as

---

16 8 Wigmore, Evidence 309 (3d ed., Little, Brown & Co., Boston 1940).

17 Steven A. Drizin and Richard A. Leo, The Three Errors: Pathways to False Confession and Wrongful Conviction, in Police Interrogations and False Confessions: Current Research, Practice, and Policy Recommendations, 9, 13–21 (Daniel Lassiter and Christian Meissner eds., American Psychological Association, Wash. D.C. 2010) (reporting 125 such cases).

fact, questioning "steadily and without relent," and engaging in other psychological tactics. A second response to the overenforcement criticism is that many other Supreme Court criminal procedure decisions are similarly "prophylactic," in the sense that they provide rights whether or not they are needed (with Gideon v. Wainwright's application of the right to counsel to all cases involving potential imprisonment being a prime example). In any event, in Dickerson v. United States,[18] decided in 2000, the Supreme Court confirmed that Miranda is a "constitutional rule," not merely a court-created doctrine.

Dickerson was a surprise to many, given the post-Warren Court's oft-demonstrated willingness to nip away at Miranda's edifice. But perhaps those adjustments to Miranda, in addition to the steady-state confession rate suggesting that police have been able to work around its restrictions, made the case easy for the Court to affirm. The modifications imposed by the post-Warren Court are apparent with respect to each of Miranda's key components: (1) the definition of custodial interrogation; (2) the warnings requirement; and (3) when a waiver of Miranda rights is valid. This rest of this chapter discusses these components and then describes the Court's separate Sixth Amendment and due process regimes for regulating interrogations and the somewhat related rules governing the entrapment defense.

5.2 Custodial interrogation

Miranda held that its warning requirement applies when the police engage in "custodial interrogation." Warnings need not be given before "[g]eneral on-the-scene questioning as to facts surrounding a crime or other general questioning of citizens in the factfinding process." But they must be given when questioning occurs after a custodial arrest, as well as when, in the words of Miranda, the person has "otherwise [been] deprived of his freedom of action in any significant way."

Despite this language, the warnings need not be given in connection with a Terry stop, whether of a pedestrian or of a driver in a car.[19] And the Supreme Court has intimated that even more significant encounters do not implicate Miranda. While waking up an individual in his

18 530 U.S. 428 (2000).

19 Berkemer v. McCarty, 468 U.S. 420 (1984).

home at 4:00 a.m. to question him clearly triggers Miranda,[20] questioning an individual in his home during the daytime for three hours does not.[21] Questioning at the stationhouse will often require warnings, but not if the individual comes there voluntarily;[22] that is so even if presence at the station is at the request of the person's probation or parole officer, as long as the interview is "arranged by appointment at a mutually convenient time."[23] If the questioning takes place in prison, warnings may be required,[24] but not if the person is removed from the general population, questioned about events that occurred outside the prison, and told he can go back to his cell whenever he wants.[25] Age may also be relevant to the custody question. In J.D.B. v. North Carolina,[26] 30 to 45 minutes of questions directed at a 13-year-old youth at his school required warnings. However, per Yarborough v. Alvarado,[27] the interrogation of a 17-year-old for two hours, during which he was twice told he could take a break and see his parents in the lobby, did not. As in the Fourth Amendment context, the Court has made clear that the subjective views of the suspect and the officer are irrelevant; rather, the "objective circumstances of the interrogation" determine when the individual is in custody, regardless of the individual's, or officer's, perceptions.[28]

Custody by itself is not enough to trigger Miranda. There must also be interrogation by the police which, the Supreme Court held, in Rhode Island v. Innis,[29] "must reflect a measure of compulsion above and beyond that inherent in custody itself." Thus, for instance, custodial interrogation did not occur in Illinois v. Perkins,[30] where an undercover agent planted in Perkins' jail cell elicited incriminating statements, because Perkins believed he was talking to a fellow criminal, not an agent of the police. Innis also held that, while actions as well as words can constitute interrogation, they only do so if they are not "normally attendant to arrest and custody" and if "police should know [they] are

20 Orozco v. Texas, 394 U.S. 324 (1969).

21 Beckwith v. United States, 425 U.S. 341 (1976).

22 California v. Beheler, 463 U.S. 1121 (1983).

23 Oregon v. Mathiason, 429 U.S. 492 (1977); see also Minnesota v. Murphy, 465 U.S. 420 (1984).

24 Mathis v. United States, 391 U.S. 1 (1968).

25 Howes v. Fields, 565 U.S. 499 (2012).

26 564 U.S. 261 (2011).

27 541 U.S. 652 (2004).

28 Stansbury v. California, 511 U.S. 318 (1994).

29 446 U.S. 291 (1980).

30 496 U.S. 292 (1990).

reasonably likely to elicit an incriminating response from the suspect." Thus, in Innis, the Court held that interrogation did not occur when three officers, sitting in a squad car with Innis, engaged in a conversation with each other about the danger a missing murder weapon would pose to "handicapped children running around in this area," and one stated "God forbid one of [the children] might find a weapon with shells and . . . hurt themselves" (which led Innis to take them to the weapon). The dissent argued that, even though Innis was not directly questioned, the purpose of the officers' exchange was to elicit a response from him, as evidenced by the fact that police interrogation manuals recommend appealing to a suspect's sense of morality. According to the Court, however, the officers' conversation was "nothing more than a dialogue between the . . . officers to which no response from [Innis] was invited." Similarly, in Arizona v. Mauro,[31] the Court held that interrogation did not occur when officers brought the suspect's wife into the interrogation room at her request and taped the ensuing conversation between her and Mauro, since police "do not interrogate a suspect simply by hoping that he will incriminate himself."

In all three of these cases the police exploited the situation. At the same time, one can make the argument that, at most, the police disguised their identity or their motives, without exerting any direct pressure on the suspect. As the language of the Fifth Amendment seems to demand, these decisions focused on whether the police act coercively, not on whether their conduct was deceptive or offensive.

5.3 Warnings requirement

Miranda declared that all persons subject to custodial interrogation must be informed of all four of their rights, with no exceptions, on the ground that "giving a warning is too simple and the rights involved too important" to hold otherwise. However, since Miranda the Court has permitted "de minimis" variations on the language of the warnings, and created two exceptions to the warnings requirement.

In both California v. Prysock[32] and Duckworth v. Eagan,[33] the warnings never made clear that the suspect was entitled to a court-appointed

31 481 U.S. 520 (1987).
32 453 U.S. 355 (1981).
33 492 U.S. 195 (1989).

lawyer prior to and during interrogation as well as at any subsequent court proceeding; in Eagan, for instance, the police stated at the end of the warnings, "We have no way of giving you a lawyer, but one will be appointed for you, if you wish, if and when you go to court." The Court found that this warning did not undermine Miranda, because its language correctly stated that, under Indiana procedure, a person who asks for an attorney during interrogation, thereby ending it, is not provided one until the initial appearance in front of a judge. Similarly, in Florida v. Powell,[34] the Court permitted a Miranda litany that, with respect to the right to counsel warning, stated only that the individual could obtain an attorney "before" questioning, because the warnings later stated, "You have the right to use any of these rights at any time you want during this interview."

More significantly, no warnings of any sort are required when giving them would threaten public safety. In New York v. Quarles,[35] the police, acting on information that a man with a gun had just gone into a supermarket, entered the store, cornered Quarles, and held him at gunpoint. After frisking him and finding his holster was empty, they asked him where the gun was, without giving him any warnings. Quarles answered "over there," while nodding his head toward some empty cartons. Upon retrieving a revolver, the police read him his rights for the first time. The Court refused to exclude the gun, reasoning that "the need for answers to questions in a situation posing a threat to the public safety outweighs the need for the prophylactic rule protecting the Fifth Amendment's privilege against self-incrimination." The undiscovered gun "obviously posed more than one danger to the public safety: an accomplice might make use of it, a customer or employee might later come upon it." The dissent pointed out that, at the time of the confrontation, the store was closed and that the lower court had found there were no "exigent circumstances." But the majority responded that police facing the type of "kaleidoscopic situation" involved in Quarles should not be held to rigid standards.

In her concurring opinion, Justice Sandra Day O'Connor agreed with the majority that the gun should be admissible, but on the ground that a tangible object such as a gun is not testimony and thus its use in court is not barred by the Fifth Amendment's prohibition on compelled "testimony" (see §8.4.1 for more on this point). At the same

34 559 U.S. 50 (2010).

35 467 U.S. 649 (1984).

time, she argued against a public safety exception for unwarned oral statements because "[t]he end result will be a finespun new doctrine on public safety exigencies incident to custodial interrogation, complete with the hair-splitting distinctions that currently plague our Fourth Amendment jurisprudence," a prediction that has been borne out in the lower courts.[36]

Just as importantly, Justice O'Connor pointed out that Quarles has subtly changed the conceptual basis of Miranda jurisprudence. She noted that Miranda had never prohibited the police from asking questions designed to protect the public; Miranda simply prohibits use of evidence found as a result of unwarned statements. Quarles, on the other hand, engages in the type of balancing analysis found in Fourth Amendment opinions: it says, in effect, that while the cost of prohibiting use of most unwarned statements, standing alone, can be borne, the cost of prohibiting use of unwarned statements that are needed to protect the public (and their fruits) is too high. Analogous to the effect of special needs doctrine on the warrant requirement (see §4.7), that type of balancing analysis opens the door to permitting police to forgo warnings in a host of other situations, such as, for instance, when government agents other than the police are carrying out the questioning, or when the coercive impact of custodial interrogation in a particular situation could be considered diluted.

The latter rationale seems to underlie the Supreme Court's subsequent opinion in Pennsylvania v. Muniz,[37] where the Court held Miranda does not apply when stationhouse intake officers ask "booking questions" about name, height, age, and the like. Although some justices justified Muniz on the ground that the answers to such questions are not incriminating testimony, that is not the case under all circumstances. In any event, there is now a public safety exception and a booking exception to Miranda.

5.4 Waiver

Even if the warnings are given, Miranda held, subsequent statements are not admissible unless the individual has expressly waived the rights

36 Daniel B. Yeager, The Public Safety Exception to Miranda: Careening through the Lower Courts, 40 Fla. L. Rev. 989 (1988).

37 496 U.S. 582 (1990).

to silence and counsel. The Miranda Court stated that "a valid waiver will not be presumed simply from the silence of the accused after warnings are given or simply from the fact that a confession was in fact eventually obtained." Further, "if the individual indicates in any manner, at any time prior to or during questioning, that he wishes to remain silent, the interrogation must cease," and "[i]f the individual states that he wants an attorney, the interrogation must cease until an attorney is present." Finally, before any resulting confession is admitted, the government bears "a heavy burden" to demonstrate that the defendant "voluntarily, knowingly and intelligently" waived these rights; "any evidence that the accused was threatened, tricked, or cajoled into a waiver will, of course, show that the defendant did not voluntarily waive his privilege."

These admonitions have largely been ignored by the post-Warren Court. Of course, a waiver without first talking to counsel is rarely "intelligent," so even the Miranda Court, which appeared to contemplate that some waivers would occur, probably did not expect rigid application of that part of its waiver test. But the post-Warren Court has also found valid many waivers that were not "knowing," in the sense that they were given by suspects who clearly did not have a complete understanding of their rights. Instead, the focus has been on whether post-warning conduct by the police is "voluntary," as that concept was defined in the Court's early due process cases; further, voluntariness need only be proven by a preponderance of the evidence,[38] which is hardly a "heavy" burden. This stance has meant that, while threats are generally not permitted, deception, trickery, and other psychological tactics are generally allowed. Even when the suspect invokes the right to silence or the right to counsel, questioning need not cease under all circumstances. In short, as the following discussion details, after the warnings are given, the analysis is virtually identical to the case-specific due process analysis that Miranda was meant to replace.

5.4.1 Questioning in the absence of invocation

Most people subjected to interrogation do not invoke their rights, for reasons discussed in §5.1. If an individual signals a willingness to talk but is not immediately forthcoming with incriminating statements, interrogation manuals of the type described in Miranda recommend that police engage in a number of tactics, including: showing sympathy

38 Lego v. Twomey, 404 U.S. 477 (1972); Colorado v. Connelly, 479 U.S. 157 (1986).

(by, for instance, pretending to have been in a similar "pickle" or pretending to be the suspect's friend); providing rationalizations for the offense (by suggesting, for instance, that drugs, alcohol, or another individual is really responsible for the crime, or that a confession will make the suspect feel better); fabricating evidence (by falsely claiming, for instance, that a co-defendant has confessed, that forensic evidence was found at the crime, or that the police have all the evidence they need and know the individual is guilty); and offering benefits for confessing (by noting, for instance, that offenders often receive treatment, or that cooperation might reduce the charge).[39]

Some commentators consider all of these interrogation techniques impermissibly coercive.[40] Even if that is so, some of these practices seem less "coercive" than others; for instance, showing sympathy or providing rationalizations may merely lead individuals to lose sight of the fact that what they say can be used against them, and fabrication may exert no more pressure to talk than occurs when a suspect is confronted with real evidence. In contrast, offering benefits for a confession is, in effect, threatening to make things worse if one is not forthcoming, and is hard to square with any prohibition on coercion.

In any event, lower court decisions have tended to permit all of these tactics, unless they morph into direct threats or promises or involve blatant fabrication of evidence.[41] The Supreme Court itself has permitted a version of the sympathy tactic in Illinois v. Perkins (the case discussed in §5.2 involving questioning by an undercover agent), as well as lies about finding the suspect's fingerprints at the scene of the crime[42] and about whether a co-suspect has confessed.[43] It is also worth noting that both plea bargaining and the sentencing rules in many jurisdictions formally offer reductions in charge in exchange for self-incriminating statements[44] (albeit only after counsel or the court have signed off on the deal, which is significantly different than "deals" offered by police before the suspect has consulted with a lawyer).

39 Fred Inbau, John Reid, Joseph P. Buckley, and Brian Jayne, Criminal Interrogations and Confessions 210–50 (5th ed., Jones & Bartlett Learning, Burlington, Mass. 2013).

40 Welsh White, Police Trickery in Inducing Confessions, 127 U. Pa. L. Rev. 582 (1979).

41 Paul Marcus, It's Not Just about Miranda: Determining the Voluntariness of Confessions in Criminal Prosecutions, 40 Val. U. L. Rev. 601, 612–14 (2006).

42 Oregon v. Mathiason, 429 U.S. 492 (1977).

43 Frazier v. Cupp, 394 U.S. 731 (1969).

44 See, e.g., U.S. Commission Sentencing Guidelines §3E1.1.

Research leaves little doubt that the negotiation techniques just described, whether deceptive or not, increase the probability of a false confession from suspects by leading them to believe a confession will somehow benefit them or at least will not significantly hurt them.[45] Nonetheless, as a constitutional matter, the possibility that certain techniques are more likely to cause false confessions is probably irrelevant. Even the Court's pre-Miranda cases had been moving toward a focus on compulsion rather than reliability, a trend the post-Miranda Court has accelerated. Indeed, in Colorado v. Connelly,[46] the Court declared that "[t]he sole concern of the Fifth Amendment, on which Miranda was based, is governmental coercion." And while due process analysis, technically separate from Miranda analysis, might at one time have been focused on reliability, that concern is now, according to Connelly, "a matter to be governed by the evidentiary laws of the forum, . . . not by the Due Process Clause." The only tactics that the Due Process Clause might prohibit that the Fifth Amendment does not are non-coercive tactics that are particularly "offensive" (such as, perhaps, an officer posing as the suspect's lawyer, or the fabrication of physical evidence that is shown to the suspect). In short, constitutional analysis of interrogation is focused on whether coercion occurred, not on whether any statements made are reliable.

Even techniques that take advantage of suspects' ignorance or confusion about their rights are often permissible. For instance, in North Carolina v. Butler[47] and Connecticut v. Barrett,[48] the suspects appeared to believe that as long as nothing is put in writing or signed, their incriminating statements could not be used. And in Colorado v. Spring,[49] the police told Spring that they wanted to question him about a minor crime and then, after he had waived his rights and begun talking, they suddenly asked him about a murder. The Supreme Court concluded that, in each of these cases, the incriminating statements were admissible; it stated that as long as the suspect understands "the basic privilege guaranteed by the Fifth Amendment" and "the consequences of speaking freely to law enforcement officials," Miranda

45 Christopher Slobogin, Manipulation of Suspects and Unrecorded Questioning: After 50 Years of Miranda, Still Two (or Maybe Three) Burning Issues, 97 B.U. L. Rev. 1157, 1161–4 (2017).

46 479 U.S. 157 (1986).

47 441 U.S. 369 (1979).

48 479 U.S. 523 (1987).

49 479 U.S. 564 (1987).

is not violated. It could certainly be contended, to the contrary, that these defendants did not understand the basics of the privilege or all of the consequences of talking, and thus that their waivers were not "knowing." But the Court's focus was on whether the defendants were compelled to talk by the police, not on whether they were mistaken about their rights.

Further, even if the suspect experiences compulsion to talk, it must stem from police conduct; otherwise, it does not trigger constitutional protection. While the state action requirement usually involves an inquiry into whether the actor is an agent of the police (see §2.2), in interrogation cases it can require a more subtle inquiry, as demonstrated in Connelly, which involved a murder confession to police by a person with severe mental illness. While the Court was willing to assume that Connelly's mental problems "compelled" his confession (a mental health professional later testified that his statements were the result of "command hallucinations" from God telling him to confess), it stressed that the police did not take advantage of Connelly's condition, and in fact were not aware of it at the time of the statements. Then, consistent with the general proposition that criminal procedure rights can only be violated by state actors, the Court held that Connelly's statements were not caused, much less compelled, by the police; unless a confession is the product of police "overreaching," it is admissible under the Fifth Amendment and the Due Process Clause. This state action requirement might also help explain the results in Butler, Barrett and Spring: the confusion that produced the confessions in those cases, it could be argued, was the defendant's fault, not the state's. Justice Antonin Scalia justified this position with the observation that "a rule that foolish mistakes do not count would leave most defendants not only unconvicted but undetected."[50]

5.4.2 Questioning after invocation

Approximately 20 percent of suspects subjected to interrogation invoke their rights. Miranda held that, when invocation occurs, questioning must stop. But several post-Miranda decisions have permitted post-invocation questioning under certain conditions.

Post-invocation questioning is most likely to be impermissible when a suspect invokes the right to counsel (as opposed to the right to

---

50 Minnick v. Mississippi, 498 U.S. 146 (1990) (Scalia, J., dissenting).

silence). But even here, waiver doctrine favors the state. In Edwards v. Arizona,[51] the Court confirmed that if an individual asserts the right to counsel, police are not permitted to reopen questioning in the absence of counsel, unless the defendant voluntarily reinitiates contact. And in later decisions the Court made clear that this is so even if the renewed questioning is about another crime,[52] or the suspect has consulted with counsel in the meantime.[53] The rationale for these decisions was that police should not be allowed to "badger" a person who has indicated a desire "to deal with police only through counsel." However, Edwards left open two questions: (1) what types of conduct constitute invocation? and (2) what types of conduct constitute reinitiation by the suspect?

As to the first issue, in a case decided soon after Edwards, the Court held that stating, "Yeah, I'd like to do that," after being told about the right to counsel, is an invocation, even if the statement occurs before the warnings are completely finished.[54] However, in Davis v. United States,[55] the Court held that the statement, "Maybe I should have a lawyer," was not an invocation; according to the Court, a suspect "must articulate his desire to have counsel present sufficiently clearly that a reasonable police officer in the circumstances would understand the statement to be a request for an attorney." Furthermore, police are not required to clarify ambiguous requests. Rather, consistent with its waiver cases suggesting that misunderstanding of the warnings is not the state's fault, Davis allows police to proceed with questioning of suspects who are confused about the benefits of counsel. Nor is Edwards triggered if the suspect asks for someone other than counsel,[56] or makes the request for counsel at a court hearing instead of interrogation itself,[57] because in neither case has the suspect stated a desire "to deal with police [interrogation] only through counsel." Similarly, the Court has held that refusing to sign a waiver form or remaining uncommunicative throughout most of an interrogation is not an invocation of the right to remain silent.[58]

---

51 451 U.S. 477 (1981).

52 Arizona v. Roberson, 486 U.S. 675 (1988).

53 Minnick v. Mississippi, 498 U.S. 146 (1990).

54 Smith v. Illinois, 469 U.S. 91 (1984).

55 512 U.S. 452 (1994).

56 Fare v. Michael C., 442 U.S. 707 (1979).

57 McNiel v. Wisconsin, 501 U.S. 171 (1991).

58 Berghuis v. Thompkins, 560 U.S. 370 (2010).

The Court has been similarly expansive in defining when a defendant initiates contact with the police. A few moments after invoking the right to counsel, the defendant in Oregon v. Bradshaw[59] asked an officer, "Well, what is going to happen to me now?" Distinguishing this request from one "arising out of the incidents of the custodial relationship," such as asking for water or a telephone, the Court held that Bradshaw had reinitiated contact with the police and that subsequent interrogation was permissible, at least if the warnings are given again. And in Maryland v. Shatzer,[60] the Court did away with the reinitiation rule entirely if there has been a "break in custody" that lasts two weeks or longer after invocation of the right to counsel. This is so even if during that time the suspect is in prison, so long as during the two weeks the prisoner is in the general population rather than in isolation where the interrogators have "power to increase the duration of incarceration."

If the suspect only invokes the right to silence, the post-Miranda Court has evidenced even less allegiance to Miranda, because in this situation the individual has only declined to talk, not signaled an unwillingness to proceed without counsel. In Michigan v. Mosley,[61] the Court held that as long as the police "scrupulously honor" the "right to cut off questioning," they may reinitiate interrogation after such an invocation. In Mosely, that meant that waiting two hours after the first interrogation attempt and interrogating Mosely in a separate room about a different crime was permissible. Similarly, in Moran v. Burbine,[62] the Court permitted interrogation that took place approximately five hours after invocation of the right to silence. That result was not affected by the fact that during the intervening period the police erroneously informed Burbine's attorney that Burbine would not be subjected to any questioning that day, or by the fact that police did not tell Burbine about the attorney's call; the only relevant fact for Fifth Amendment purposes, the Court stressed, was that Burbine had been told of his rights before the interrogation and had voluntarily waived them. Nor did the police's misstatement to the attorney "shock the conscience" sufficiently to amount to a due process violation. The idea behind the Court's waiver analysis seems to be that the warnings are the only information a rational defendant needs in order to make a voluntary decision about confessing.

59 462 U.S. 1039 (1983).

60 559 U.S. 98 (2010).

61 423 U.S. 96 (1975).

62 475 U.S. 412 (1986).

5.5 Sixth Amendment rules

Two years before Miranda, the Supreme Court decided Massiah v. United States.[63] There the government persuaded one Colson, who had been indicted along with Massiah on a drug smuggling charge, to engage Massiah in conversation while in Colson's car, which had been bugged. The Court excluded the ensuing incriminating statements on the ground that the Sixth Amendment's guarantee of the right to counsel "in all criminal prosecutions" prohibited use of statements "deliberately elicited from [a defendant] after he had been indicted and in the absence of his counsel."

Note that exclusion would not have been required under the Court's Miranda doctrine, given Massiah's belief he was talking to a colleague in crime, which meant that the "inherent coercion" of custodial interrogation was absent. The Court's focus in Massiah was not compulsion. Rather, the Court emphasized that the period from arraignment to trial is as "critical . . . as trial itself," because of the need for "consultation, thorough-going investigation and preparation." Once that critical period has begun, questioning in the absence of counsel without an explicit waiver of that right violates the Sixth Amendment's separate guarantee of "the assistance of counsel." Thus, there is both a Fifth Amendment right to counsel, recognized in Miranda and applicable solely to custodial interrogation, and a Sixth Amendment right to counsel during any questioning that occurs after criminal prosecution begins.

The Miranda decision two years later pushed Massiah to the side for some time. It was not until Brewer v. Williams,[64] 13 years after Massiah, that the Supreme Court next applied the Sixth Amendment to police questioning. There, after Williams had been arraigned on charges of killing a young girl and appointed an attorney, he was taken by a detective named Leaming from Davenport, Iowa to Des Moines. Despite the defense attorney's demand that Leaming not question Williams during the trip, once in the car alone with Williams the detective delivered what has since been called the "Christian burial speech," during which he falsely stated he knew the girl's body would be lying along the route they were taking, noted that snowfall anticipated that night might cover it, and opined that "the parents of this little girl should be

63 377 U.S. 201 (1964).

64 430 U.S. 387 (1977).

entitled to a Christian burial." Williams led Leaming to the body soon afterward. The case could have been analyzed under Miranda, since it did not involve undercover questioning, as in Massiah, and since Williams was clearly in custody. But instead the Court, noting that Williams had already been arraigned, looked to the Sixth Amendment, and found that Leaming had "deliberately and designedly set out to elicit information from Williams just assuredly as, and perhaps more effectively than—if he had formally interrogated him," yet had "made no effort to ascertain whether Williams wished to relinquish" the right to counsel.

Massiah and Brewer indicate that Sixth Amendment regulation of interrogation requires the answer to three questions: (1) when does criminal prosecution begin? (2) when has the government "deliberately elicited" information from the accused? and (3) in what ways, if any, is waiver analysis in the Sixth Amendment setting different from waiver of Fifth Amendment rights?

In Rothgery v. Gillespie County, Texas,[65] the Court firmly held what Williams had already implied, that "criminal prosecution" for Sixth Amendment purposes begins at the first appearance in front of a judicial officer ("arraignment") even in the absence of a formal charge from the prosecutor or a grand jury indictment. However, as Burbine indicates, the Sixth Amendment does not apply at arrest, even if the individual already has an attorney; while one could argue that an arrested person has as much need for the assistance of counsel as one who has been arraigned, the Court has insisted that the protection afforded by the Sixth Amendment (as opposed to Fifth Amendment) is triggered only after the government's role "shifts from investigation to accusation."

It follows that the Sixth Amendment's reach is charge-specific. In Maine v. Moulton,[66] the Court excluded statements obtained by an undercover agent relevant to charges for which the defendant was indicted, but refused to exclude statements made during the same encounter relevant to other, uncharged, crimes. Even when the crimes are very closely related, this rule applies. In Texas v. Cobb,[67] for instance, statements about a murder that occurred during a burglary

65 554 U.S. 191 (2008).
66 474 U.S. 159 (1985).
67 532 U.S. 162 (2001).

were admissible because, although the defendant had been formally charged with the burglary and counsel appointed, formal prosecution had not yet commenced on the murder.

If, however, the questioning is about a charged crime, custody is not required to trigger the Sixth Amendment. That fact was emphasized by the Court in Fellers v. United States,[68] where it held that the Sixth Amendment was violated by police questioning of an indicted defendant for 15 minutes in his home during the daytime, a scenario that probably would not have triggered Miranda's protection given the narrow definition of "custody." Again, the different outcome stems from the different rationale underlying the Sixth Amendment, which is to prevent interference with the attorney-client relationship, not deter compulsion.

"Deliberate elicitation" is obviously analogous to "interrogation" under Miranda. Again, however, compulsion is not the issue under the Sixth Amendment; rather motive is. Thus, in United States v. Henry,[69] the Supreme Court held that the test under the Sixth Amendment is whether the government "intentionally creates a situation likely to induce [the defendant] to make incriminating statements without the assistance of counsel." In Henry the Court concluded that this test was met because the police placed an informant in Henry's cell, told him to be alert to statements Henry made about his charges, and made clear to the informant that he would only be paid if he produced useful information. However, on the very similar facts of Kuhlmann v. Wilson,[70] statements Wilson made to a jail-cell informant were not excluded—even though the informant had at one point told Wilson his earlier denial of the crime "didn't sound too good"—because at the time of the confession the informant had "only listened" to the defendant's "spontaneous" and "unsolicited" statements, which the Court attributed to a visit from his brother, not to the informant's importunings. Wilson notwithstanding, the Sixth Amendment's focus on preventing interference with the attorney-client relationship clearly provides more protection from jailhouse snitches than the Fifth Amendment, which, as Perkins demonstrates, is not triggered by covert questioning.

---

68 540 U.S. 519 (2004).

69 447 U.S. 264 (1980).

70 477 U.S. 436 (1986).

The same difference in rationales has affected waiver analysis, although only marginally. For instance, in Patterson v. Illinois,[71] the Court indicated that while police obstruction of an attorney's access to a client, as in Burbine, does not violate the Fifth Amendment, it would violate the Sixth Amendment if it occurs after prosecution has begun. Further, since compulsion is not driving the analysis in the latter context, obtaining statements through trickery may be more likely to lead to exclusion. At the same time, the Court has made clear that the rules governing invocation of counsel in the Fifth Amendment setting also govern invocation in Sixth Amendment cases.[72] Thus, even after prosecution has begun, as long as they give the usual warnings (which of course include the admonition that the individual is entitled to counsel), police need not discontinue questioning unless the defendant unequivocally asks for counsel during interrogation, and they may resume questioning if the defendant reinitiates, as defined in Bradshaw.

5.6 Due process limitations

If police carry out their questioning prior to charging, thus avoiding the Sixth Amendment, and before taking an individual into custody, thus avoiding Miranda's dictates, their conduct is generally immune from constitutional challenge. However, in addition to informing waiver analysis under the Fifth and Sixth Amendments, the Supreme Court's due process doctrine also prohibits manifestly coercive questioning anytime it occurs. That fact was illustrated by Arizona v. Fulminante,[73] which involved an informant's questioning of Fulminante, in prison for possession of a firearm, about the murder of his step-daughter. Knowing that Fulminante, who was slight of build and of low-average intelligence, was "starting to get some tough treatment" from other prisoners, the informant told Fulminante, "You have to tell me about [the killing,] ... for me to give you any help." Neither Miranda nor Massiah applied, since the questioning was covert and Fulminante was not charged with the murder. Nonetheless, calling it a "close question," a five-member majority held Fulminante's subsequent incriminating statements were obtained in violation of the Due Process Clause.

71 487 U.S. 285 (1988).

72 Id.; Montejo v. United States, 556 U.S. 778 (2009).

73 499 U.S. 279 (1991).

5.7 Entrapment and regulation of undercover activity

As construed by the Supreme Court, the Constitution has little impact on undercover work. The technique of posing as a friend or co-conspirator can involve significant intrusions into privacy, but the Fourth Amendment does not apply because of the assumption of risk doctrine (see §2.3.4). The Fifth Amendment is inapposite because custody and compulsion are not involved. The Sixth Amendment, when triggered, prohibits elicitation of statements by an undercover agent and, as Fulminante indicates, the Due Process Clause could limit some undercover activity as well. But the Sixth Amendment only applies post-prosecution, and, as described in more detail below, the Due Process Clause only prohibits particularly egregious misconduct.

In contrast, the entrapment defense, although not constitutional in origin, can have an impact on undercover investigative activity regardless of when it occurs, in situations where coercive conduct by government agents falls short of the compulsion banned by the Due Process Clause. The Supreme Court has held that the entrapment defense is available in federal cases as a matter of inferred congressional intent. In Sorrells v. United States,[74] for instance, the Court stated "[w]e are unable to conclude" that Congress would countenance conviction of an "otherwise innocent" person who is lured into committing crime by government agents. However, the Court only recognizes an entrapment defense when the defendant can show that he or she was "otherwise innocent," or, as the courts put it, was not "predisposed" to commit the crime charged. Applying the predisposition test, the Court has held that entrapment occurred when a government agent convinced the defendant to sell him whiskey during the Prohibition era only after two previous, unsuccessful solicitation attempts,[75] and when the defendant provided drugs to an informant, at cost, only after repeated attempts to get him to do so.[76] But the Court held the defense was not available when an agent posing as a narcotics distributor offered to supply ingredients for methamphetamine production to an individual who had previously been an "active participant in an illegal drug manufacturing enterprise,"[77] and where a drug user agreed to find

74 287 U.S. 435 (1932).

75 Id.

76 Sherman v. United States, 356 U.S. 369 (1958).

77 United States v. Russell, 411 U.S. 423 (1973).

a supplier for the informant (even when the supplier turned out to be a government agent as well!).[78]

The most difficult entrapment case at the Supreme Court level may have been Jacobson v. United States.[79] There the Court reversed Jacobson's conviction for purchasing two magazines containing photographs of nude preteen and teenage boys, after the government had spent 2½ years—using five different fictitious organizations touting pornographic images—trying to get him to buy such material. Despite the fact that the defendant had on several occasions expressed an interest in seeing pictures of preteen sex, and despite conceding that the defendant probably had "certain personal inclinations" toward viewing such pictures even before his contact with the government, the majority did not find evidence of predisposition to buy pornographic material prior to the government's inducements. The dissent complained that this result in effect requires the government to have "reasonable suspicion of criminal activity before it begins an investigation" using surreptitious ploys, an assertion which, if true, would be consonant with a Fourth Amendment approach to undercover activity. However, Jacobson is probably best explained as a reaction to the uniquely inefficient and wasteful efforts undertaken by the government in the case, which aimed at getting Jacobson to commit conduct that had not even been criminalized until shortly before the government's inducement campaign began.

In contrast to the federal predisposition test for entrapment is the conduct of authorities test, which at one time was adopted in a number of states.[80] Under the latter test, the entrapment defense is viewed as a means of sanctioning police misconduct rather than as a tool for assessing the defendant's culpability; the defense is available whenever the government's conduct was reprehensible, even if the defendant was predisposed to commit the crime. Under one version of this test, for instance, the Florida Supreme Court found objectionable a decoy operation in a high crime area using an officer posing as an unconscious "drunk" with money sticking out of his pocket.[81]

While the Supreme Court has refused to adopt the conduct of authorities formulation, it has intimated that, independently of entrapment

---

78 Hampton v. United States, 425 U.S. 484 (1976).

79 503 U.S. 540 (1992).

80 State v. Wilkins, 473 A.2d 295 (Vt. 1983) (listing cases).

81 Cruz v. State, 465 So.2d 517 (Fla. 1995), over'd Munoz v. State, 629 So.2d 90 (Fla. 1993).

doctrine, the Due Process Clause might be violated in cases involving atrocious police conduct. Thus, in one majority opinion, Justice William Rehnquist stated that "we may someday be presented with a situation in which the conduct of law enforcement agents is so outrageous that due process principles would absolutely bar the government from invoking judicial processes to obtain a conviction,"[82] and in a concurring opinion in another case, Justice Lewis Powell stated that "it would be unthinkable, for example, to permit government agents to instigate robberies and beatings merely to gather evidence to convict other members of a gang of hoodlums."[83] While the Court has never found this due process principle to be violated, one lower federal court so held when the government not only supplied the defendant with much of the paraphernalia and ingredients necessary to manufacture illegal drugs, but also provided an isolated farmhouse as a manufacturing site.[84]

82 United States v. Russell, 411 U.S. 423 (1973).

83 Hampton v. United States, 425 U.S. 484 (1976) (Powell, J., concurring).

84 United States v. Twigg, 588 F.2d 373 (3d Cir. 1978).

6 Eyewitness identification procedures

6.1 Reliability of eyewitness identifications

The term "identification procedures" encompasses a wide array of investigative techniques, ranging from eyewitness identifications using lineups, one-on-one confrontations (showups), and photo arrays, to fingerprinting, DNA, and other types of forensic analyses that attempt to determine whether characteristics associated with a particular person match evidence obtained from a crime scene. This chapter will focus on eyewitness identification procedures, usually conducted by police and prosecutors. Later chapters will address in more detail forensic techniques normally conducted by laboratory technicians (see §§8.4.3; 11.4.3).

Eyewitness-driven identifications are the leading cause of wrongful convictions.[1] Years of research explain why.[2] Perception of a crime can be obscured not only by poor eyesight or bad lighting, but by the stress associated with the crime, a focus on weapons rather than faces, short observation time, and "seeing" what the witness expected or wanted to occur rather than what actually occurred; cross-racial perceptions are particularly likely to be inaccurate. Even if the initial perception is unadulterated, memory of an event begins decaying immediately, and gaps in memory are often filled with images based on preconceptions and biases, or with post-event information provided by the police or others. Finally, even if witnesses accurately perceive and remember an event, they may have difficulty describing it or be influenced by the manner in which the description is elicited; for instance, a witness may feel compelled to identify someone in a lineup because of conscious or unconscious pressure from the police, the victim, or other witnesses,

1 Michael J. Saks and Jonathan. Koehler, The Coming Paradigm Shift in Forensic Science, 309 Science 892 (2005).

2 See Ralph N. Haber and Lyn Haber, Experiencing, Remembering and Reporting Events, 6 Psychol, Pub. Pol'y & L. 1057 (2000) (summarizing research).

or because the identification procedure does not provide a "not there" option.

While police and prosecutors can do nothing about perception problems or memory decay, they can minimize the extent to which their actions influence memory, recall, and the ultimate identification.[3] Most experts agree that one-on-one confrontations with a suspect should be avoided whenever possible, and that lineups and photo arrays should generally have at least six options, including a "blank" option; otherwise witnesses tend to assume the perpetrator is present and pick the person who looks most like the culprit. Witnesses should be required to describe the perpetrator before the identification procedure, and "distractors" (i.e., people who are not the suspect) should resemble that description to ensure the suspect is not the only one who does so; further, every attempt should be made to avoid a lineup or array in which the suspect is the only one with a salient characteristic (such as a scar). Administration of the identification procedure should be "blind" (meaning that those conducting it should not know who the suspected perpetrator is) and, when there is more than one witness, a separate identification procedure should be conducted for each, to avoid witnesses influencing one another. Witnesses who are uncertain whether they can identify the perpetrator should not be pressured to do so and, if they do make an identification, they should be asked to state their confidence level, which can be compared to (and should be roughly the same as) the confidence expressed at trial.

While some lower courts have required or strongly encouraged these types of procedures,[4] the Supreme Court has taken a more flexible approach. It has held that the Due Process Clause requires that state-conducted identifications have indicia of reliability, but has been unwilling to prescribe any particular identification procedure. It has concluded that the Sixth Amendment requires counsel during some types of procedure but not others. And it has concluded that the Fourth and Fifth Amendments place virtually no constraints on governmental use of any force that is necessary to get a suspect to participate in identification procedures.

3 Gary L. Wells, Mark Small, Steven Penrod, Roy S. Malpass, Solomon M. Fulero, and C.A.E. Brimacombe, Eyewitness Identification Procedures: Recommendations for Lineups and Photospreads, 22 L. & Hum. Beh. 1 (1998).

4 See, e.g., State v. Henderson, 27 A.3d 872 (N.J. 2011).

6.2 Due process limitations

In contrast to the Supreme Court's search and seizure caselaw, which focuses on protecting privacy and autonomy, and its caselaw on interrogation, which primarily addresses compulsion, "reliability is the linchpin in determining the admissibility of identification testimony," a principle that derives from the Due Process Clause.[5] The Warren Court signaled that, to minimize the possibility of unreliable eyewitness testimony, it would exclude all identifications produced by a "suggestive" procedure, unless extenuating circumstances made the procedure necessary. The post-Warren Court has been less willing to restrict eyewitness identifications.

One example of the Warren Court's approach comes from Stovall v. Denno,[6] where the victim of a vicious assault identified Stovall as the perpetrator after a group of police brought him to her hospital room. The Court noted that such one-on-one confrontations are "widely condemned" because they strongly imply the police think they have the perpetrator. At the same time, the Court upheld the identification because it was "necessary," given the fragile state of the witness and the difficulty of arranging a lineup in such circumstances (although a photo array certainly would have been possible). Similarly, in Simmons v. United States,[7] the Court stated that a six-photo array police showed to witnesses to a robbery was "short of the ideal," but upheld the identification because "[i]t was essential for the FBI agents swiftly to determine whether they were on the right track." In contrast, in Foster v. California,[8] the necessity requirement resulted in exclusion of an identification of Foster made during a five-person lineup, after the witness had declined to identify him in a three-person lineup and remained tentative even after a highly suggestive but uncalled for one-on-one confrontation with him.

The post-Warren Court quickly dispensed with any necessity requirement, however. In Neil v. Biggers,[9] the witness, a rape victim, identified Biggers, a 16-year-old African-American youth, in a one-on-one

5 Manson v. Brathwaite, 432 U.S. 98 (1977). As with invasions of privacy and compulsion, the cause of unreliability must be the government, not factors beyond the government's control. Perry v. New Hampshire, 565 U.S. 228 (2011).

6 388 U.S. 293 (1967).

7 390 U.S. 377 (1968).

8 394 U.S. 440 (1969).

9 409 U.S. 188 (1972).

confrontation, after he was asked to speak the same words—"Shut up or I'll kill you"—that were spoken by the rapist. Since a lineup probably could have been arranged, the Court essentially conceded that the procedure had been unnecessarily suggestive, but it went on to conclude the identification had sufficient indicia of reliability after considering five factors:

> [t]he opportunity of the witness to view the criminal at the time of the crime; the witness' degree of attention; the accuracy of the witness' prior description of the criminal; the level of certainty demonstrated by the witness at the confrontation; and the length of time between the crime and the confrontation.

According to the Court, concerns about the suggestive nature of the one-on-one confrontation and the several-month lapse between the rape and the identification did not outweigh the length of the witness' encounter with the perpetrator (over 15 minutes), the fact that the witness had declined to accuse several other "suspects" prior to identifying Biggers, the fit between her earlier description of the rapist and Biggers' appearance, and her immediate certainty that he was the perpetrator. Similarly, in Manson v. Braithwaite,[10] the case that affirmed reliability as the "linchpin" of due process analysis, the Court dismissed concerns about an identification of a drug dealer based on one photo shown to the witness two days after the encounter, because the witness was a trained police officer who viewed the seller for two to three minutes, and who described him a few minutes later to the officer who subsequently produced the photo.

Justice Thurgood Marshall's dissenting opinion in Brathwaite argued that, given the need to look for signs of danger, the witness had only directly observed the dealer's face for under 30 seconds, that the two-day lapse before viewing the photo could easily have undermined the witness' memory (which was likely influenced by the other officer's certainty that Braithwaite was the dealer), and that witness confidence is not necessarily correlated with accuracy (an assertion that is corroborated by research[11]). Justice Marshall also suggested that exclusion of a suggestive identification like the one that occurred in Braithwaite does not have to lead to disqualification of the witness, if he or she subsequently identifies the defendant during a properly constructed procedure. But there is a problem with Justice Marshall's proposal as

10 432 U.S. 98 (1977).

11 Wells et al., supra note 3, at 17–20.

well, since research strongly suggests that new identifications are often heavily influenced by previous ones.[12] The best approach is to avoid the suggestive procedure in the first place if at all possible.

6.3 Sixth Amendment limitations

A second method of regulating identification procedures is by providing counsel, who can observe the procedure, recommend changes in how it is carried out, and describe it in subsequent court proceedings. As indicated in the previous chapter, however, the Sixth Amendment only applies after criminal prosecution has begun, so there is no right to counsel at identification procedures that occur prior to that point. Additionally, while post-charge lineups and showups are "critical stages" that trigger the right,[13] United States v. Ash[14] held that photo arrays do not, because the defendant—who is obviously elsewhere during such a procedure—is not faced with an "adversarial" or "trial-like confrontation" of the type that occurs during interrogation and preliminary hearings.

One could argue that, even at lineups and showups, there is no adversarial confrontation of the type contemplated in Ash, since no decisions or arguments are made during such procedures and since, at least with lineups, the defendant's only encounter with government officials may be through a one-way mirror. At the same time, if counsel is considered an important means of ensuring a reliable procedure during lineups, the same would seem to hold true at photo arrays, perhaps even more so, precisely because otherwise no one from the defense side is present to observe how it is conducted. But the Ash majority responded that "[t]he primary safeguard against abuses [of the photo array process] is the ethical responsibility of the prosecutor" (despite the fact that police alone conduct most photo array procedures). Perhaps more responsive to any concerns about abuse during a photo array was Justice Potter Stewart's observation, in a concurring opinion, that attorneys should have little trouble reconstructing the array at a later hearing (as compared, for instance, to challenging the construction of a lineup without having seen it).

12 Nancy K. Steblay, Maintaining the Reliability of Eyewitness Evidence: After the Lineup, 42 Creighton L. Rev. 643, 647–51 (2009).

13 United States v. Wade, 388 U.S. 218 (1967); Moore v. Illinois, 434 U.S. 220 (1977).

14 413 U.S. 300 (1973).

In theory, an attorney who is present during the identification procedure could do more than simply observe it. For instance, if confronted with a very suggestive or inadequate procedure, the attorney might make recommendations for changing it, and perhaps even seek a court order to do so, especially in non-exigent circumstances. Cognizant of the research described in §6.1, an attorney might also want to compare witness descriptions with distractors, make sure that the procedure is blindly and neutrally administered, and insist that witnesses are kept separate and are told that they have the option to say the perpetrator is not present in the lineup. But most courts, following Ash's description of counsel's role as that of a passive observer, have held that attorneys are entitled only to view the lineup and then argue at later proceedings that the resulting identification was unreliable.[15]

6.4 Fourth and Fifth Amendment limitations

If the police want to bring a person who has yet to be arrested to the stationhouse for a lineup procedure, the Supreme Court has signaled that the seizure can be justified on something short of probable cause. In Hayes v. Florida,[16] the Court stated in dictum:

> there is . . . support in our cases for the view that the Fourth Amendment would permit seizures for the purpose of fingerprinting, if there is reasonable suspicion that the suspect has committed a criminal act, if there is a reasonable basis for believing that fingerprint will establish or negate the suspect's connection with that crime, and if the procedure is carried out with dispatch.

The Court added, however, that if the seizure is from the individual's home, some sort of judicial authorization would be required. It is likely the same set of rules applies to seizures for the purpose of conducting lineups. If instead, as is often the case, the participants in a lineup are already in custody, no Fourth Amendment issue is likely to arise.

Nor is the Fifth Amendment violated by forcing a person to appear for observation or to utter words purportedly spoken by the perpetrator of the crime (as in Biggers). In both instances, the exposure is considered

15 See, e.g., People v. Sharp, 942 N.Y.S.2d (Sup. Ct. 2012) (quoting People v. Hobson, 348 N.E.2d 894 (N.Y. 1976); United States v. Bierey, 588 F.2d 620 (8th Cir. 1978).

16 Hayes v. Florida, 470 U.A. 811 (1985).

"nontestimonial"; even in the latter case, the individual's voice is used "as an identifying physical characteristic, not to speak his guilt."[17] For the same reason, forcing a person to submit to a blood alcohol test, upon pain of having a refusal brought up at a later trial for drunk driving, does not violate the Fifth Amendment.[18]

17 Dionisio v. United States, 410 U.S. 1 (1973).

18 South Dakota v. Neville, 459 U.S. 553 (1983). Although it violates the Fourth Amendment if conducted without a warrant. See Birchfield v. North Dakota, 136 S.Ct. 2160 (2016).

7 The exclusionary rule and other remedies for police misconduct

7.1 Rationale for the exclusionary rule

The exclusionary rule—the rule that evidence obtained in violation of the Fourth, Fifth, Sixth, and Fourteenth Amendments is inadmissible at trial—is probably the most controversial topic in all of criminal procedure. Opponents of the rule point not only to the obvious fact that the suppression of evidence obtained through searches and seizures, interrogations, and identification procedures can result in dismissal or reduction of charges against a clearly guilty person. They also argue that exclusion often fails to achieve its goal of deterring police misconduct, because its most direct impact falls on prosecutors, not law enforcement officers. Yet the rule's proponents insist that, despite its flaws, the rule is still the optimal method of ensuring obedience to the Constitution's mandates, and that allowing courts to use evidence obtained through unconstitutional means undermines the integrity of the judicial system.

No constitutional provision specifically requires exclusion. However, the Fifth Amendment's declaration that "no person . . . shall be compelled to be a witness against himself" does suggest that compelled statements and testimony should not be admitted into evidence. In the 1886 decision of Boyd v. United States,[1] the Supreme Court relied on that language in suppressing invoices obtained through compulsory process (i.e., a subpoena), and declared that this compulsion was also "the equivalent of search and seizure—an unreasonable search and seizure—within the meaning of the Fourth Amendment." As a result, in federal courts exclusion eventually became the remedy not only when the Fifth Amendment was infringed, but also for violations of the Fourth Amendment, which until that time had been redressed through damages actions.[2] While the Fifth Amendment basis for

1 116 U.S. 616 (1886).

2 Weeks v. United States, 232 U.S. 383 (1914).

exclusion in search and seizure cases is suspect when the evidence is non-testimonial, especially when the target is not compelled to produce it (see §8.4.1), that concern soon became moot. Justice Oliver Wendell Holmes' declaration in 1921 that the Fourth Amendment would be a "mere form of words" if exclusion were not the remedy for its infringement established that the Fourth Amendment alone was sufficient basis for the rule.[3] Seven years later Justice Louis Brandeis added that "the government itself would become a lawbreaker" if it relied on illegally seized evidence to convict someone.[4]

These latter two rationales for the rule reappeared decades later in Mapp v. Ohio,[5] the Warren Court decision that applied the Fourth Amendment exclusionary rule to the states. Citing Justice Holmes, the Court stated that allowing the use of illegally obtained evidence "is to grant the right but in reality to withhold its privilege and enjoyment"; it also noted that other sanctions for illegal searches and seizures had proven "worthless and futile." And citing Justice Brandeis, the Court opined that "[n]othing can destroy a government more quickly than its failure to observe its own law, or worse, its disregard of the charter of its own existence."

Thus, at its genesis, exclusion of illegally seized evidence was based on the twin notions that constitutional rights must be meaningfully vindicated and that judicial reliance on such evidence besmirches the entire system. Post-Warren Court cases, however, developed a third rationale for the rule, one that soon became the dominant focus of exclusionary rule jurisprudence and led to a significant reduction in the rule's scope. Twelve years after Mapp the Court declared, in United States v. Calandra,[6] that "the rule's prime purpose is to deter future unlawful police conduct." And ten years after Calandra it explicitly rejected Justice Brandeis' systemic integrity rationale—and by implication Holmes' vindication rationale as well—when it stated that "our cases establish that the question whether the use of illegally obtained evidence in judicial proceedings represents judicial participation in a Fourth Amendment violation and offends the integrity of the courts is essentially the same as the inquiry into whether exclusion would serve

3 Silverthorne Lumber Co. v. United States, 251 U.S. 385 (1920).

4 Olmstead v. United States, 277 U.S. 438 (1928) (Brandeis, J., dissenting).

5 367 U.S. 643 (1961).

6 414 U.S. 338 (1974).

a deterrent purpose."[7] While these words were aimed at the Fourth Amendment exclusionary rule, they have turned out to have almost equal applicability in Fifth and Sixth Amendment cases.

Given the Court's current approach, some sense of the rule's deterrent impact on the police would be useful. Sociological research observing typical search and seizure practices suggests that, in the average, quickly developing case, the police are not particularly concerned about exclusion.[8] Rather, they are more interested in meeting arrest quotas, removing drugs and weapons from the streets, and impressing their supervisors. Any concern they do have about exclusion may also be eroded by knowledge that their description of a search, interrogation, or lineup is more likely to be believed than the defendant's (although taping has diminished that advantage in the interrogation and identification settings, and body cameras are beginning to have the same impact in the search and seizure context). Perhaps most importantly, as noted above, exclusion has its most direct impact on the prosecutor; in many cases, police may never find out their conduct has resulted in exclusion or only learn about it months later.

The Supreme Court has also clearly been mindful of the "cost" of exclusion. Most studies show that exclusion only results in dismissal of somewhere around 1 percent of all criminal cases, and that most of these cases involve minor crimes, such as possession of small amounts of drugs and petty larceny.[9] Even so, in absolute terms, thousands of cases are dismissed or undermined because probative evidence has been excluded. Given its consequences, in particular its harm to the prosecution's case, the rule may also make judges reluctant to give expansive interpretation to constitutional provisions. Further, contrary to Mapp's assertion, it may actually diminish the average citizen's respect for a legal system that frees guilty people on "technicalities."

Nonetheless, there is no doubt that the rule does have a significant cautionary impact on many police, especially in important cases involving prolonged investigations where prosecutors are monitoring their

---

7 United States v. Leon, 468 U.S. 897 (1984).

8 See Christopher Slobogin, Why Liberals Should Chuck the Exclusionary Rule, 1999 U. Ill. L. Rev. 363, 368–71, 391–2.

9 Craig D. Uchida and Timothy S. Bynum, Search Warrants, Motions to Suppress and "Lost Cases": The Effects of the Exclusionary Rule in Seven Jurisdictions, 81 J. Crim. L. & Criminol. 1034, 1064–5 (1991); Peter Nardulli, The Societal Costs of the Exclusionary Rule Revisited, 1987 U. Ill. L. Rev. 223, 226, 236.

actions. And if Mapp is right that other remedies—such as damages actions brought against police departments and individual officers—are "worthless and futile," the exclusionary rule may be the best among imperfect options for remedying constitutional violations. It should also be noted that, even if a good alternative remedy were developed, the government would probably still "lose" a sizeable number of cases because of the Fourth, Fifth, and Sixth Amendments; an aggressive damages remedy, for instance, might deter risk-averse police from carrying out any action that is not clearly permissible. The difference between the rule and other remedies is that it more obviously "flaunts before us the costs we pay for [constitutional] guarantees."[10]

The current Court is clearly hostile to an expansive exclusionary rule. The following discussion focuses on the many ways in which the Court has eroded the suppression remedy, not only in the search and seizure context, but in connection with Miranda and other constitutional doctrines as well. It ends with a description of the main alternatives to the rule, so that a proper evaluation can be made of whether they are in fact "worthless," and whether they, or some variation thereof, could effectively replace exclusion as the predominant remedy for constitutional violations by the police.

7.2 Secondary process exception

Relying on the deterrence rationale, the Supreme Court has made clear that the exclusionary rule applies only to criminal trials, not in any other type of secondary proceeding, criminal or civil. In Calandra, for instance, the Court held that evidence seized in violation of the Fourth Amendment may be considered by a grand jury in deciding whether to indict someone. Ignoring the claim that use of such evidence would taint the criminal process, the Court concluded that, because exclusion would still occur at Calandra's trial, "[a]ny incremental deterrent effect which might be achieved by extending the rule to grand jury proceedings is uncertain at best." At the same time, it noted, extending the rule to that proceeding "would seriously impede the grand jury" in its historical role as an investigatory body. Using similar reasoning, the Court has held that the Fourth Amendment exclusionary rule should not operate in post-conviction proceedings,[11] parole revocation

10 John Kaplan, The Limits of the Exclusionary Rule, 26 Stan. L. Rev. 1027, 2037 (1974).

11 Stone v. Powell, 428 U.S. 465 (1976).

hearings,[12] civil tax proceedings,[13] and civil deportation proceedings.[14] In some of these situations, the likelihood of a criminal trial and the concomitant influence of exclusion on the police can be very remote, a fact recognized in the civil deportation case when four justices in the majority stated they might change their opinion "if there developed good reason to believe that Fourth Amendment violations by [immigration] officers were widespread." But to date the Court's secondary process cases have been more concerned with the "deflection of truth-finding" that the rule incurs than the possibility its absence will tempt police misconduct.

The Court has treated the exclusion of confessions and eyewitness identifications under the Fifth and Sixth Amendments in a similar fashion. In part, of course, that is because the explicit reference in those amendments to the criminal process means that they do not apply at all in civil proceedings. But the Court has also indicated that these amendments do not require exclusion at some stages of the criminal process.[15] As the following discussion will make clear, while the Court has distinguished the Fourth Amendment exclusionary rule from the exclusionary rule in Fifth and Sixth Amendment cases by insisting that the former rule is merely a "judicially-created remedy" that is subject to adjustment depending upon the deterrence rationale, the Court has often treated all of these rules as eminently manipulable.

7.3 Impeachment exception

Even at the criminal trial, unconstitutionally seized evidence is often admissible. One such situation is when the defendant takes the stand and the prosecutor wants to use the evidence to impeach (contradict) the witness. Consistent with its secondary process cases, the Court has reasoned that as long as police know that illegally seized evidence will be excluded in the prosecution's case-in-chief, extension of the rule to impeachment is unnecessary for deterrence purposes, while doing so would allow the defendant to fabricate stories without fear of exposure. The first case to so hold involved evidence obtained in violation

12 Pennsylvania v. Scott, 524 U.S. 357 (1998).

13 United States v. Janis, 428 U.S. 433 (1976).

14 INS v. Lopez-Mendoza, 468 U.S. 1032 (1984).

15 See Lawn v. United States, 355 U.S. 339 (1958) (grand jury may consider statements obtained in violation of the Fifth Amendment).

of Miranda, with the Court reasoning that the privilege against self-incrimination "cannot be construed to include the right to commit perjury."[16] The Court subsequently reached the same conclusion in cases involving impeachment using evidence obtained in violation of the Fourth[17] and Sixth Amendments.[18]

The principal limitation on the impeachment exception to the rule is that the prosecutor may only use the illegally seized evidence if it contradicts something the defendant said or implied during direct examination; attempting to get the defendant to make an impeachable statement for the first time on cross-examination would violate the general rule that cross-examination must stay within the scope of direct examination.[19] The Court also appears unwilling to permit impeachment with evidence obtained in violation of the Due Process Clause, at least if it consists of statements that are truly "involuntary" (meaning involuntary because of physical or legal threats rather than involuntary in Miranda's sense).[20] Finally, the Court has held that witnesses other than the defendant may not be impeached using illegally obtained evidence, largely on the ground that people who are not on trial are sufficiently deterred by the threat of perjury charges, much more so than defendants fighting against conviction.[21]

A separate type of impeachment issue arises when the prosecutor wants to use a person's silence as impeachment evidence. For instance, the prosecutor might want to imply that the defendant's trial testimony that he acted in self-defense is fabricated, because he did not mention anything about self-defense at the time of arrest or at any other point prior to trial. The Court has held, as a matter of due process, that if the pretrial silence occurs after the defendant has been given Miranda warnings—which of course specifically state that there is a right to remain silent—this type of impeachment is impermissible, because the person's silence is "insolubly ambiguous."[22] However, if after receiving the warnings a suspect decides to talk, a post-warning story that is

16 Harris v. New York, 401 U.S. 222 (1971).

17 United States v. Havens, 446 U.S. 620 (1980).

18 Kansas v. Ventris, 556 U.S. 586 (2009). The one exception is when the testimony is given under a grant of immunity. New Jersey v. Portash, 440 U.S. 450 (1979).

19 United States v. Havens, 446 U.S. 620 (1980).

20 Harris v. New York, 401 U.S. 222 (1971).

21 James v. Illinois, 493 U.S. 307 (1990).

22 Doyle v. Ohio, 426 U.S. 610 (1976).

different from the trial story is still admissible.[23] And the admissibility of pre-warning silence is merely a matter of relevance, not an issue of constitutional significance.[24] Thus, in Salinas v. Texas,[25] the Court held that the Constitution was not violated when the prosecution introduced into evidence the fact that during questioning Salinas, who was not in custody at the time and therefore was not given warnings, looked down at the floor and remained silent for a few moments when asked about whether his shotgun would match the shells found at the crime scene. The Court concluded that his silence would have been inadmissible only if Salinas had explicitly asserted his right to remain silent at the time; otherwise, the prosecution was entitled to argue that his hesitation in answering was consistent with an attempt to think up a lie or with consciousness of guilt.

7.4 Good faith exception

A second exception to the general rule that unconstitutionally obtained evidence is inadmissible at criminal trials has, to date, arisen only in search and seizure cases. In United States v. Leon,[26] the Court held that if an officer reasonably relies on a warrant when conducting a search or seizure, a subsequent finding that the warrant is invalid should not result in exclusion. Although called the "good faith" exception to exclusion, this doctrine is in fact objectively defined; as in other areas of Fourth Amendment law, the officer's subjective belief about whether the warrant is valid is irrelevant. Rather, the exception applies as long as the warrant is issued by a neutral and detached magistrate, is not facially invalid, and is not "so lacking in indicia of probable cause as to render official belief in its existence entirely unreasonable," as might occur, the Court explained, if the officer provides the magistrate with information he or she knows or should know is false.[27] The Court reasoned that, when this reasonable reliance test is met, exclusion would be unlikely to deter violations of the Fourth Amendment, yet would result in the loss of a significant number of convictions.

---

23 Anderson v. Charles, 447 U.S. 404 (1980).

24 Jenkins v. Anderson, 447 U.S. 231 (1980).

25 570 U.S. 178 (2013).

26 468 U.S. 897 (1984).

27 Franks v. Delaware, 438 U.S. 154 (1978).

The dissenters in Leon noted that, even if an officer's good faith reliance on a warrant could be proven, exclusion in this situation would still provide an incentive for magistrates to be careful about probable cause determinations. An even more telling point from the dissent was the observation that the majority's rule in effect creates two Fourth Amendment standards: probable cause and the not "entirely unreasonable" cause necessary to avoid exclusion. The latter standard now governs warrant-based searches, a fact dramatically illustrated by lower court decisions that avoid analyzing whether a warrant was based on probable cause once they find that a reasonable officer could have believed it was.[28] In Leon itself, the Court never determined whether partially corroborated five-month-old information from an unnamed confidential informant constituted probable cause, but rather ended its analysis once it concluded that the good faith exception applied.

The same dynamic occurred in Leon's companion case, Massachusetts v. Shepard,[29] which involved a search of Shepard's house for evidence of murder, pursuant to a standardized "controlled substances" warrant form; because of an oversight by the magistrate, the form did not have those words crossed out, nor mention the murder-related items that the warrant application stated the police wanted to seize, nor cross-reference that application. Although the defendant argued that this warrant violated the Particularity Clause, the Court did not respond to that argument (until ten years later when, in another case, it agreed that this situation violates the Clause[30]). Rather, Shepard held that the officer, who had told the magistrate the warrant needed some changes, reasonably relied on the warrant, despite the fact that the warrant was literally "facially deficient." Like Leon, Shepard emphasized that exclusion should occur only when likely to deter misconduct by the police; deterrence of other actors in the system, such as magistrates, is not its objective.

That rationale explains why the Court subsequently held, in Arizona v. Evans,[31] that drugs found incident to an arrest, based on a misdemeanor warrant that had been quashed 17 days earlier, should not be

28 See David Clark Esseks, Errors in Good Faith: The Leon Exception Six Years Later, 89 Mich. L. Rev. 625 (1999).

29 468 U.S. 981 (1984).

30 Groh v. Ramirez, 540 U.S. 551 (2004), discussed in §3.4.

31 514 U.S. 1 (1995).

excluded, and why it held in Herring v. United States[32] that exclusion was not appropriate for evidence found pursuant to a warrant that should have been withdrawn five months before. In both cases, the police were not at fault; rather, they relied on other actors—in the first case, court clerks, and in the second, clerks within the police department. Dictum in Evans even calls into question older caselaw that requires exclusion when the arresting officer relies on a faulty bulletin from police in another police department.[33]

Good faith reasoning has also been the basis for decisions holding that exclusion should not occur when police rely on laws that turn out to be illegitimate. Thus, searches during arrests based on statutes later declared to be unconstitutional do not trigger exclusion.[34] Nor does a police action based on judicial precedent that is subsequently overturned.[35] To the argument that this latter rule would mean litigants would have no incentive to challenge existing caselaw (since they could not benefit from exclusion if they win), the majority responded that deterrence, not facilitating the overruling of precedent, is the goal of the exclusionary rule; at most, the Court stated, it might grant exclusion to a litigant who can show that otherwise "ossification" of the law would result.

All of these cases suggest significant hostility to the Fourth Amendment exclusionary rule. In Herring, the Court did state that if a record-keeping error was "flagrant," "knowing," "reckless," or "systemic" then a different result might be warranted. But this language—in a case where the mistake was made by an employee of the police department, not another branch of government—also suggests that the Court is unwilling to exclude evidence even when the police action is objectively unreasonable, so long as it does not involve reckless or flagrant violation of the Constitution. It is not out of the question that the Court will eventually hold admissible evidence obtained in violation of the Fourth Amendment by officers who are not relying on some outside legal source but rather can show their own judgment or the judgment of fellow officers on which they relied was not "entirely unreasonable." In the meantime, while the good faith exception at present applies solely in Fourth Amendment cases, the Court has developed analogous

32 555 U.S. 135 (2009).

33 Whiteley v. Warden, 401 U.S. 560 (1971); United States v. Hensley, 469 U.S. 221 (1985).

34 Michigan v. DeFillippo, 443 U.S. 31 (1979); Illinois v. Krull, 480 U.S. 340 (1987).

35 Davis v. United States, 564 U.S. 229 (2011).

doctrine in the Fifth Amendment context, in cases more profitably described below (see §7.6)

7.5 Standing

"Standing" rules define who is legally entitled to bring a lawsuit. Without some limitation on who has standing, people could bring claims about matters that do not affect them in any way; for instance, any citizen, even one having nothing to do with the crime in question, could ask for exclusion of evidence. While that rule is far too broad, one could argue that, since deterrence is the goal of exclusion, any criminal defendant who is the "target" of the government's investigation should have standing to contest its legality.

However, the Supreme Court has adhered to the position developed in non-criminal cases that only those whose constitutional interests are directly affected by the government's action have standing. That means, for instance, that a defendant cannot exclude a confession obtained in violation of a co-defendant's Miranda rights, even if the purpose of the interrogation was to get incriminating information about the defendant. It also means that a defendant cannot contest a search of someone else's premises and property if the evidence discovered there is used against the defendant. This is so even if the government illegality is perpetrated by officers who know standing rules will prevent challenge to their actions. Thus in United States v. Payner,[36] the Court held that Payner did not have standing to contest a break-in of a bank official's apartment by federal agents, even though the agents admitted Payner was the target of their investigation and that they carried out the illegal entry expecting that he would not have standing to contest it.

Defined in terms of whether the claimant's own rights are at stake, standing in Fifth, Sixth, and Fourteenth Amendment cases is an easy inquiry, since the only issue is whether it was the defendant or someone else who was allegedly denied the right to remain silent, have counsel present, or avoid coercion. Similarly, deciding whether a person has standing to contest an arrest or stop depends solely on whether he or she was seized. The task is somewhat more difficult when the defendant wants to challenge a search, because the scope of

36 447 U.S. 727 (1980).

Fourth Amendment search doctrine is more inchoate. While target standing of the type described above might best effectuate the exclusionary rule's deterrent purpose in such cases, the Court, once again emphasizing that the rule "exacts a substantial cost for the vindication of Fourth Amendment rights," held in Rakas v. Illinois[37] that only those whose "legitimate expectations of privacy" were infringed by the search have standing to contest it. In Rakas, this meant that the defendants, who were passengers in a car that they did not own, did not have standing to challenge a search of the car's glove compartment or the area under the seat.

Rakas also indicated, however, that the legitimate expectation of privacy formulation—which the reader of §2.3 will recognize resonates with the modern definition of "search" that eschews a rigid property-based orientation—provides standing not only to owners of searched property but also to those who have a "right to exclude" others from the searched area or property. Thus the Court's cases have granted standing to non-owners who are legitimately present in a residence or office and whose possessions are searched and seized,[38] as well as to people who are not on the premises but have continuing legitimate access to them (because, for instance, they have a key) and have their possessions searched and seized.[39] The Court has even held, unanimously, that a person who is driving a car in violation of a rental agreement has standing to contest search of the car, as long as the person who rented the car has given the defendant permission to use it.[40] Defendants may also have standing to contest seizure of their property when it is found in someone else's possession, if they have effected a lawful bailment to that person. The Court recognized this possibility in Rawlings v. Kentucky,[41] although in that case it held that, because Rawlings, aware that police had arrived on the scene, had hurriedly stuffed his drugs into his friend's purse without her consent, a valid bailment did not occur.

37 439 U.S. 128 (1978).

38 Jones v. United States, 362 U.S. 257 (1960) (affirmed in Rakas); Mancusi v. DeForte, 392 U.S. 364 (1968); Minnesota v. Olson, 495 U.S. 91 (1990). But see Minnesota v. Carter, 525 U.S. 83 (1998) (no standing to contest observation through window).

39 United States v. Jeffers, 342 U.S. 48 (1951) (affirmed in Rakas).

40 Byrd v. United States, 138 S.Ct. 1518 (2018).

41 448 U.S. 98 (1980).

7.6 Fruit of the poisonous tree

While earlier cases encompassed the idea, Nardone v. United States[42] was the first Supreme Court decision to use the colorful fruit of the poisonous tree language that has since permeated exclusionary rule jurisprudence. As Justice Felix Frankfurter imagined it in that case, any evidence (the fruit) discovered as a result of an unconstitutional action by the police (the poisonous tree) should generally be excluded. Thus, for instance, not only will evidence found incident to an illegal arrest or stop be excluded, but so will any evidence discovered during a later inventory of the person or a confession the arrested person makes at the stationhouse, because "but for" the illegality the evidence would never have been found. Although deterrence was not yet the rationale for the exclusionary rule at the time of Nardone, fruit of the poisonous tree doctrine is consistent with it, because it provides a disincentive to engage in an illegal action, such as an arrest on less than probable cause, in the hope something useful will eventually turn up.

However, there are several exceptions to the fruit of the poisonous tree exclusionary principle. Justice Frankfurter himself stated that fruit should still be admitted if the connection between the poisonous tree and the fruit becomes "so attenuated as to dissipate the taint," an idea which came to be called attenuation doctrine. Further, he pointed out that if the evidence is not, in fact, fruit of an illegality but instead came from a legitimate source, exclusion is not necessary, a notion that came to be called the independent source doctrine. And out of the latter doctrine arose the hypothetical independent source (or inevitable discovery) exception to fruit of the poisonous tree exclusion, which posits that exclusion should not occur if the evidence, although fruit of an illegality, would eventually have been found through a legal source. All of these exceptions could, in theory, be consistent with a deterrence rationale, since they could be construed to allow admission only of fruit that is unanticipated or that did not require an illegal act to obtain. However, the Court's more recent cases have interpreted these exceptions expansively or, in cases where it concludes that the exclusion remedy is not a good fit for the violation involved, have ignored their dictates altogether.

42 308 U.S. 338 (1939).

7.6.1 Attenuation

A classic example of a situation in which fruit of the poisonous tree doctrine extends the reach of the exclusionary rule is Brown v. Illinois,[43] where the police broke into Brown's apartment, searched it, and then arrested Brown, all without probable cause or a warrant. Brown was taken back to the station house, given Miranda warnings and, within an hour of his arrest, made incriminating statements. A few hours later, after another search by the police and another set of warnings, Brown provided more incriminating statements. Assuming the interrogations were properly carried out under Miranda, the Court nonetheless excluded both confessions on the ground that they were fruit of the poisonous arrest. The government had argued that the Miranda warnings "broke the causal chain" between the arrest and the confessions. But, citing Nardone, the Court held that the warnings did not sufficiently attenuate the taint of the arrest, as measured by "the temporal proximity of the arrest and the confession, the presence of intervening circumstances, and, particularly, the purpose and flagrancy of the official misconduct." Here the confessions occurred soon after an arrest that was a gross violation of the Fourth Amendment, and the only intervening events were the Miranda warnings, which the Court held were insufficient.

In Taylor v. Alabama,[44] the Court similarly held that the six-hour period between an illegal arrest and the confession, three sets of Miranda warnings, and a visit from friends did not sufficiently attenuate the original illegality, the oppression of being jailed, and the frequent confrontations with police in the meantime. In contrast, a "spontaneous" unsolicited confession, made after a 45-minute "congenial" home detention that was based on a good faith mistake by the police, was held to be admissible fruit.[45] Similarly, a volunteered confession made two days after release from the station house was considered untainted by an illegal arrest.[46]

Not all fruits are confessions, nor are all poisonous trees Fourth Amendment violations. In United States v. Ceccolini,[47] the fruit was a witness. There, an officer illegally looked in a package he saw in

43 422 U.S. 590 (1975).

44 457 U.S. 687 (1982).

45 Rawlings v. Kentucky, 448 U.S. 98 (1980).

46 Wong Sun v. United States, 371 U.S. 471 (1963).

47 435 U.S. 268 (1978).

the shop of a friend named Hennessey; the contents of the package eventually linked Hennessey to Ceccolini and resulted in Hennessey testifying against him. The Court noted that the officer had not been looking for evidence against Ceccolini at the time, that the testimony took place over a year after the search and, most importantly, that the witness testified on her own volition. The Court strongly implied that witnesses will rarely be considered inadmissible fruit, either because of attenuation or because there is a good chance they would have been discovered through legal means.

In Oregon v. Elstad,[48] the fruit was a confession, but the poisonous tree was also a confession. The first confession was obtained in violation of Miranda; the second came after Elstad received warnings. Elstad argued that the only reason he confessed the second time was because he thought the "cat was out of the bag." But the Court held that, when the poisonous tree is a mere "procedural" Miranda violation, the warnings are a sufficient "intervening" event, in contrast to when the poisonous tree is an illegal arrest. According to the Court,

> [i]t is an unwarranted extension of Miranda to hold that a simple failure to administer the warnings, unaccompanied by any actual coercion or other circumstances calculated to undermine the suspect's ability to exercise his free will, so taints the investigatory process that a subsequent voluntary and informed waiver is ineffective for some indeterminate period.

Subsequent cases made clear that if the first, unwarned confession is obtained through flagrant coercion "calculated to break the suspect's will," or if there is evidence that the interrogation officers deliberately took advantage of the cat-out-of-the-bag dynamic, for instance, by questioning the person in the same location immediately after the unwarned confession, a subsequent confession must be excluded, even if preceded by warnings.[49] However, when the fruit of a Miranda violation is "non-testimonial" (such as a gun), then even a deliberate effort to take advantage of an unwarned suspect does not result in exclusion.[50] As previous discussion has suggested (see §§3.6.1; 7.1), the latter result can be said to follow from the Fifth Amendment's language, which only prohibits government compelling a person to be a self-incriminating "witness."

48 470 U.S. 298 (1985).
49 Missouri v. Seibert, 542 U.S. 600 (2004); Bobby v. Dixon, 565 U.S. 23 (2011).
50 United States v. Patane, 542 U.S. 630 (2004); Wisconsin v. Knapp, 542 U.S. 952 (2004).

The Court has relied on the concept of attenuation not only in the sense of the fruit's proximity to the illegality, as in Brown, Taylor, Ceccolini, and Elstad, but also in terms of the link between the exclusionary remedy and the substantive right in question. This idea first appeared in New York v. Harris,[51] where the police arrested Harris in his home without a warrant, obtained a confession from him after giving him Miranda warnings, then took him to the station house and obtained another statement, again after warnings. Here the illegality was a violation of the Fourth Amendment, so Elstad did not apply; rather, on first impression, the case seems more like Brown. But the Court still admitted the second confession; the difference between this case and a case like Brown, the Court explained, was that the police in Harris had probable cause at the time of the arrest; the failure to obtain a warrant only required suppression of the confession in the home, where an arrest warrant is required (see §4.2), not suppression of the confession obtained at the station, where a warrant is not required. As the Court put it, "[b]ecause the officers had probable cause to arrest Harris for a crime, Harris was not unlawfully in custody when he was removed to the station house."

This notion of "substantive" attenuation resurfaced in Hudson v. Michigan,[52] where the Court refused to exclude evidence obtained in violation of the knock and announce rule, because "the interest protected by the constitutional guarantee that has been violated would not be served by suppression of the evidence obtained." According to the Court, the knock and announce rule "has never protected . . . one's interest in preventing the government from seeing or taking evidence described in a warrant" (which the police had in this case) but rather is meant to protect against the violence that might be provoked by unannounced entry, the destruction of property that could be avoided if the occupants open the door, and the "privacy and dignity . . . destroyed by a sudden entrance." It is likely the same idea will undermine the rule's relevance when police violate other warrant execution rules (see §3.5). In such cases, damages are the only remedy.

A third interpretation of the attenuation doctrine that relies neither on temporal nor substantive attenuation—and in fact seems to have more in common with independent source doctrine (discussed below) than

51 494 U.S. 14 (1990).

52 547 U.S. 586 (2006).

with attenuation—appeared in Utah v. Strieff.[53] There an officer, who admitted he was merely on a fishing expedition, stopped Strieff on less than reasonable suspicion, but after discovering there was a warrant for his arrest on a traffic violation, arrested him and found drugs incident to the arrest. Despite the fact that the Fourth Amendment violation was intentional and that the fruit was discovered immediately thereafter, the Court held that the warrant, which predated the stop, was an "intervening event" that dissipated the taint. Justice Sonia Sotomayor wrote in dissent that, given the huge number of outstanding arrest warrants (over 7.8 million nationally), many for minor offenses such as Strieff's, the majority's ruling will encourage police to stop people randomly with the hope of discovering admissible evidence, a scenario she surmised would disproportionately affect minorities.

7.6.2 Independent source and hypothetical independent source

The other two exceptions to the fruit of the poisonous tree doctrine—the independent source exception and the hypothetical independent source or inevitable discovery exception—were summarized in Nix v. Williams.[54] There the Supreme Court explained that evidence that comes from a legal source, or that would have come from such a source had the illegal action not occurred, is admissible, because exclusion "would put the police in a worse position than they would have been in absent any error or violation"; in other words, without these exceptions, the police would be deprived of evidence that they actually did obtain, or would have obtained, legally.

Williams involved application of the hypothetical independent source doctrine. Recall that, in Brewer v. Williams (§5.5), the police were led to the body of the murder victim by the defendant, who was influenced by a detective's speech about the need to give the body a Christian burial that the Court found violated the Sixth Amendment. When the case returned to the Court seven years later, the Court did not revisit the Sixth Amendment issue, but rather held that, had the illegal interrogation not occurred, the body would have eventually been found through legal means, specifically a search party that had been scouring the vicinity for the body. Furthermore, the Court held that the state need only prove the "inevitability" of the legitimate discovery by a preponderance of the evidence, and that the motives of the detective

53 136 S.Ct. 2056 (2016).

54 467 U.S. 431 (1984).

(including whether he knowingly engaged in the illegality hoping that the evidence might later be declared admissible because of a hypothetical independent source) were irrelevant.

The majority thus rejected the dissent's contention that, given the deterrence rationale behind exclusion, the government should have to meet a heavier burden on the inevitability question and that bad faith should always result in exclusion. However, the phrase "hypothetical independent source" does suggest that the hypothetical source should be truly independent of the illegal police action, like the search party in Williams. For instance, the government presumably would not be able to argue that police with probable cause can enter a house without a warrant because those same police "inevitably" would have obtained one; if that argument were successful, the warrant requirement would be emasculated.

The sensibleness of the related independent source exception might seem obvious—if fruit is in fact found legally, why would exclusion be an issue? But the Court's cases illustrate how the matter can become complicated. In United States v. Crews,[55] the Court held that an in-court identification was admissible, despite two previous identifications that were possible solely because of an illegal arrest of Crews, on the ground that the in-court identification was based on an "independent" recollection of Crews, formed before the illegal arrest. As Chapter 6 explained, previous identifications can heavily influence subsequent ones such as the in-court identification in Crews, in ways that are difficult to discern. But the Court held that the in-court identification was not tainted by the earlier identifications.

Another example of the independent source doctrine comes from Segura v. United States,[56] where the police, with probable cause but without a warrant, entered Segura's apartment and arrested him; they then secured the apartment and returned 19 hours later with a warrant and found drugs. Although assuming that the warrantless entry was illegal, the Court found that the drugs were admissible because the probable cause for the search pursuant to the warrant had preexisted the illegal entry and thus was independent of it; to the dissent's argument that the decision would encourage warrantless entries and securals, the Court stated "[w]e are unwilling to believe that officers

---

55 445 U.S. 463 (1980).

56 468 U.S. 796 (1984).

will routinely and purposely violate the law as a matter of course." Similarly, in Murray v. United States,[57] the police entered a warehouse illegally and found drugs and related items, and then later "rediscovered" the drugs pursuant to a warrant. The Court concluded that the police had probable cause before they entered the warehouse the first time, and thus that the second, warranted search was based on an independent legal source—the pre-existing probable cause—over a dissent that argued that police can too easily fabricate for the magistrate what they "knew" prior to the illegal entry once they find what is in the premises.

7.7 Other remedies

In several of its decisions limiting the scope of the exclusionary rule, the Supreme Court has noted that other remedies—in particular damages, the usual remedy in the colonial era—might provide deterrence or vindication of constitutional rights. As the Supreme Court recognized in Hudson, compared to when Mapp was decided, civil rights claims are much more common, and are now authorized by specific statutes that also provide for attorney's fees in certain types of cases. The Court also asserted that "the professionalization of police forces" is a second reason exclusion that may be less necessary than it once was. However, the Court itself has imposed a number of restrictions on damages actions that diminish their effectiveness, and administrative remedies have a mixed track record to say the least.

Damages actions are most commonly brought against state officers and police departments under 42 U.S.C. §1983, and against federal officers and the federal government under Bivens v. Six Unknown Named Agents[58] and the Federal Tort Claims Act of 1946, respectively.[59] Studies indicate that the success rate of these suits is significantly lower than for typical civil plaintiffs.[60] Perhaps suits against the police are less meritorious, or the plaintiffs who bring them are less palatable to juries. But there are also serious legal obstacles to such damages claims.

57 487 U.S. 533 (1988).

58 403 U.S. 388 (1971). While Bivens clearly provides relief in search and seizure cases, in Hernandez v. Mesa, 140 S.Ct. 735 (2020), the Court made clear that it is unlikely to extend Bivens to "new contexts."

59 28 U.S.C. §§1346(b); 2680(h) (1946).

60 Theodore Eisenberg, Section 1983: Doctrinal Foundations and an Empirical Study, 67 Cornell L. Rev. 842 (1982).

To ensure that officers are not deterred from doing their job, the Court has held that individual officers can claim a good faith or "qualified immunity" defense, which immunizes them from liability unless it can be shown they violated a rule that was "clearly established" at the time of the act and that the officer's interpretation of that rule was unreasonable.[61] Because many constitutional rules—like those defining when police may use deadly force or when they have probable cause—are very fact-specific, officers can often successfully argue that they did not violate any established rule. The situation is exacerbated by the fact that, after Pearson v. Callahan,[62] courts may dismiss a case once qualified immunity is found, without having to establish a governing rule that could apply in future cases.

If instead suit is brought against the police agency, on a respondeat superior theory, other hurdles must be cleared. State-level agencies, as opposed to police departments run by municipalities, are completely immune from §1983 actions for historical reasons.[63] Federal agencies are not immune from suit, but may have a good faith defense.[64] While local municipalities cannot rely on that defense, they are only liable if the plaintiff can show that they have a policy or endorse a custom that is unconstitutional.[65] Thus, while proof that police acted under instructions from a city official is a sufficient basis for finding municipal liability,[66] a city cannot be found liable for a single incident of "unusually excessive force" unless the plaintiff can show that the city has a policy that on its face authorizes inadequate training, or that the city is in some other way "deliberately indifferent to the rights of persons with whom the police come into contact."[67] Finally, neither federal nor city departments can be sued for punitive damages.[68]

Similar limitations are placed on attempts to enjoin a police department from engaging in illegal actions under §1983. In Los Angeles v. Lyons,[69] the Court concluded that the plaintiff's allegations that he had been rendered unconscious when police applied a chokehold to

61 Anderson v. Creighton, 483 U.S. 635 (1987); Malley v. Briggs, 475 U.S. 335 (1986).

62 555 U.S. 223 (2009).

63 Will v. Michigan Dept. of State Police, 491 U.S. 58 (1989).

64 Norton v. United States, 581 F.2d 390 (4th Cir. 1978), cert. denied 439 U.S. 1003 (1978).

65 Monell v. Dept. of Social Services of New York, 436 U.S. 658 (1978).

66 Pembaur v. Cincinnati, 475 U.S. 469 (1986).

67 Oklahoma City v. Tuttle, 471 U.S. 808 (1985).

68 Newport v. Fact Concerts, Inc., 453 U.S. 247 (1981).

69 461 U.S. 95 (1983).

his neck and that police routinely applied such chokeholds to others fell "far short" of what is necessary to state a claim for an injunction. Rather, Lyons

> would have had not only to allege that he would have another encounter with the police but also to make the "incredible" assertion either, (1) that all police officers in Los Angeles always choke any citizen with whom they happen to have an encounter, whether for purposes of arrest, issuing a citation or for questioning, or, (2) that the city ordered or authorized police officers to act in such a manner.

While this restrictive language is not inconsistent with the persistence requirement found in other injunction settings, it is also explained in part by the Court's reluctance to authorize federal court oversight of state entities.[70]

Other remedies for illegal police actions include criminal and administrative sanctions against the offending officers. Criminal sanctions, at least under the criminal analogue to §1983, are uncommon, however, since the prosecutor must prove beyond a reasonable doubt that the officer had the specific intent to deprive the alleged victim of his or her constitutional rights.[71] Moreover, prosecutors are usually very reluctant to bring criminal charges against officers with whom they work on a daily basis. For similar reasons, research suggests that meaningful internal discipline for illegal searches and seizures or interrogations, even those that result in exclusion, is rare, and that civilian review boards, which are often reliant on the cooperation of the police, have had uneven success at monitoring them.[72]

If the exclusionary rule were eliminated, even the combination of these remedies would probably not be able to achieve whatever deterrent effect the rule has, unless those remedies are modified substantially. In particular, adjustments to the current damages regime would be necessary. The typical illegal stop or search does not result in significant compensatory damages, individual officers are usually indemnified by the department, and departments can often claim a "policy and custom" defense. If instead, damages were liquidated (say, a percentage

---

70 Rizzo v. Goode, 423 U.S. 362 (1976).

71 Screws v. United States, 325 U.S. 91 (1945) (construing 18 U.S.C. §242).

72 See Samuel Walker, Governing the American Police: Wrestling with the Problems of Democracy, 2016 U. Chi. Legal F. 615, 636–7 (2016).

of the officer's salary) when the injury is to inchoate interests such as dignity, autonomy, or privacy, officers were held directly liable for bad faith illegalities, and departments were always liable for other illegalities regardless of their policies, officers might be effectively deterred and departments might be encouraged to minimize their payouts by improving training programs. This judicial sanctioning of police misconduct might also be considered a viable way of achieving the now-ignored original rationales for the exclusionary rule—vindication of constitutional rights and maintenance of judicial integrity. But there is also the possibility that such a damages regime would overdeter liability-wary officers in the run-of-the-mill case, while at the same time under-deter police and prosecutors willing to "pay" for illegality they think is necessary to solve a serious case. It may be that exclusion is the optimal remedy even from the deterrence perspective taken by the Court.

8 The pretrial process

8.1 Overview

After arrest, the suspect, who is now more aptly called the defendant, is often taken into custody. If so, and the arrest is not based on a warrant or indictment, the defendant is entitled to a hearing (variously called the initial appearance, the probable cause hearing, or the arraignment) to determine whether the arrest is based on probable cause; the defendant is also appointed counsel if one is not already involved, and, in very minor cases, may be tried. Also considered at this hearing, or at a separate hearing near this point in time, is whether the individual should be released pending trial and, if so, under what conditions. Soon thereafter, the defense attorney may make various motions, seeking, for example, exclusion of illegally seized evidence, psychiatric evaluation of the defendant, or discovery of information from the prosecution's files.

In the meantime, the prosecutor will formalize charges. The charging decision will be affected by a number of considerations, including the strength of the case (which, if too weak, may lead to dismissal), whether multiple charges or defendants should be joined together in one proceeding, and the proper venue for the case. The charging decision will usually be subjected to review at another preliminary hearing or by a grand jury, or both, depending on the jurisdiction.

This chapter describes this pretrial process. All of these stages are designed to winnow out weak cases, control the prosecutor's power, and ensure that the ultimate adjudication is based on all the relevant facts. As this chapter will make clear, however, the extent to which they do so is open to question. It should also be kept in mind that plea bargaining, which is the dominant means of resolving cases, often takes place at a fairly early stage of the process, sometimes before discovery has occurred or the admissibility of evidence has been adjudicated. Plea bargaining and guilty pleas are discussed in Chapter 9.

8.2 Probable cause hearing

In Gerstein v. Pugh,[1] the Supreme Court held that the Fourth Amendment requires a probable cause hearing in front of a judge for any defendant who is arrested or subject to any other significant restraint on liberty, unless the arrest has already been authorized by a warrant or an indictment. In the latter two instances, there has already been an official determination of probable cause. But in the absence of a warrant or indictment, the Gerstein Court reasoned, the seizure involved in pretrial detention must be judicially authorized.

In Riverside County v. McLaughlin,[2] the Court held that this hearing must take place within 48 hours of arrest, although some justices argued strongly that any period longer than 24 hours should be considered presumptively unreasonable. Not clear is whether release is required if the hearing does not occur in a timely fashion, or if a confession is admissible when obtained after release should have occurred. Furthermore, because the hearing is, in essence, equivalent to the warrant process, it need not involve trial-like procedures; hearsay and written testimony is permissible, and even the presence of the defendant and defendant's counsel is not required. While this hearing is often combined with the hearing on pretrial release, even there the presence of counsel is not necessarily required, as the next section explains.

8.3 Pretrial detention

There are at least three types of pretrial detention schemes. Most prominent is the detention of individuals charged with crime, which often involves what is commonly called the bail determination. But the federal government also detains illegal aliens pending deportation hearings, and the federal government and many states have material witness statutes that prevent individuals thought to have useful information from leaving the jurisdiction.

8.3.1 Bail and pretrial release of criminal suspects

Bail refers to the procedure allowing defendants to post a certain amount of money, usually according to a preset bail schedule, as a

1 420 U.S. 103 (1975).

2 500 U.S. 44 (1991).

guarantee that they will return for trial or some other stage in the criminal process. In many jurisdictions, bail bondsmen agree to cover the amount of bail in exchange for a small percentage of that amount from defendants, who lose that sum whether or not they show up in court; the incentive to return for trial comes not from the bond but from fear that bail bondsmen will track them down if they do not appear.

In Schilb v. Keubel,[3] the Supreme Court upheld this type of scheme against an equal protection claim that it unfairly taxed indigent defendants who, because they could not afford full bail, were forced to forfeit the bondsman's fee (in this case 10 percent of the bail) if they wanted release; the Court stated: "It should be obvious that the poor man's real hope and avenue for relief is the personal recognizance provision." As this language indicates, most jurisdictions also authorize a judge to opt for release on personal recognizance (essentially, a promise to return), or release with or without financial or other conditions. But when the judge does not choose this option, many unconvicted defendants often end up in jail for months simply because they cannot pay the bondsman, with the result that perhaps 40 percent of pretrial detainees are low-risk defendants who are poor.[4]

Pretrial detention can harm defendants in obvious ways; in addition to the negative physical and psychological effects of spending time in jail, jobs can be lost, families disrupted, and preparation for trial compromised. But the Supreme Court has held that defendants do not have a right to pretrial release, through bail or any other mechanism, and that only minimal process is due in making the release decision. The Eighth Amendment states that "[e]xcessive bail shall not be required." But in Carlson v. Landon[5] the Court concluded that this language means only that "bail shall not be excessive in those cases where it is proper to grant bail." Similarly, arguments that there should be a right to pretrial release because of the "presumption of innocence" have failed. In Bell v. Wolfish,[6] the Court held that the presumption of innocence is merely "a doctrine that allocates the burden of proof in criminal trials telling the factfinder to judge the defendant on the evidence rather than the

3 404 U.S. 357 (1971).

4 Kyle Harrison, SB10: Punishment before Conviction? Alleviating Economic Injustice in California Bail Reform, 49 U. Pac. L. Rev. 533, 537–42 (2018).

5 342 U.S. 524 (1952).

6 441 U.S. 520 (1979).

fact of being charged." And, despite the significant consequences that can result from denial of pretrial release, many jurisdictions do not provide counsel at the bail hearing, taking a cue from the Supreme Court's reminder in United States v. Salerno[7] that, at the analogous probable cause hearing, counsel and cross-examination rights "far exceed what we found necessary" in Gerstein. As a result, defendants can be detained for long periods of time through a fairly informal process, limited only by speedy trial rights (which are discussed further in §10.2).

Until the 1970s, the only ground that authorized pretrial detention, at least in theory, was fear of flight. As the Court stated in Stack v. Boyle,[8] "the modern practice of requiring a bail bond or the deposit of a sum of money subject to forfeiture serves as additional assurance of the presence of an accused." The law of every state and the federal Bail Reform Act of 1966 reflected this view. However, research at the time showed that judges often intentionally set bail at a level that defendants could not afford, even when a bail bondsman was available.[9] Despite Stack's admonition that judges should consider "the financial ability of the defendant to give bail" in setting bond, the implication of the research was that judges were sometimes using bail as a means of keeping defendants perceived to be dangerous off the streets.

Beginning in the 1970s, some states dealt with this subterfuge by expressly permitting preventive detention on the basis of dangerousness. Following this lead, the federal Bail Reform Act of 1984, while prohibiting the judge from imposing "a financial condition that results in pretrial detention of the person," permits detention if no condition "will reasonably assure the . . . safety of any other person and the community."[10] In Salerno,[11] the Supreme Court explicitly condoned this practice, stating that "[n]othing in the text of the Bail Clause limits permissible government considerations solely to the question of flight." To the argument that prevention detention of this sort results in punishment in the absence of conviction, the Court responded that pretrial detention is regulatory rather than punitive in nature, given

7 481 U.S. 739 (1987).

8 342 U.S. 1 (1951).

9 See, e.g., John Mitchell, Bail Reform and the Constitutionality of Preventive Detention, 55 Va. L. Rev. 1223 (1969).

10 18 U.S.C. §§3141–50.

11 481 U.S. 739 (1987). See also, Schall v. Martin, 467 U.S. 253 (1984).

that its duration is limited by speedy trial rules and is driven by a preventive, not a retributive, motivation. The Court also dismissed the claim that risk assessments are unreliable. Noting that dangerousness determinations inform decisions throughout the criminal process, the Court concluded, "from a legal point of view, there is nothing inherently unattainable about a prediction of future criminal conduct."

Research suggests that, if defendants are reminded of their reappearance date and assisted with transportation, failures-to-appear can be significantly reduced; similarly, research indicates that only a small proportion of arrestees pose a high risk of serious crime pending trial.[12] Given these considerations and the negative consequences of pretrial detention, most scholars argue that it should be used sparingly. In the meantime, cash bail is on the decline, in some jurisdictions almost completely replaced by release decision-making based on risk assessment instruments that rely on an actuarial approach to help inform judges about the risk a defendant will fail to appear or commit crime.[13]

8.3.2 Detentions pending deportation

The government detains aliens when they attempt to enter or re-enter the country, when they have been found deportable but are unable to find a country in which to reside, and pending deportation proceedings. In all of these situations, the government has very wide-ranging discretion. As the Supreme Court put it in Demore v. Kim,[14] "this Court has firmly and repeatedly endorsed the proposition that Congress may make rules as to aliens that would be unacceptable if applied to citizens." Thus, in Kim, the Court held that the government did not need to demonstrate that Kim was either a flight risk or dangerous in order to detain him prior to his deportation proceeding. While the Court indicated that, when the alien being detained is trying either to enter the country or to re-enter it, a hearing must be held within six months of detention, it also stated that, if Congress passed a statute explicitly granting the Attorney General the power to detain an alien indefinitely, "the Court would be required to give it effect."

---

12 Megan Stevenson, Assessing Risk Assessment in Action, 103 Minn. L. Rev. 303 (2018).

13 Id.

14 538 U.S. 510 (2003).

8.3.3 Detentions of material witnesses

Under federal law and the law of most states, a person may be "arrested" as a "material witness" if, in the words of the federal statute, "it appears from an affidavit filed by a party that the testimony of a person is material in a criminal proceeding, and if it is shown that it may become impracticable to secure the presence of the person by subpoena." Detention as a material witness must be authorized in writing by a judge, and is limited to a "reasonable period of time necessary to take a deposition," although detention may continue if the person refuses to be deposed or if "necessary to prevent a failure of justice."[15] Although the statute does not require even a probable cause showing with respect to the crime, the materiality of the witness' testimony, or the necessity of the detention, it has been upheld against Fourth Amendment challenge in the lower courts.[16]

While rare, detentions under these statutes can be quite prolonged; after 9/11, for instance, the federal statute was the basis for holding some individuals as long as one year. In Ashcroft v. al-Kidd,[17] al-Kidd was prevented from leaving for Saudi Arabia and was detained for over a week on the allegation that he possessed information relevant to another person's prosecution. Al-Kidd argued that the real reason for his detention was that the government suspected he was consorting with terrorists, despite the facts that he had cooperated with the government on several occasions and that his parents, wife, and children were all U.S. citizens and residents. The Supreme Court held that, even if his detention as a material witness was a pretext, the government had enough individualized suspicion about his potential as a witness to hold him, citing Whren v. United States (see §3.5.3). Unfortunately, al-Kidd did not provide any more detail about the standard that must be met before a person can be held as a material witness.

8.4 Discovery

Once criminal prosecution has begun, both the defense and prosecution want to find out about, or discover, the evidence that the other side possesses. Discovery can lead to more accurate and efficient

15 18 U.S.C. §3142(a) and §3144.

16 See, e.g., United States v. Awadallah, 349 F.3d 42 (2d Cir. 2003).

17 563 U.S. 731 (2011).

criminal proceedings in several ways. It can: facilitate rational decision-making during pretrial negotiations; conserve attorney resources that would otherwise be diverted through investigatory efforts; enhance preparation for trial; and minimize surprises at trial that cannot be adequately countered or would require inefficient continuances to do so. However, the Fifth Amendment's prohibition of compelled self-incrimination (which affects discovery from the defense) and the sometimes overblown fear that witnesses will be intimidated (which mostly affects discovery from the prosecution) have led to significant limitations on discovery. Additionally, even when disclosure appears to be mandated, aggressive adversarialism sometimes results in one or both parties withholding pertinent information.

The discovery process is governed largely by statute and rule. Rule 16 of the Federal Rules of Criminal Procedure provides that, upon request, the prosecution must provide the defense: (1) any written statements or transcriptions of oral statements made by the defendant that are in the prosecution's possession; (2) the defendant's prior criminal record; and (3) documents, photographs, tangible objects, results of physical and mental examinations, and test reports in the prosecution's possession that the prosecution intends to use as evidence or that are deemed "material" to the defense's trial preparation. If the defendant requests any of the items in the latter two categories, Rule 16 grants the prosecutor "reciprocal discovery" of documents, objects, and test results that the defense intends to introduce at trial. "Work product" that might be found in documents and reports (i.e., descriptions of trial strategy or attorney opinion) is protected, however.

Most state rules are much broader in scope. For example, over half the states not only provide for discovery of the items covered in Rule 16, but also require the prosecution to provide names and addresses of all persons known to have information relevant to the offense charged, as well as any statements about the offense these persons have made. In most of these states, the defense must reciprocate, either by providing a list of all persons whom the defense expects to call as witnesses and any recorded statements they have made, or by simply providing a list of witnesses. In many states, the defense must provide this information even if it has not requested information from the prosecution. A smaller number of states have adopted "open file" discovery by the defense, which requires disclosure of all tangible objects and all statements from witnesses and expert reports in the prosecution's possession that will not be introduced at trial, as well as information about any agreements with witnesses whom the prosecution intends to call.[18]

All of these rules have been shaped by constitutional concerns. Defendants have argued that requiring defense disclosure of information prior to trial can implicate both the prohibition on compelled self-incrimination and the Sixth Amendment's right to effective assistance of counsel. More successfully, they have argued that the Due Process Clause and the right of confrontation requires the prosecution to produce evidence that is material to the defense, even if it will not be used at trial. Finally, the courts have also recognized a limited duty on the part of the prosecution to preserve evidence.

8.4.1 Constitutional limitations on discovery by the prosecution

Both the Fifth Amendment and the attorney-client privilege prevent the prosecution from obtaining incriminating statements made by the defendant to defense counsel. One could argue that the defense should be able to withhold all information in its possession, even evidence the defense plans to disclose at trial, because it might provide leads to unknown witnesses, or help the prosecution gather impeachment evidence. But the Supreme Court has held that:

> [n]othing in the Fifth Amendment privilege entitles defendants as a matter of constitutional right to await the end of the State's case before announcing the nature of his defense, any more than it entitles him to await the jury's verdict on the State's case-in-chief before deciding whether or not to take the stand himself.[19]

In other words, the type of discovery contemplated by provisions such as Federal Rule 16 does not violate the Fifth Amendment because it merely accelerates disclosures that the defense will voluntarily make in any event, a notion called the acceleration doctrine. While pretrial disclosure may give the prosecution some advantages over trial disclosure, in all likelihood, the Court has noted, the prosecution would be granted a continuance if it needed more time to counter the defense evidence. Thus, recognizing a Fifth Amendment right to prevent

---

18 For an example of such a regime and discussion of these various approaches, see American Bar Association, Criminal Justice Discovery Standard 11-2.1 and commentary.

19 Williams v. Florida, 399 U.S. 78 (1970).

pretrial discovery would simply make the adjudication process more inefficient. This reasoning first surfaced in cases challenging "notice-of-alibi" statutes that require the defense to notify the prosecution, within a certain time prior to trial, of alibi claims and the supporting witnesses.[20] But it can easily be extended to other notice requirements (such as notice of an intent to raise an insanity defense), as well as to more general rules requiring lists of witnesses and other items the defense plans to introduce at trial.

The one type of information about trial evidence that the defense might be permitted to keep close to the vest until trial is whether the defendant will testify. In Brooks v. Tennessee,[21] the Supreme Court invalidated a statute that required a defendant who wanted to testify to do so just after the state rested. The Court concluded that the defendant should be able to delay deciding whether to exercise the right to testify until after assessing the impact of the rest of the defense's evidence. While Brooks involves trial disclosure, rather than discovery, the same rationale would apply in the latter context.

More difficult issues arise when the prosecution seeks tangible evidence (such as a weapon) or documents (such as expert reports) that the defense does not want to introduce at trial. Here the acceleration rationale obviously does not apply. In Fisher v. United States,[22] the Supreme Court made clear that the prosecution cannot force either the defendant (who is protected by the Fifth Amendment) or the defense attorney (because of the attorney-client privilege) to admit the existence of items it has in their possession. But if the prosecution already knows the defendant possesses a particular weapon or a certain document, it can compel its production through a subpoena or discovery demand unless the "act of production" must be proven to establish a link with the defendant.

The reasoning behind this last conclusion rests on the language of the Fifth Amendment. While that amendment clearly bars compelled testimony from the defendant, tangible evidence like a weapon is not "testimony."[23] And while documents are testimony for Fifth Amendment purposes, if they pre-exist the discovery request, the

20 See id.

21 406 U.S. 605 (1972).

22 425 U.S. 391 (1976).

23 See, e.g., United States v. Patane, 542 U.S. 630 (2004).

state has not compelled their creation or their content. Thus, the only testimonial act compelled by a subpoena is the act of producing the evidence. While that act can be incriminating if it is introduced to show authorship or guilty knowledge on the part of the defendant, in many cases the prosecution can authenticate the gun or document and its source in other ways. If so, or if the fact of the item's existence or its possession by the defendant is a "foregone conclusion" (as is likely to be the case with tax records, for instance), Fisher held that the Fifth Amendment is not applicable. Again, however, to avoid the Fifth Amendment challenge, the state must be able to show with relative precision and certainty what the defense has in its possession, akin to the type of showing that is made for a warrant, before it can obtain items in the defense's possession. Otherwise, the state would be compelling the defendant to reveal the "contents of his own mind," in a way that resembles "telling an inquisitor the combination to a wall safe."[24]

Under certain circumstances, the Sixth Amendment might also prevent prosecution discovery of evidence in the possession of the defense that it will not use at trial. This second argument against broad discovery by the prosecution posits that such discovery undermines the defendant's right to effective assistance of counsel because it will chill investigation by defense attorneys fearful that they will produce witnesses or other evidence for the prosecution. Thus, for instance, some lower courts have held that defense attorneys do not need to reveal the identities of experts they have consulted but decided not to use at trial, even though this information does not come from the defendant and thus does not implicate either the Fifth Amendment or the attorney-client privilege.[25] In this sense, Sixth Amendment protection reinforces the work-product protection.

However, in United States v. Nobles,[26] the Supreme Court concluded that, in some circumstances, the Sixth Amendment does not permit the defense to withhold information gathered by the defense attorney when it might be relevant to witnesses the defendant does call. In Nobles, the Court upheld a trial judge's ruling barring testimony from an investigator hired by the defense because the defense would not disclose the portions of the investigator's report that were the basis of his testimony. What remains unsettled after Nobles is whether a court

24 United States v. Hubbell, 530 U.S. 27 (2000).

25 See, e.g., United States v. Alvarez, 519 F.2d 1036 (3d Cir. 1975).

26 422 U.S. 225 (1975).

could require pretrial discovery of information the defense does not plan to introduce but which is relevant to a defense witness' testimony. Allowing such discovery might chill defense investigative efforts in a way that requiring disclosure at trial (as in Nobles) would not. At the least, Nobles itself made clear, attorney work-product is protected under the Constitution.

8.4.2 Constitutional entitlement to discovery by the defense

Many courts and prosecutors have expressed concern about revealing certain types of information to the defense. For instance, in State v. Eads,[27] an Iowa court listed four reasons for refusing to grant broad defense discovery:

> (1) It would afford the defendant increased opportunity to produce perjured testimony and to fabricate evidence to meet the State's case; (2) witnesses would be subject to bribe, threat and intimidation; (3) since the State cannot compel the defendant to disclose . . . evidence [protected by the Fifth Amendment], disclosure by the State would afford the defendant an unreasonable advantage at trial; and (4) disclosure is unnecessary in any event because of the other sources of information which defendant has under existing law.

Based on these types of concerns, many jurisdictions do not permit defense depositions of witnesses except to preserve the testimony of witnesses who will not be available at trial. In federal court, the Jencks Act of 1957 prohibits prosecution disclosure of witness identities and statements until the witness has testified at trial, a rule followed in many states.[28]

Each of Eads' reasons for limiting discovery in these ways can be challenged, however. If defendants are willing to perjure themselves, they can do so effectively even without pretrial discovery, because they see the state's evidence before they testify. Witness intimidation and bribery can be curbed through protective orders in those few cases where such fears are realistic. The Fifth Amendment is a constitutional right and, as the preceding section made clear, it is hardly a bar to prosecutorial discovery of evidence the defense intends to use at trial. And other sources of evidence—primarily preliminary hearings

27 166 N.W.2d 766 (Iowa 1969).

28 18 U.S.C. §3500 (1957).

or bills of particulars—are neither dependable sources of evidence nor routine (see §§8.6; 8.7.6). For these reasons, several federal courts have held that, despite the Jencks Act, trial courts have inherent authority to require pretrial disclosure of prosecution witness identities under appropriate circumstances, an authority that is frequently exercised.[29]

In any event, these concerns do not override constitutional protections. In Wardius v. Oregon,[30] the Court struck down a notice-of-alibi statute that required defense notice of an alibi and the associated witnesses, but did not require the prosecution to provide the defense with a list of its alibi rebuttal witnesses. The Court reasoned that, under the Due Process Clause, "in the absence of a strong showing of state interests to the contrary, discovery must be a two-way street." This logic suggests that, in jurisdictions that require that the defense provide witness lists prior to trial, application of Jencks Act-type provisions delaying disclosure of prosecution lists and statements until trial would be unconstitutional, barring a "strong" reason for adhering to them.

An even more important constitutional entitlement to defense discovery comes from a line of cases construing the Due Process Clause to require prosecution disclosure of "exculpatory" evidence (which presumably is generally not evidence the prosecution would use at trial). In several early cases, the Supreme Court held that due process was violated when the prosecutor failed to correct testimony known to be perjured.[31] In Brady v. Maryland,[32] the Court broadened the prosecutor's discovery obligations beyond these obvious situations, and made clear that the duty to disclose extends to information relevant at sentencing. In Brady, a murder case, the defense requested the pretrial statement of Brady's co-defendant, but only received that part of the statement that indicated the co-defendant had committed the actual killing. The prosecution indicated it withheld other parts of the statement describing Brady's small role in the offense in part because, under state law, accomplices to murder (as Brady was alleged to be) are still guilty of it. But the Court found that the withheld statement would still have been "material" to Brady's punishment, and that "irrespective of the good faith or bad faith of the prosecution," a new sentencing hearing was required with the previously undisclosed statement.

29 See, e.g., United States v. Jackson, 508 F.2d 1001 (7th Cir. 1975).

30 412 U.S. 470 (1973).

31 See, e.g., Mooney v. Holohan, 294 U.S. 103 (1935); Napue v. Illinois, 360 U.S. 264 (1959).

32 373 U.S. 83 (1963).

The key issue after Brady is the definition of "materiality." A definition that would align with the harmless error standard applied when constitutional error occurs would focus on whether the undisclosed evidence would have created a reasonable doubt in the factfinder (see §12.3.2). But the Court has settled on a more prosecution-friendly standard that asks whether there is "a reasonable probability that, had the evidence been disclosed to the defense, the result of the proceeding would have been different."[33] In Kyles v. Whitley,[34] the Court held that this test was met because the prosecutor did not disclose that the government's informant and one of its eyewitnesses had given several contradictory statements, nor disclose that the initial statement of another eyewitness described a perpetrator who looked more like the informant than the defendant; perhaps also relevant was the fact that the defendant's first trial had resulted in a hung jury.[35]

In most cases involving Brady claims, however, the Court has found for the prosecution. In a case in which the defendant was claiming self-defense, the Court held immaterial, and thus not necessary to disclose, the fact that the victim had convictions for assault and carrying a deadly weapon,[36] in another case it held not subject to mandatory disclosure the fact that a key prosecution witness had initially experienced significant difficulty in recalling important events surrounding a murder,[37] and in another it refused to call evidence tending to show that others committed the crime "material."[38] In United States v. Bagley,[39] the case that announced the reasonable probability test, the Court strongly implied that due process was not violated when, despite forwarding affidavits that two witnesses had not received rewards or promises of rewards for their testimony, the prosecution failed to disclose that the witnesses had in fact received financial inducements to testify.

The analysis in each of these cases was highly fact-specific and contingent on the government's proof, as it must be under the Court's "reasonable probability" of impact on the outcome test. The effect, Justice Marshall argued in Bagley, is to create an incentive for prosecutors "to gamble, to play the odds, and to take a chance that evidence

33 United States v. Bagley, 473 U.S. 667 (1985).
34 514 U.S. 419 (1995).
35 See also Banks v. Dretke, 540 U.S. 668 (2004).
36 United States v. Agurs, 427 U.S. 97 (1976).
37 Strickler v. Greene, 527 U.S. 263 (1999).
38 Turner v. United States, 137 S.Ct. 1885 (2017).
39 473 U.S. 667 (1985).

will later turn out not to have been potentially dispositive." The significant number of lower court decisions reversing convictions on Brady grounds, in spite of the Court's narrow definition of materiality, suggests that many prosecutors in fact make that gamble.[40] But the Court has declined to require, as a constitutional matter, that prosecutors open their files to the defense.

One possible compromise short of an open file policy is to involve the judge in the determination of whether evidence in the file is "material." In Pennsylvania v. Ritchie,[41] the Supreme Court suggested that, if the defense can provide a specific basis for its claim that the prosecution possesses material information, the trial judge can be required to review the undisclosed file in camera. Although it did not involve pretrial discovery, a decision along these lines is DeMarco v. United States,[42] where the Court directed that an evidentiary hearing be held on a defense claim that, based on remarks made by the prosecutor during sentencing, the prosecutor appeared to have made an undisclosed promise of leniency to a witness prior to his testimony.

Another important limitation on defense discovery is that it usually may seek only that information that combats the prosecution's case-in-chief. In United States v. Armstrong,[43] the Court held that Rule 16's requirement that the prosecution provide the defense with information "material to the preparation of the defendant's defense" does not encompass information about charging patterns that might bolster a claim of selective prosecution on racial grounds, because such information would only be used as a "sword" against the prosecution rather than a "shield" designed to "refute the Government's arguments that the defendant committed the crime charged." The Court did indicate that discovery of such information might still be possible, outside of the discovery rules, upon a sufficient showing that the "essential elements" of the claim were present. But it did not think this showing was made in Armstrong. The trial court had required the prosecution to disclose the race of defendants it had charged with crack cocaine distribution over the previous three years, because the defense had shown that whites and blacks used crack cocaine at roughly equal rates but that

40 Adam M. Gershowitz, The Challenge of Convincing Prosecutors that Their Profession Has a Brady Problem, 16 Ohio St. J. Crim. L. 307, 310–11 (2019) (providing a summary).

41 480 U.S. 39 (1987).

42 415 U.S. 449 (1974).

43 517 U.S. 456 (1996).

prosecutors in the relevant jurisdiction could not name a single white person who had been prosecuted for crack cocaine distribution. The Court concluded that this showing about non-disparity in drug use (as opposed to drug distribution) was insufficient and that the lower court ruling could be ignored; instead, the defense needed "to identify individuals who were not black and could have been prosecuted for the offenses for which respondents [who were black] were charged, but were not so prosecuted."

Assuming information in the prosecution's file is material under Brady, a final question is when it must be revealed to the defense. Since most cases are resolved through plea bargaining, ideally the information would be provided before the bargaining process begins. But in United States v. Ruiz,[44] the Court held that the prosecutor is not obligated to provide the defense with impeachment evidence or information supporting an affirmative defense prior to bargaining, at least when the bargaining is under the federal "fast track" scheme that provides a discount in sentence if the defendant agrees to engage in bargaining early in the process. At the same time, Ruiz intimated that if the evidence goes to "factual innocence" rather than the type of information sought in that case, disclosure is required before any type of bargaining occurs. Consistent with this view, when the defendant is going to trial rather than pleading guilty, most lower courts require that Brady material be provided in a "timely fashion" rather than at trial.

8.4.3 Right to preservation of evidence

With the advent of DNA testing, preservation of physical evidence has become particularly important. Nonetheless, the Supreme Court ruled in California v. Trombetta[45] that evidence destruction does not violate due process unless the defense can show the evidence: (1) could have played "a significant role in the suspect's defense"; (2) was of "such a nature that the defendant would be unable to obtain comparable evidence by other reasonably available means"; and (3) was destroyed because of "official animus toward [the defendant] or . . . a conscious effort to suppress exculpatory evidence." This standard is more demanding than the Brady test both because it requires a greater showing of materiality and because it requires bad faith on the part of the government. It was nonetheless appropriate, the Court explained,

44 536 U.S. 622 (2002).

45 467 U.S. 479 (1984).

to avoid imposing "an undifferentiated and absolute duty to retain and to preserve all material that might be of conceivable evidentiary significance in a particular prosecution."

In Trombetta, where the state failed to preserve a breath sample from a suspected drunk driver, the Court held that the defense did not provide sufficient evidence of either exculpatory value or official animus. It also noted that, in such cases, the defense could always try to show that the breath-testing machine malfunctioned or was used improperly. Similarly, in Arizona v. Youngblood,[46] where the defendant was convicted of sexual assault of a ten-year-old boy, the state's failure to preserve semen on the boy's clothing was considered merely "negligent" by the Court, which noted that the state's test had been inconclusive and that the defense was free to argue that a more sophisticated test would have been exculpatory. In dissent, Justice Blackmun asserted that "it makes no sense to ignore the fact that a defendant has been denied a fair trial because the State allowed evidence that was material to the defense to deteriorate beyond the point of usefulness, simply because police were inept rather than malicious." That point was dramatically brought home 15 years later, when more sophisticated DNA testing exonerated Youngblood.

8.4.4 Sanctions for violation of discovery rules

If Brady is violated, the usual remedy is a new trial with the undisclosed evidence. If the jurisdiction's other discovery rules are violated, the typical discovery provision provides for a wide variety of sanctions. For instance, under the federal rules, upon finding that a party has failed to comply with a discovery rule a court may order "discovery or inspection [of the item]; specify its time, place, and manner; . . . grant a continuance; . . . or enter any other order that is just under the circumstances."[47] One type of order sometimes relied upon—one that might be particularly useful when the prosecution fails to preserve evidence—is a charge telling the jury that a requested piece of evidence was not produced and that it may draw whatever conclusion it wishes from that fact. There may also be sanctions available outside the discovery rules. For instance, the Supreme Court has recognized that proof that a particular prosecutor's office has routinely engaged in Brady violations might lead to liability under §1983 on a failure-to-train

46 488 U.S. 51 (1988).

47 Fed. R. Crim. P. 16(d).

theory. However, consistent with §1983 jurisprudence in other areas (see §7.7), the violations must be "so persistent and widespread as to practically have the force of law," and the failure to train must be due to "deliberate indifference" to constitutional rights.[48]

The primary constitutional issue that has arisen in connection with discovery sanctions is whether the defense may be prevented from presenting evidence that it should have provided the prosecution during discovery. In Taylor v. Illinois,[49] the trial court excluded the testimony of a defense witness who was not listed on the defense's witness list, after finding that counsel had been aware of the witness' existence at least a week before trial. Noting that it had upheld a similar trial court sanction in Nobles, the Supreme Court found that the sanction did not violate the Sixth Amendment's Compulsory Process Clause's guarantee of the right to present evidence (see §11.5). To the defense's argument that a continuance or a disciplinary action against the attorney would better balance the defendant's interests with the state's, the Court responded that the trial court was "reasonable to assume that there is something suspect about a defense witness who is not identified until after the eleventh hour has passed," especially when the failure to list the witness is "willful and blatant," as the trial court found in this case.

In interesting contrast to the materiality requirement under Brady, Taylor also stated that, given the legitimate concern about accuracy, the trial court considering exclusion of defense evidence need not find that the defense's failure to disclose it resulted in prejudice to the prosecution. Nor need it be concerned that exclusion might make the defendant pay for the lawyer's mistakes, since investigation into the relative responsibilities of client and lawyer for the failure would be "impractical." In Michigan v. Lucas[50] the Court went further, indicating that, even when concerns about the reliability of the undisclosed evidence are absent, exclusion is permitted as a discovery sanction. There, the Court upheld trial court exclusion of a sexual assault victim's past sexual conduct with the defendant because the defense willfully failed to give notice of an intent to use the evidence as required by state rule. The fact that, in contrast to the witness testimony in Taylor, the evidence was clearly reliable did not give the Court pause.

48 Connick v. Thompson, 563 U.S. 51 (2011).

49 484 U.S. 400 (1988).

50 500 U.S. 145 (1991).

8.5 Constraints on the prosecutor's charging decision

The prosecutor usually formalizes the charge against the defendant early in the process. But those charges can change as a result of plea bargaining, or as the prosecutor gains more evidence. The prosecutor's decisions in this regard are given wide berth. As the Supreme Court stated in Bordenkircher v. Hayes,[51] "so long as the prosecutor has probable cause to believe that the accused committed an offense defined by statute, the decision whether or not to prosecute, and what charge to file or bring before a grand jury, generally rests entirely in his discretion." However, both the Constitution and legislative or administrative rules put some limits on this discretion.

8.5.1 Decisions to forgo prosecution

In some jurisdictions, prosecutors dismiss charges in three-quarters of the cases brought before them, and the average dismissal rate is approximately 25 percent.[52] Prosecutors might dismiss charges not only due to insufficient evidence, but also because, for instance, they believe the crime is not weighty enough to warrant expenditure of resources, the defendant does not deserve criminal punishment, alternatives to punishment (such as diversion) better suit the government's goals, or the defendant is an informant who merits a reward for helping the prosecution.

Generally, charge dismissal is unreviewable. Some jurisdictions make provision for judicial approval of a nolle prosequi, which is a formal prosecutorial declaration, explained in writing, that no prosecution will be sought on a particular charge, a procedure meant "to protect a defendant against prosecutorial harassment, e.g., charging, dismissing and recharging, when the Government moves to dismiss an indictment over the defendant's objection."[53] But the Supreme Court has expressed misgivings with a more general requirement of judicial review over charge dismissals, because "[s]uch factors as the strength of the case, the prosecution's general deterrence value, the Government's enforcement priorities, and the case's relationship to the Government's overall enforcement plan are not readily susceptible to the kind of analysis the courts are competent to make," and because law enforcement might

---

51 434 U.S. 357 (1978).

52 See, e.g., Adam M. Gershowitz, Prosecutorial Screening before Arrest, [2019] Ill. L. Rev. 293.

53 Rinaldi v. United States, 434 U.S. 22 (1977).

be "chilled" if the prosecutor's motives and actions were subject to outside scrutiny and government enforcement policies were revealed publicly.[54]

8.5.2 Discriminatory prosecution

Despite the wide-ranging prosecutorial authority recognized in Hayes, the Court has indicated that, under limited circumstances, a defendant can successfully challenge even a charge that is clearly based on probable cause. One basis for such a challenge is the Equal Protection Clause, which requires that, as a general matter, similarly situated individuals should be treated similarly, at least when the differential treatment is based on race, gender, religion, speech, or some other suspect classification. For instance, in Yick Wo v. Hopkins,[55] the Supreme Court overturned a conviction under a statute that criminalized the operation of laundries housed in wooden buildings unless the owners first obtained permission from the board of supervisors. Finding that permission was only denied to those laundries operated by Chinese, the Court concluded that the law was "applied and administered by a public authority with an evil eye and an unequal hand."

The Court later held that a "selective prosecution claim" lies under the Equal Protection Clause if the defendant can show: (1) a failure to prosecute those who are similarly situated (2) that is intentionally based on (3) an arbitrary rather than a rational classification using "an unjustifiable standard such as race, religion, or other arbitrary classification."[56] These requirements are difficult to meet. In Oyler v. Boles, the case that declared this formulation, the Court rejected the defendant's equal protection claim—to the effect that he was the only person in the county among those similarly situated who had been charged as an habitual offender—because he could not show his charge was the result of a deliberate policy or focused on a suspect class such as race. In Wayte v. United States,[57] the Court rejected an equal protection claim against a deliberate policy of enforcing the draft laws selectively—specifically against those who publicly disclosed their unwillingness to register for the draft or were reported by others—because, the Court concluded, these non-registrants were easier to identify than other

54 Wayte v. United States, 470 U.S. 598 (1985).

55 118 U.S. 356 (1886).

56 Oyler v. Boles, 368 U.S. 448 (1962).

57 470 U.S. 598 (1985).

non-registrants, not "because" of their protest activity. To the argument that selective prosecution decisions were therefore made on the basis of speech in violation of the First Amendment, the Court noted that not only vocal non-registrants but all non-registrants who were publicly identified were prosecuted, and that these prosecutions were based as much on conduct (non-registration) as they were on speech (protesting the draft).

Similarly, lower courts have held that singling out "conspicuous lawbreakers" (e.g., "individuals who have achieved notoriety as tax protesters"[58]) or pursuing only "significant lawbreakers" (e.g., bookmakers but not those who place bets[59]) does not violate the Equal Protection Clause. As one court put it, "the prosecutor may conserve resources for more important cases."[60] However, lower courts have found constitutional violations when the government prosecutes only protesters even when non-protesters are also easily identifiable (unlike in Wayte), focuses only on members of a suspect class (e.g., female nude dancers at a male private club), or is unable to offer any rational basis for the selective prosecution (e.g., prosecution of private detectives but not government officials for illegal wiretapping[61]).

A final situation that might raise discrimination claims arises when the prosecutor appears to have charged the defendant with a relatively minor crime solely because evidence of the real crime of interest cannot be developed. These so-called "pretextual prosecutions" are particularly prevalent in cases involving individuals thought to be part of an organized crime syndicate; most famously, Al Capone was prosecuted for tax fraud. Analogous to the Supreme Court's approach to pretextual searches and seizures, such prosecutions are generally permissible unless, perhaps, the defendant can show that he or she was targeted primarily because of ethnicity.[62]

---

58 United States v. Catlett, 584 F.2d 864 (8th Cir. 1968).

59 People v. Garner, 139 Cal.Rptr. 838 (1977).

60 Falls v. Town of Dyer, Ind. 875 F.2d 146 (7th Cir. 1989).

61 Federov v. United States, 580 A.2d 600 (D.C. App. 1990); State v. McCollum, 464 N.W.2d 44 (Wisc. 1990); United States v. Robinson, 311 F.Supp. 1063 (W.D. Mo. 1969).

62 Compare United States v. Sacco, 428 F.2d 264 (9th Cir. 1970) with United States v. Cammisano, 413 F.Supp. 886 (W.D. Mo. 1976).

8.5.3 Vindictive prosecution

In Blackledge v. Perry[63] the Supreme Court held that, if the prosecutor raises the charge after a defendant has been convicted and successfully appeals, the Due Process Clause requires recognition of a "presumption of vindictiveness," on the ground that otherwise exercise of legal rights (such as the right to appeal) would be chilled. However, the presumption can be overcome if the prosecutor can show that the greater charge could not have been brought before the trial because, for instance, the victim of an assault has since died. And in Texas v. McCullough,[64] the Court intimated that the presumption might be rebuttable if any new information about the offense develops.

Furthermore, a vindictive prosecution claim generally is not available if the prosecutor raises the charge prior to trial,[65] and is probably foreclosed altogether if the change in charge occurs as part of the plea negotiation process. In Bordenkircher v. Hayes (noted above) the prosecutor told Hayes that if he did not plead guilty to a forgery charge with a recommended sentence of five years, he would be charged under an habitual offender statute (given Hayes' two previous forgery convictions), which carried a mandatory life sentence. The Court held that due process was not violated by this threat because "the conduct engaged in by the prosecutor . . . no more than openly presented the defendant with the unpleasant alternatives of foregoing [*sic*] trial or facing charges on which he was plainly subject to prosecution." The Court may well have been concerned that a contrary decision would seriously undermine plea bargaining. But Justice Powell argued in dissent that a claim of vindictiveness should nonetheless be cognizable in a case such as this, where "the admitted purpose" of the prosecutor "was to discourage and then to penalize with unique severity [the defendant's] exercise of constitutional rights."

Closely related to the plea bargaining scenario is a decision by a prosecutor to charge the defendant under the harsher of two statutes that penalize the same conduct. In United States v. Batchelder,[66] the defendant received a five-year sentence under one statute despite the fact that another statute, more recently passed, provided for a maximum

63 417 U.S. 21 (1974).

64 475 U.S. 134 (1986) (although this case involved resentencing by a judge).

65 United States v. Goodwin, 457 U.S. 368 (1982).

66 442 U.S. 114 (1979).

of two years for defendants in the same situation. The Supreme Court rejected Batchelder's due process claim, stating it could find "no appreciable difference between the discretion a prosecutor exercises when deciding whether to charge under one of two statutes with different elements and the discretion he exercises when choosing one of two statutes with identical elements."

8.5.4 Joinder of charges

Another constraint on the prosecutor's charging decision affects the number of charges that can be litigated, or joined, at one trial. Under the federal rules, charges against the same defendant may be joined as separate counts in the same indictment or information when the charges arise out of: (1) the same transaction (e.g., burglary of a house, theft in the same house, and assault while escaping); (2) two different transactions that are "connected together" or are part of a "common scheme or plan" (e.g., burglarizing a gun store to obtain a gun later used in a bank robbery); and (3) two or more different acts that are "the same or similar in character" (e.g., two robberies committed in a very similar way).[67] Virtually every state allows joinder in the first two situations and about a third allow joinder in the third situation. It should also be noted that, when two crimes are considered the "same offense" for double jeopardy purposes (see §12.5.3), they must be joined or the prosecutor forfeits the ability to try the second charge after jeopardy has attached on the first one.

However, both federal and state rules also provide that either the defense or the prosecution can make a motion to sever properly joined charges if "prejudice" would result.[68] At the federal level, such prejudice exists if the joinder could have, or (in the appeal setting) did have, "a substantial and injurious effect or influence in determining the jury's verdict."[69] If such a severance occurs on the defendant's motion the defendant cannot subsequently argue that the second trial is barred by the double jeopardy prohibition.[70]

The reason most states do not recognize the third type of joinder (for similar crimes) is primarily due to fear that the factfinder will infer

67 Fed. R. Crim. P. 8(a).

68 Id. Rule 14.

69 Kotteakos v. United States, 328 U.S. 750 (1946).

70 Jeffers v. United States, 432 U.S. 137 (1977).

criminal disposition from the fact that the crimes are alike, and will not consider the specific evidence against the accused. In Drew v. United States,[71] the D.C. Circuit Court of Appeals held that joinder of two robbery charges against the defendant was improper because the two crimes, while similar, were not similar enough. In the first robbery a black male wearing sunglasses pulled a gun from his pocket. In the second, a black man wearing sunglasses asked to buy some peanuts, and then demanded the store's money, but left when the clerk refused to give him any. The court held that joinder of these two crimes might have been permissible had the manner of their commission demonstrated identical modi operandi, of the type required by the rules of evidence when a party seeks to introduce evidence of a prior conviction of the defendant to show he committed the crime charged. But where, as in Drew, the modi operandi are not identical, the potential for prejudice is great; the jury might convict without individualized consideration of the charges (and, in fact, in Drew the record showed repeated confusion as to which of the two crimes was at issue).

An analogous argument could be made with respect to the first two types of joinder (same transaction and common scheme joinder). However, it is much less likely to prevail. In United States v. Adams,[72] for instance, the defendant was charged with both selling heroin to an undercover agent and possession of heroin, charges separated by nine months. Adams argued that the jury's conviction on the distribution charge could have been influenced by proof of the drug possession, despite the time difference. The court disagreed, stating that "the pattern here was typical of conduct in the narcotics traffic" and thus the two crimes could be joined as parts of "a common scheme or plan"; further, it concluded that prejudice did not occur, because the trial court was careful to delineate the elements of each charge for the jury and because the evidence for each charge was substantial and "simple."

8.5.5 Joinder of defendants

The joinder situation most likely to raise concerns about prejudice involves not joinder of charges but joinder of defendants. Under the federal rules, such joinder is allowed if the defendants "are alleged to have participated in the same act or transaction or in the same series of acts or transactions constituting an offense or offenses," and

71 331 F.2d 85 (D.C. Cir. 1964).

72 434 F.2d 756 (2d Cir. 1970).

is most likely to occur when two or more defendants are alleged to be co-conspirators or accomplices.[73] Unlike joinder of charges, which can sometimes benefit defendants who want to avoid two trials, joinder of defendants will usually benefit only prosecutors interested in efficiency. The negative consequences for defendants are several: (1) a co-defendant's confession that also implicates the defendant might be introduced without the defendant being able to cross-examine the co-defendant because of the latter's refusal to take the stand under the Fifth Amendment; (2) also for Fifth Amendment reasons, a co-defendant's account tending to exculpate the defendant (while inculpating the co-defendant) may not be introduced; (3) the factfinder may convict merely out of the confusion or disgust created by conflicting defense strategies (e.g., the defendants accuse one another of the crime); or (4) the factfinder may convict merely because the defendant is associated with other clearly guilty defendants.

The first situation may run afoul of the Sixth Amendment's Confrontation Clause and often results in severance (see §11.4.3). When confronted by the other three situations, the courts sometimes grant severance motions. But they are usually reluctant to do so. In part, this may be due to a valid concern that severance will allow defendants to prevent accurate factfinding. For instance, granting severance in an attempt to avoid the second type of prejudice (exclusion of exculpatory information) might occasionally present an opportunity for defendants to "swap alibis" (e.g., X falsely exculpating Y at Y's trial, and then Y—now acquitted and protected against retrial by the Double Jeopardy Clause—returning the favor at X's trial).

Similarly, severance to avoid the third type of prejudice (contradictory defenses) runs counter to the notion that differing stories are most effectively tested when all of the players put on their best defense in the same room. As one court put it, "conflicting versions of what took place, or the extent to which [the defendants] participated in it," is "a reason for rather than against a joint trial" because "it is easier for the truth to be determined if all are required to be tried together."[74] In Zafiro v. United States,[75] a unanimous Supreme Court agreed that, under the federal rules, severance is not automatically required when co-defendants disclaim knowledge of the crime and try to blame each

73 Fed. R. Crim. P. 8(b).

74 Ware v. Commonwealth, 537 S.W.2d 174 (Ky. 1976).

75 506 U.S. 534 (1993).

other. Rather, it should be granted only when the trial court finds "a serious risk that a joint trial would compromise a specific trial right of one of the defendants [such as the previously mentioned right to confront accusers], or prevent the jury from making a reliable judgment about guilt or innocence."

The fourth type of prejudice is reflected in the Supreme Court's observation that "[i]t is difficult for the individual to make his own case stand on its own merits in the minds of jurors who are ready to believe that birds of a feather are flocked together."[76] Yet even when "guilt-by-association" is a strong possibility, courts may refuse to find that joinder prejudicial, as illustrated by Schaffer v. United States,[77] involving a trial with seven defendants. After conviction of all seven, four of them—the two Schaffer brothers and Marco and Karp—appealed on the ground they should not have been tried with the other three, the Stracuzzas. The state's theory was that the Stracuzzas had been the "brains" of a group involved in transporting across state lines clothing stolen from a New York establishment: they and the Schaffers had transported goods to Pennsylvania, they and Marco had transported goods to West Virginia, and they and Karp had transported goods to Massachusetts. But the trial court, despite allowing joinder, ended up dismissing the conspiracy charge linking these defendants together, which the Schaffers argued meant that severance should have been automatic. The Supreme Court disagreed, finding insufficient prejudice to warrant severance. During trial, the Court noted, the evidence against each petitioner "was carefully compartmentalized" because proof of each shipment was related to a specific petitioner and proven by different witnesses with respect to each shipment. Furthermore, the judge's instructions "meticulously set out separately the evidence as to each of the petitioners and admonished the jury that they were 'not to take into consideration any proof against one defendant and apply it by inference or otherwise to any other defendant.'" The dissent insisted that "where, as here, there is no nexus between the several crimes, the mounting proof of the guilt of one is likely to affect another."

8.5.6 Venue

A final constraint on the prosecutor's charging decision comes from Article II, section 2 of the Constitution, which states that the trials

76 Krulewitch v. United States, 336 U.S. 440 (1949).

77 362 U.S. 511 (1960).

of all crimes are "to be held in the State where said crimes shall have been committed," and from federal and state rules that provide that trial should occur in the jurisdiction (federal district or state county) where the offense was committed. In every jurisdiction, venue is an element of the crime and must be alleged in the charging instrument. According to the Supreme Court, the "locus delicti must be determined from the nature of the crime alleged and the location of the act or acts constituting it."[78]

Occasionally, this requirement can pose difficult issues, particularly in the federal courts, where interstate crimes are often tried. In federal court, Congress mooted some of these issues in 1948 when it declared in 18 U.S.C. §3237(a) that a criminal case can be tried "in any district in which such offense was begun, continued, or completed." Nonetheless, challenging inquiries persist, because the defendant can always move for a change of venue and cite the federal rules, which obligate courts to "set the place of trial within the district with due regard for the convenience of the defendant and the witnesses, and the prompt administration of justice."[79]

Two Supreme Court cases illustrate the problem. In United States v. Cabrales,[80] the Court held that a prosecution for laundering money obtained through drug dealing could only take place where the money was laundered, in Florida, not where the laundered funds were generated, in Missouri, despite government arguments that the underlying drug dealing offense was an essential element of and facilitated by the laundering charge and that the major harm from the offense occurred in Missouri. In contrast, in United States v. Rodriguez-Moreno,[81] the Court held that the crime of "using or carrying" a firearm "during and in relation to any crime of violence"—in this case kidnapping—could be tried in New Jersey, even though the kidnapping occurred in Texas and the kidnappers only stayed in New Jersey a short while before moving to Maryland, where the defendants used a gun on the kidnapping victim for the first time. The defendants conceded that the venue for kidnapping lies in every jurisdiction in which the victim is taken, but argued that the firearm charge was properly tried only in Maryland. However, the Court concluded that the gun was used "during and in

78 United States v. Anderson, 328 U.S. 699 (1946).

79 Fed. R. Crim. P. 18.

80 524 U.S. 1 (1998).

81 526 U.S. 275 (1999).

relation to" the kidnapping, which occurred in a number of states, including New Jersey.

8.6 The preliminary hearing

The preliminary hearing discussed here is to be distinguished from the initial, or Gerstein, hearing and from the bail hearing, both of which occur soon after arrest (see §§8.2, 8.3). The purpose of the preliminary hearing, which can occur weeks later, is to prevent "hasty, malicious, imprudent, and oppressive prosecutions" and to assure that "there are substantial grounds upon which a prosecution may be based."[82] Thus, while the earlier hearings are primarily a check on the police, the preliminary hearing is a check on the prosecutor.

While the preliminary hearing is not constitutionally required,[83] almost all jurisdictions provide for one, at least in felony cases. However, the defendant may waive the hearing (and often does). Moreover, in jurisdictions where the prosecutor must obtain an indictment, doing so may obviate the hearing. For example, under the federal rules, a "preliminary examination" must be held no later than ten days after the initial appearance if the defendant is in custody and no later than 20 days if the defendant is not in custody, unless an indictment occurs before that time.[84] In other jurisdictions, discussed further in §8.7, the prosecutor has the option of either seeking an indictment or proceeding on an "information" (a formal charging document filed by the prosecutor). Although in these jurisdictions as well, a timely indictment obviates the hearing, if the prosecutor decides to proceed via information, the charges usually must be presented at a preliminary hearing.

The hearing is presided over by a judge or magistrate, and the defendant is entitled to counsel under the Sixth Amendment.[85] However, counsel may have only a small role. The Supreme Court has held that there is no constitutional right to cross-examination at the preliminary hearing,[86] and, although the federal rules allow such questioning, they

82 Thies v. State, 189 N.W. 539 (Wisc. 1922).

83 Lem Woon v. Oregon, 229 U.S. 586 (1913).

84 Fed. R. Crim. P. 5.1(a)(2).

85 Coleman v. Alabama, 399 U.S. 1 (1970).

86 Goldsby v. United States, 160 U.S. 70 (1895).

do not explicitly allow the defense to call its own witnesses.[87] In many jurisdictions the rules of evidence do not apply, and illegally seized evidence is also usually admissible. Use of hearsay is justified on the ground that it avoids exposing victims and witnesses to the defendant, and use of illegally seized evidence is justified for the same reasons that the Supreme Court had held that the exclusionary rule does not apply at other secondary proceedings (see §7.2).

Practical considerations also explain these restrictions. If preliminary hearing judges were required to make admissibility determinations, significant delay might result that would undercut other rules; recall that, in the federal system, the hearing is to take place within 10 to 20 days of arrest. More generally, restrictions on preliminary hearings are justified on the ground that they are designed to determine only whether the prosecution has enough evidence to "bind" the case over the grand jury (in indictment jurisdictions) or to proceed to trial (in information jurisdictions), a standard courts often describe as "probable cause," which suggests a fairly low threshold of proof. Allowing a full-blown adversarial proceeding before trial may also be premature, duplicative, and wasteful of judicial resources. Furthermore, expansive preliminary hearings might undermine the jurisdiction's limitations on discovery (see §8.4.2).

Some courts nonetheless are unwilling to impose substantial limitations on the preliminary hearing. As one court noted, "probable cause to arrest does not automatically mean that the [state] has sufficient competent legal evidence to justify the costs both to the defendant and to the [state] of a full trial."[88] If it did, there would be no point to having a preliminary hearing after the Gerstein hearing determines that probable cause exists. Accordingly, these courts require that the prosecution make out a prima facie case for conviction, meaning that the prosecutor must present enough evidence to convince the magistrate that the defendant would not win a directed verdict motion at trial after the state rests.

That standard does not necessarily bar hearsay if the prosecution can show that the out-of-court declarant will be available at trial, nor does it contemplate allowing the defense to put on witnesses supporting affirmative defenses. But it arguably does require exclusion of illegally

87 Fed. R. Crim. P. 5.1(e).

88 Myers v. Commonwealth, 298 N.E.2d 819 (Mass. 1973).

seized evidence. Moreover, in Coleman v. Alabama,[89] the case that held that the Sixth Amendment guarantees counsel at preliminary hearings, the Supreme Court emphasized that cross-examination at the preliminary hearing can expose weaknesses in the prosecution's witnesses and obtain answers that can be used for impeachment at trial, neither of which is possible if the prosecution's case at the hearing consists solely of hearsay. The concern about duplication of effort may also be overblown because, as one court noted, for strategic reasons both sides "will usually withhold as much of their case as possible."[90] And as another court pointed out, if a jurisdiction's discovery rules are very restrictive (see §8.4.2), the preliminary hearing "may provide the defendant with the most valuable discovery technique available to him,"[91] an aspect of the hearing that Coleman also recognized.

8.7 The grand jury

The Fifth Amendment states in part "No person shall be held to answer for a capital, or otherwise infamous crime, unless on a presentment or indictment of a grand jury." Under English common law, the grand jury was usually composed of 23 or 24 people; an indictment was sought by a government official, while a presentment came directly from the grand jury. The Framers of the Constitution saw the grand jury as a "bulwark against oppression," because colonial grand juries had often charged British soldiers and other royal officers with crimes against the citizenry, while at the same time refusing to indict colonists for perceived "political" crimes; they also frequently issued reports critical of England's policies.[92]

In theory, the grand jury is well-equipped to be both an independent investigative entity and a mechanism for checking prosecutorial charging decisions, because it has wide-ranging investigative powers, operates in secret, can issue subpoenas for testimony and documents, and can refuse to indict. Today, however, the grand jury's usefulness as a bulwark against government misuse of power is much diminished. While its lay composition can act as a counter to the government,

89 399 U.S. 1 (1970).

90 Myers v. Commonwealth, 298 N.E.2d 819 (Mass. 1973).

91 Wheeler v. Flood, 269 F.Supp. 194 (E.D.N.Y. 1967).

92 See generally, Richard Younger, The People's Panel (Brown University Press, Providence, R.I. 1963).

typically the grand jury is dominated by the prosecutor, who usually controls the witnesses the grand jury hears and the subpoenas it issues. Grand juries rarely initiate investigations on their own, and even more rarely refuse to return an indictment; rather, they almost always find a "true bill" (thus the saying, "A prosecutor can get a grand jury to indict a ham sandwich"). Some have argued that the grand jury may even serve as a shield for prosecutors who want to pursue illegitimate or questionable investigations or who want cover for unpopular decisions (such as, for instance, a decision about whether to charge police officers with use of excessive force).

Perhaps wisely, then, the Supreme Court has held that the Indictment Clause in the Fifth Amendment is not applicable to the states if a preliminary hearing, conducted in open court with counsel, is available to screen the prosecutorial charging decision.[93] Today, only about 20 states and the federal government require that felonies be prosecuted based on indictments, with the remaining states giving the prosecution the option of proceeding on either an indictment or information. In the latter jurisdictions ("information jurisdictions"), most cases are investigated by the prosecutor and police, not the grand jury, and screening occurs through the preliminary hearing. However, prosecutors often choose the indictment option when a case is of great public interest or particularly sensitive politically, when the grand jury's investigative powers are useful (as in organized crime and corruption cases), when the grand jury process is speedier (as might be the case when multiple defendants are involved), when the grand jury's secrecy enables the prosecutor to coax a scared or reluctant witness to provide evidence, or when its immunity and contempt powers facilitate coercion of testimony.

8.7.1 Structure and composition

As a formal matter, the court convenes the grand jury in most jurisdictions, but the decision to impanel a grand jury is, in fact, usually the prosecutor's, and some jurisdictions allow the prosecutor to impanel the grand jury directly. Once summoned, a grand jury sits for a specific term, which can last from a month to several months or, in the case of special grand juries charged with investigating particularly complicated crimes, even several years. The term of federal grand juries is limited to 18 months, but can be extended for 6 months at

93 Hurtado v. California, 110 U.S. 516 (1884).

a time, "upon a determination that such extension is in the public interest."[94]

While federal grand juries continue to consist of 23 members, in some states they can be as small as five. Members are selected through a two-stage process similar to the selection process for petit juries (see §10.3.3). The jury pool (or "venire") is usually randomly drawn from population-wide sources, such as voting lists, tax returns, or telephone directories, and whittled down based on statutory exclusions that bar, for instance, non-citizens, non-residents, ex-felons, and people with mental illness; individual grand jury members are then chosen through a judicial questioning process analogous to petit jury voir dire. While the Sixth Amendment's guarantee of an "impartial jury" applies only to petit juries, not grand juries, the Court has held that, as a matter of due process, the grand jury pool must represent a fair cross-section of the community and has implied that the grand jury itself must be impartial, as with trial juries.[95] At the same time, even in those cases where the target of the grand jury is apparent, no jurisdiction allows the target's defense attorney to conduct a pre-indictment voir dire of the grand jury like that conducted in choosing petit juries. And a post-indictment voir dire by the defense is unlikely to be granted because of fear it will expose how grand jurors voted, a fact that is supposed to be secret. At most, the defense can ask the judge to question potential grand jurors and remind them of their oath to avoid basing their decision on antipathy to the defendant.

8.7.2 Grand jury secrecy

The modern justifications for grand jury secrecy were spelled out by the Supreme Court in Pittsburgh Plate Glass Co. v. United States:[96]

> (1) to prevent the escape of those whose indictment may be contemplated; (2) to insure the utmost freedom to the grand jury in its deliberations, and to prevent persons subject to indictment or their friends from importuning the grand jurors; (3) to prevent subornation of perjury or tampering with the witnesses who may testify before the grand jury and later appear at the trial of those indicted by it; (4) to encourage free and untrammeled disclosures by persons who have information with respect to the commission of crimes;

94 Fed. R. Crim. P. 6(g).

95 Hobby v. United States, 468 U.S. 339 (1984); Beck v. Washington, 369 U.S. 541 (1962).

96 360 U.S. 395 (1959).

(5) to protect the innocent accused who is exonerated from disclosure of the fact that he has been under investigation, and from the expense of standing trial where there was no probability of guilt.

Prior to the 1960s, reasons like these were invoked to deny the defendant and third parties access to evidence produced for the grand jury. However, exceptions to the general rule of secrecy now arise in three separate situations.

First, despite the dangers listed above, grand jury witnesses are generally allowed to disclose their own testimony, principally on the ground that preventing them from doing so is too difficult, and perhaps also as a means of monitoring how grand jury witnesses are treated. Further, the First Amendment may bar prohibiting witnesses from recounting their testimony under certain circumstances. In Butterworth v. Smith,[97] the Supreme Court struck down a statute establishing such a bar even after the grand jury's term ended. The Court reasoned that, after the term has ended, secrecy is not necessary to prevent escape of suspects or manipulation of the grand jury, at the same time such a rule could keep vital information from the public forever. To the argument that the statute could prevent unfair stigmatization of an exonerated target, the Court stated that "reputational interests alone cannot justify the proscription of truthful speech."

A second exception to grand jury secrecy involves disclosure to the defendant, in one of two situations. The first occurs when, as the federal rules put it, the defendant can make "a showing that a ground may exist to dismiss the indictment because of a matter that occurred before the grand jury." As discussed in §8.7.5, however, these grounds are very narrow. The second situation is when the defendant makes a discovery request for a particular witness' testimony. Consistent with the discovery rules (see §8.4), most jurisdictions allow such discovery only when the witness will testify at trial, and some require a special showing even in that limited situation. However, a substantial minority of states provide the full transcript, on the ground that, after an indictment, most of the dangers associated with disclosure have dissipated. Consistent with this line of reasoning, the Supreme Court has stated that "[i]n our adversary system for determining guilt or innocence, it is rarely justifiable for the prosecution to have exclusive access to a

97 494 U.S. 624 (1990).

storehouse of relevant fact. Exceptions to this are justifiable only by the clearest and most compelling considerations."[98]

Finally, various third parties may be entitled to part or all of a grand jury transcript under special circumstances, which the Supreme Court has summarized as a showing that the material sought "is needed to avoid a possible injustice to another judicial proceeding, that the need for disclosure is greater than the need for continued secrecy, and that [the] request is structured to cover only material so needed."[99] Illustrating the narrowness of this test is United States v. Proctor & Gamble Co.,[100] where the Court denied a request by defendants in an antitrust suit for transcripts of a grand jury proceeding that had targeted them (but which had not resulted in an indictment). The Court pointed out that the defendants had not made a "particularized" showing that the transcript would be needed "to impeach a witness, to refresh his recollection, to test his credibility and the like." It also noted that some of the witnesses at the grand jury had been employees and customers of the defendant companies who might face some retaliation if their identities became known.

However, if the *government* is seeking disclosure in another criminal or civil case, the showing need not be particularly strong, because such disclosure "typically implicates few, if any, of the concerns that underlie the policy of grand jury secrecy."[101] Additionally, the Supreme Court noted in United States v. John Doe, Inc., I,[102] such disclosure could "sav[e] the Government, the potential defendants and witnesses, the pains of costly and time consuming depositions and interrogatories which might later have turned out to be wasted if the Government decided not to file a civil action after all." The danger here is that the government will use the grand jury process as a way of circumventing civil discovery rules. Thus, it was important in John Doe that the grand jury attorneys, who had been unable to secure an indictment, had submitted an affidavit attesting to their good faith in conducting the investigation.

98 Dennis v. United States, 384 U.S. 855 (1966).

99 Douglas Oil Co. of California v. Petrol Stops Northwest, 441 U.S. 211 (1979).

100 356 U.S. 677 (1958).

101 United States v. Sells Engineering, Inc. 463 U.S. 418 (1983).

102 481 U.S. 102 (1987).

8.7.3 Rights of grand jury witnesses

People called to testify at the grand jury do not have the rights witnesses are provided at trial, or even the rights witnesses receive at a preliminary hearing. Given the desire to maintain secrecy and avoid alerting suspects, most states do not grant targets of grand jury investigations the right to testify and explain their side. Nor does the Constitution require that witnesses be told of their right to remain silent or that they are the target of the investigation, on the ground that a grand jury proceeding is not as inherently coercive as interrogation (although many states statutorily mandate Miranda-type warnings for either targets or for all witnesses).[103] Further, the Supreme Court has implied that grand jury proceedings precede the initiation of the "criminal prosecution" referred to in the Sixth Amendment, and thus that even targets of the grand jury do not have a right to counsel.[104]

These restrictions on witness rights can all be criticized, especially if the grand jury is acting as a check on an already-made decision to prosecute rather than as an investigatory body. In jurisdictions that require a preliminary hearing to bind over the defendant to the grand jury, a restriction on the right to testify makes little sense, because the defendant already knows he or she is the target. A grand jury proceeding may not be as coercive as an interrogation, but because defendants and targets do not have a right to counsel, they may not be aware of the scope of their Fifth Amendment rights in the absence of Miranda warnings. And, for that reason, one can argue that, even if there is no Sixth Amendment right to counsel at the grand jury, there should be a Fifth Amendment right, analogous to the right recognized in Miranda. Furthermore, the Court's interrogation cases indicate that criminal prosecution for Sixth Amendment purposes can begin as early as arraignment (see §5.5), which often precedes the grand jury process when it is used as a screening mechanism rather than an investigatory body. Most jurisdictions allow witnesses to consult with counsel outside the grand jury room, and many allow counsel inside the grand jury room.

---

103 Cf. United States v. Mandujano, 425 U.S. 564 (1976) (distinguishing the grand jury from custodial interrogation).

104 Id. See also In re Groban's Petition, 352 U.S. 330 (1957).

8.7.4 Subpoena and immunity powers

As the Supreme Court stated in Branzburg v. Hayes,[105] the grand jury has "a right to every man's evidence," meaning that it may compel evidence subject only to "constitutional, common law or statutory privilege." This right exists, the Court later explained in United States v. Dionisio,[106] because the "obligation of every person to appear and give testimony [to the grand jury] is indispensable to the administration of justice." The grand jury's power is manifested in its ability to subpoena testimony (through a subpoena ad testificandum) and documents (through a subpoena duces tecum); to grant, at the prosecutor's request, immunity from prosecution; and to hold in contempt a person who refuses to comply with a subpoena or to testify after being immunized. In modern times, these powers are largely controlled by the prosecutor, although a court might be called upon for enforcement of a contempt order.

Generally, so long as the subpoena is aimed at investigating criminal activity and is not used as a ruse to gain discovery for civil litigation or for the purpose of harassment, it will be upheld.[107] Given the right to every man's evidence, a subpoena ad testificandum does not require probable cause or any level of suspicion, but rather can be issued, in the words on Dionisio, on the basis of "tips, rumors, evidence offered by the prosecutor, or [the jurors'] own personal knowledge." While such a subpoena may be "inconvenient" or "burdensome," it is not a seizure for Fourth Amendment purposes because its command is not as abrupt or physically coercive as an arrest or stop, is flexible enough to accommodate the witness' schedule, and involves questioning by a prosecutor and laypeople rather than police in the field. Nor can a subpoena ad testificandum be resisted on Fifth Amendment grounds, because the witness cannot know what the grand jury will ask (indeed, it might be seeking evidence about another person or even exculpatory information about the witness), and thus cannot make an intelligent assertion of the right to silence until the appearance before the grand jury.

A subpoena duces tecum is subject to somewhat more constitutional regulation. Like a subpoena ad testificandum, as a constitutional

105 408 U.S. 665 (1972).

106 410 U.S. 1 (1973).

107 Blair v. United States, 250 U.S. 273 (1919).

matter a subpoena duces tecum can issue merely to satisfy "official curiosity."[108] Consistent with this language, the federal rules provide that a subpoena may only be quashed if "there is no reasonable possibility that the category of materials the Government seeks will produce information relevant to the general subject of the grand jury's investigation," an extremely low standard.[109] At the same time, in Hale v. Henkel,[110] the Court held that the Fourth Amendment does prohibit subpoenas that are "too sweeping" or that fail to state with "particularity" the items to be produced, and thus demand so much material that they might compromise an entity's ability to conduct business. Many courts follow the lower court decision in United States v. Gurule in stating that, to be "reasonable" under the Fourth Amendment "the subpoena may command only the production of things relevant to the investigation being pursued; specification of things to be produced must be made with reasonable particularity; and production of records covering a reasonable period of time may be required."[111] The courts have also indicated that subpoenas demanding some types of intimate material, such as blood samples or medical records, may require more justification.[112] Finally, the Supreme Court's decision in Carpenter v. United States,[113] which held that a warrant is required to obtain cell-site location information from a common carrier (see §2.3.4), could eventually upend this entire area of the law, by requiring more robust justification for certain types of subpoenas.

Furthermore, when the subpoena is aimed at obtaining material from the target of an investigation rather than a third party, the Fifth Amendment may impose more significant limitations. As recounted in §8.4.1, a subpoena does not compel creation of the sought-after documents, but it does compel the act of producing the document, which may be considered incriminating testimony if the act of production is used against the target to prove knowledge of the document's existence or authenticity. Moreover, if the subpoena is not particularized, but instead in effect requires the target to find the relevant incriminating information for the state, the Fifth Amendment may impose Fourth Amendment-like restrictions on the subpoena,

108 United States v. Morton Salt, 338 U.S. 632 (1950).

109 United States v. R. Enterprises, Inc., 498 U.S. 292 (1991).

110 201 U.S. 43 (1906).

111 437 F.2d 239 (10th Cir. 1970).

112 See United States v. Mara, 410 U.S. 19 (1973); Doe v. Broderick, 225 F.3d 440 (4th Cir. 2000).

113 138 S.Ct. 2206 (2018).

because the state is compelling the defendant to reveal the "contents of his own mind."[114]

Even a valid Fifth Amendment claim can be overridden, however, if the prosecutor, acting through the grand jury, grants the witness immunity. Immunity comes in two types, transactional immunity, which bars the witness' future prosecution with respect to any transaction relating to the testimony, and "use and derivative use" immunity, which bars only the subsequent use of the specific testimony of the witness, as well as any evidence derived from that testimony. Under the latter type of immunity, if the prosecution can show that a subsequent prosecution is based on evidence independent of the immunized witness' testimony, it may proceed. In Kastigar v. United States,[115] the Supreme Court held that use and derivative immunity is permissible under the Fifth Amendment despite the lesser protection it affords, because it prohibits any use of compelled statements. But the Court also emphasized that the burden of proof is on the government to show that any new evidence against the defendant is derived from "a legitimate source wholly independent of the compelled testimony." Thus, most individuals granted immunity are minor players whose testimony is needed to prosecute criminals further up the chain, or are individuals against whom the government has already developed a significant amount of evidence. Even a grant of immunity does not prevent a witness' testimony from being used in a perjury prosecution, however; as the Court stated in United States v. Apfelbaum,[116] the Fifth Amendment has never permitted "false swearing."

The grand jury's ability to issue subpoenas and grant immunity is backed up by the court's authority to impose civil and criminal contempt citations on those who refuse to respond. Civil contempt, which is the usual sanction, results in a fine or jail until the witness is "purged" of contempt by providing the sought-after evidence or testifying. If the evidence is not produced by the end of the grand jury's term, the witness is released, but a new grand jury can once again hold the witness in civil contempt. If civil contempt fails, criminal contempt, which results in a fixed sentence or fine, may be imposed.

---

114 United States v Hubbell, 530 U.S. 27 (2000).

115 406 U.S. 441 (1972).

116 445 U.S. 115 (1980).

8.7.5 Challenges to the basis of an indictment

If, after its investigation, the grand jury finds a true bill, its indictment can be challenged on a number of grounds, but such challenges are rarely upheld. In Costello v. United States,[117] the Supreme Court stated that "an indictment returned by a legally constituted and unbiased grand jury, . . . if valid on its face, is enough to call for a trial of the charge on the merits." Thus, Costello held, an indictment based on evidence that would be inadmissible at trial is valid. Such evidence can still have probative value, and any objections to the evidence can be remedied at trial. Determining whether such evidence is admissible would delay the investigation, and require an adversarial proceeding antithetical to the grand process.

For similar reasons, evidence obtained in violation of the privilege against self-incrimination or the Fourth Amendment can be a valid basis for an indictment[118] (although, for statutory reasons, grand jury questions based on information obtained through an illegal wiretap need not be answered).[119] Even a failure to provide the grand jury exculpatory information that the prosecutor is obligated to provide the defense under Brady v. United States (see §8.4.2) is not grounds for dismissal of indictment. In United States v. Williams,[120] the Supreme Court stated that "requiring the prosecutor to present exculpatory as well as inculpatory evidence would alter the grand jury's historical role, transforming it from an accusatory to an adjudicatory body." Thus the constitutional rules that apply to trials rarely provide a basis for challenging an indictment.

Even when a violation of constitutional or statutory rules occurs, the Court has made clear that it will almost always be harmless error if exposed after conviction. In United States v. Mechanik,[121] which involved a violation of a rule limiting who may attend grand jury proceedings, the Court stated that:

> the petit jury's subsequent guilty verdict not only means that there was probable cause to believe that the defendants were guilty as charged, but that

117 350 U.S. 359 (1956).

118 Lawn v. United States, 355 U.S. 339 (1958); United States v. Calandra, 414 U.S. 338 (1974).

119 Gelbard v. United States, 408 U.S. 41 (1972) (interpreting 128 U.S.C. §2515).

120 504 U.S. 36 (1992).

121 475 U.S. 66 (1986).

> they are in fact guilty as charged beyond a reasonable doubt. . . . [Further,] there is no simple way after the verdict to restore the defendant to the position in which he would have been had the indictment been dismissed before trial. He will already have suffered whatever inconvenience, expense, and opprobrium that a proper indictment may have spared him.

Lower courts have relied on this language in rejecting almost all other types of challenges to the indictment. In the subsequent case of Bank of Nova Scotia v. United States,[122] the Supreme Court did state that dismissal of an indictment could occur "if it is established that the violation substantially influenced the grand jury's decision to indict or if there is 'grave doubt' that the decision to indict was free from the substantial influence of such violations," or if the prosecutorial misconduct was "so systematic and pervasive as to raise a substantial question about the fundamental fairness of the process which resulted in the indictment." But in Nova Scotia itself, the Court found that the following illegal actions by the prosecutor were not grounds for quashing the indictment: (1) use of the grand jury to gather evidence for civil matters; (2) public identification of the targets; (3) imposition of secrecy oaths on witnesses; (4) permitting misleading summaries of the evidence by government agents (that the defense could not show were intentional); (5) granting immunity to witnesses with the implicit threat that they would be charged if they testified for the defendant; (6) making abusive comments to an expert witness that were overheard by grand jury members; and (7) failure to prevent two witnesses from appearing in front of the grand jury simultaneously.

However, in at least one situation an indictment challenge does not require proof of prejudice. Recall that Costello's justification for resisting most indictment challenges was predicated on the assumption that the grand jury was "legally constituted and unbiased." In Mechanik, the Court emphasized that "racial discrimination in the selection of grand jurors is so pernicious and other remedies so impractical, that the remedy of automatic reversal [is] necessary as a prophylactic means of deterring grand jury discrimination." In Bank of Nova Scotia, the Court arrived at the same conclusion with respect to violation of the due process fair cross-section requirement for selection of grand jury pools.

---

122 487 U.S. 250 (1988).

8.7.6 Challenges to the face of the indictment

A conviction can be overturned if it is based on an indictment that does not "fairly inform the defendant of the charge," or does not enable the defendant "to plead an acquittal or conviction in bar of future prosecution for the same offense" as provided under the Double Jeopardy Clause (see §12.5.3). Further, a conviction is invalid under the Fifth Amendment's Indictment Clause if the indictment fails to reflect that the grand jury found probable cause with respect to all of the "essential elements" of the alleged crime.[123] These problems can be avoided if the indictment tracks the language of the relevant statute "accompanied by such a statement of facts and circumstances as will inform the accused of the specific offense." However, as the Court noted in Russell v. United States,[124] if a defendant is "convicted on the basis of facts not found by, and perhaps not even presented to, the grand jury which indicted him," the defendant is deprived "of a basic protection which the guaranty of the intervention of the grand jury was designed to secure."

In Russell, the Court found the Indictment Clause was violated because the indictment charged the defendant with a failure to answer questions "then under inquiry" by a congressional subcommittee, without identifying the nature of the inquiry. In contrast, in United States v. Resendiz-Ponce,[125] an indictment that failed to allege a "substantial step" toward entering the country illegally, a lapse the prosecution conceded, was still sufficient because it used the word "attempt" in describing the defendant's conduct.

A violation of the Indictment Clause can also be harmless error. In United States v. Cotton,[126] the indictment properly alleged a conspiracy but failed to allege the amount of cocaine necessary to support the judge's sentence enhancement (50 grams), which the Court found was an essential element under Apprendi v. New Jersey's requirement that sentencing facts that result in enhancements must be proven at trial (see §10.3.1). Despite this finding, however, the Court concluded that the error did not "seriously affect the fairness, integrity or public reputation of judicial proceedings, given the overwhelming nature of

123 See United States v. Debrow, 346 U.S. 374 (1953).

124 369 U.S. 749 (1962).

125 549 U.S. 102 (2007).

126 535 U.S. 625 (2002).

the evidence against the defendants," and that the grand jury, having found that a conspiracy existed "surely . . . would have also found that the conspiracy involved at least 50 grams of cocaine base." Thus, this type of error is not "structural error" that requires automatic reversal (see §12.3.2 for further discussion of structural error).

A closely related issue arises when the proof offered by the prosecution at trial is at "variance" with the allegations in the grand jury's indictment. If there is substantial variance, the indictment might be quashed and the conviction reversed under the Indictment Clause, at least if the error affects the fairness and integrity of the proceeding in the manner alluded to in Cotton. Similarly, some courts have overturned petit jury convictions that are based on some, but not all, of the material allegations in the indictment, on the ground that if the grand jury had heard only the evidence related to the allegations proven at trial, it might have failed to indict. In United States v. Miller,[127] however, the Supreme Court held that when the indictment facts that the prosecution fails to prove at trial are "in no way essential to the offense on which the jury convicted," they can be regarded as "surplusage." Thus, in Miller, although the government was unable to prove the first allegation in the indictment—to the effect, that the defendant, charged with insurance fraud, had colluded in a "burglary" of his property that resulted in an insurance "loss"—it was able to prove that the defendant misrepresented the value of the loss to his insurance company, which was sufficient for conviction under the relevant statute.

127 471 U.S. 130 (1985).

9 Guilty pleas and plea bargaining

9.1 Overview

Well over 90 percent of all convictions in the United States result not from trial but from a guilty plea, which is usually the product of negotiation between the prosecutor and the defense attorney. As the Supreme Court recognized in Lafler v. Cooper,[1] "criminal justice today is for the most part a system of pleas, not of trials." Judges play only a minor role in these cases, and juries play no role at all; the lawyers, and in particular, the prosecutor, control the adjudication process. The much-vaunted ideal of the adversarial, public jury trial is simply too expensive to provide to more than a small portion of criminal defendants. Thus, in most cases, cross-examination of witnesses never occurs, and laypeople have no input into the determination of guilt and innocence. In many cases, guilty pleas may even obviate discovery, preliminary hearings, and grand jury proceedings.

To ensure that most defendants plead guilty rather than go to trial, there must be a substantial punishment differential between plea-based sentences and sentences imposed after trial. Research has found that, in state courts, the post-plea/post-trial sentence increase ranges from 13 percent to 461 percent, depending on the jurisdiction and the crime;[2] in Lafler, the increase was 350 percent. Under the federal sentencing guidelines, the formal discount for a guilty plea is 25 to 35 percent, and the informal discount is much higher.[3]

Resolution of criminal charges through plea bargaining and guilty pleas streamlines the process and allows the prosecutor and defense

1 566 U.S. 156 (2012).

2 Nancy King, David A. Soulé, Sara Steen, and Robert R. Weidner, When Process Affects Punishment: Differences in Sentences after Guilty Plea, Bench Trial, and Jury Trial in Five Guidelines States, 105 Colum. L. Rev. 959, 992 (2005).

3 Stephanos Bibas, Plea Bargaining outside the Shadow of Trial, 117 Harv. L. Rev. 2463, 2488–89 (2004).

to fine-tune the final disposition in a way that trial on specific charges connected with specific penalties may not. But given the plea-trial punishment differential, defendants with valid challenges to their charges, and even defendants who are completely innocent of the charges, may plead guilty simply to avoid trial, especially when the charges are relatively minor. Moreover, plea bargaining may encourage prosecutors to overcharge as a negotiating ploy, and it can also lead to less individualized dispositions, at least in busy urban areas where bargaining may proceed according to preset "schedules." Additionally, plea bargaining may cause defense attorneys to "devise strategies whose only utility lies in the threat they pose to the court's and prosecutor's time."[4] Nonetheless, only a few jurisdictions have successfully experimented with elimination of plea bargaining, and most enthusiastically support it. As long ago as 1971, the Supreme Court stated, "[t]he disposition of criminal charges by agreement between the prosecutor and the accused . . . is an essential component of the administration of justice. Properly administered, it is to be encouraged."[5]

The type of offer a prosecutor might make during plea negotiations comes in three varieties: (1) charge bargaining, where the prosecutor offers to lower or dismiss a charge or reduce the number of charges, or both; (2) sentence bargaining, where the prosecutor offers to recommend, stipulate to, or not contest a particular sentence or sentence range (which the judge must ultimately approve, and almost always does); or (3) fact bargaining, where the prosecutor and defense agree to a particular version of the facts. In return, the defendant offers to plead guilty, or plea nolo contendere (literally, "I do not contest," a plea that cannot be used in civil proceedings or to enhance subsequent sentences). In addition, the defendant may agree to testify against co-defendants, forgo asserting certain rights (including the right to appeal or assert ineffective assistance of counsel), or to provide other benefits to the prosecution.

9.2 Rights during bargaining

Generally, the defendant has fewer rights during the plea bargaining process than during a trial. Given the language of the Sixth Amendment, there is no right to counsel during bargaining that takes

4 Albert Alschuler, The Prosecutor's Role in Plea Bargaining, 38 Chi. L. Rev. 50, 56 (1968).

5 Santobello v. New York, 404 U.S. 257 (1971).

place prior to the onset of criminal prosecution (i.e., indictment or other formal charge), although as Chapter 5 explains, the rules governing interrogation may curtail prosecutorial or police bargaining with a counsel-less defendant at that stage of the process. And, as §11.3.4 discusses in more detail, while defendants are entitled to effective assistance of counsel when the right to counsel attaches, any failure by counsel to investigate or make particular arguments during the bargaining process, even if egregious, does not require invalidation of a guilty plea unless the defendant can show "a reasonable probability that, but for counsel's errors, he would not have pleaded guilty and would have insisted on going to trial."[6]

As recounted in §8.4.2, the defendant's right to exculpatory evidence under Brady may also be curtailed during the bargaining process. In United States v. Ruiz,[7] the Supreme Court held that, at most, defendants are entitled to information "establishing factual innocence" prior to entering a plea agreement. The Court reasoned that requiring early disclosure of other information, even if "material" under Brady, would disrupt ongoing investigations, expose prospective witnesses and informants to harm, and require the government "to devote substantially more resources to trial preparation prior to plea bargaining," thereby making bargaining a much less attractive option.

Finally, in contrast to trial, the defendant apparently does not have a right to be present during plea bargaining. As discussed in §11.4, defendants have a Sixth Amendment right to confront their accusers. But prosecution witnesses are not involved in the bargaining process. Moreover, as a practical matter, bargaining that requires the defendant's presence may be more difficult to carry out when the defendant is in jail.

9.3 Permissible inducements during bargaining

In Boykin v. Alabama,[8] the Supreme Court held that, as a matter of due process, a judge may not accept a guilty plea "without an affirmative showing that it is intelligent and voluntary." One might argue that, given the plea/trial punishment differentials described earlier,

6 Hill v. Lockhart, 474 U.S. 52 (1985).

7 536 U.S. 622 (2002).

8 395 U.S. 238 (1969).

any guilty plea induced through bargaining is involuntary under the Due Process Clause, or is "compelled testimony" barred by the Fifth Amendment. But the Court has distinguished between bargains that are illegitimately compelled and those that are induced by presenting the defendant with options authorized by statute. In Bordenkircher v. Hayes,[9] the prosecution confronted the defendant with the choice of pleading guilty and receiving a five-year sentence or going to trial on a habitual offender charge that could result in a life sentence. Hayes chose to go to trial and was convicted. As discussed in §8.5.3, the Court found that Hayes' prosecution under the habitual offender statute was not an unconstitutionally vindictive act, since it was authorized by law. By implication, the Court also affirmed that, had Hayes pleaded guilty, his plea would have been voluntary. According to the Court, "the imposition of these difficult choices [is] an inevitable—and permissible—attribute of any legitimate system which tolerates and encourages the negotiation of pleas." So long as the dispositional alternatives are "openly presented" to the defendant, and are based on reasonable interpretations of the criminal law, any resulting plea will usually be considered voluntary.

The exceptions to this rule are narrow. Of course, "the State may not produce a plea by actual or threatened physical harm or by mental coercion overbearing the will of the defendant." This latter statement comes from Brady v. United States[10] (not be confused with Brady v. Maryland, the discovery case), where the defendant pleaded guilty in part because avoiding trial meant he would not be exposed to the death penalty. Noting that Brady knew that a co-defendant had agreed to testify against him at trial, the Court found his guilty plea voluntary. But it stated that a finding of involuntariness might be appropriate had there been proof that "Brady was so gripped by fear of the death penalty or hope of leniency, that he did not or could not, with the help of counsel, rationally weigh the advantages of going to trial against the advantages of pleading guilty." In Hayes the Court also cautioned that an effort to obtain a plea by threatening, or promising lenience toward, a person other than the accused might raise constitutional issues, and in a much earlier case the Court indicated that use of deception to obtain a plea is unconstitutional.[11]

---

9 434 U.S. 357 (1978).

10 397 U.S. 742 (1970).

11 Walker v. Johnson, 312 U.S. 275 (1941).

Certain statutory, as opposed to prosecutorial, inducements to plea may also be impermissible. In United States v. Jackson,[12] the Court found unconstitutional a statute that provided for the death penalty in cases like Jackson's if conviction occurred after a jury trial, but limited his punishment to life imprisonment after a bench trial or a guilty plea. The Court struck down the statute on the ground that it "needlessly encourage[d]" guilty pleas. By contrast, a statute that permitted a sentence of either 30 years or life imprisonment after a guilty plea, but only a life sentence after trial, was upheld because the statute made a life sentence an option after both conviction by trial and conviction by plea.[13]

Judicial domination of the plea bargaining process might also raise concerns about coercion, because judges whose offers are spurned may act vindictively at trial, a possibility defendants are likely to assume. In part for that reason, the federal rules prohibit judicial involvement in plea bargaining.[14] But the Supreme Court has held that violating this rule can be harmless error.[15] The American Bar Association would allow judicial participation during bargaining at the request of the parties, provided the judge only indicates what charge or sentence concessions would be acceptable and "never through word or demeanor, either directly or indirectly, communicates to the defendant or defense counsel that a plea agreement should be accepted or that a guilty plea should be entered."[16] In many jurisdictions, judges are routinely involved in the bargaining process to an even greater extent. Some have argued that judges should always be involved in plea negotiations, in part on the ground that it will minimize guessing as to dispositions the judge is likely to accept.[17]

9.4 Legal effect of a bargain

Under contract law, an offer and an acceptance, voluntarily arrived at, usually constitute a legally binding agreement that a court must enforce. That simple rule does not apply in the plea bargaining context.

12 390 U.S. 570 (1968).

13 Corbitt v. New Jersey, 439 U.S. 212 (1978).

14 Fed. R. Crim. P. 11(e)(1).

15 United States v. Davila, 569 U.S. 297 (2013).

16 ABA Criminal Justice Standard 14-3.3(d) and (c).

17 Albert Alschuler, The Trial Judge's Role in Plea Bargaining, Part I, 76 Colum. L. Rev. 1059 (1976).

The judge presiding over the plea hearing need not accept either a sentence or fact bargain, and may not even be required to accept a charge bargain, at least if the charge is considered "an abuse of prosecutorial discretion."[18] Nor need the defendant abide by an agreement to plead guilty; the defendant may decide to plead not guilty at the plea hearing regardless of any previous bargain.

In many jurisdictions, the defendant may withdraw a bargained-for plea even after the agreement is confirmed at the plea hearing, if the judge then rejects the prosecutor's sentencing recommendation (although in other jurisdictions such withdrawal is not permitted, on the theory that the defendant knows the recommendation may not be followed and, indeed, as indicated in §9.6.1, must be told of that possibility at the plea hearing in federal courts). Under the federal rules, the defendant may also withdraw a guilty plea prior to imposition of sentence for a "fair and just reason," such as a showing of coercion, a recently discovered prosecutorial breach, or facts supporting a defense that were previously overlooked by the defendant.[19] In some jurisdictions, the trial court judge can permit withdrawal even after imposition of sentence, but only if "manifest justice" would result. Otherwise, the plea can be challenged only on appeal or collateral review, matters taken up in §9.7 and Chapter 12.

Finally, most courts also hold that the prosecutor may withdraw an offer, even after it has been accepted by the defendant, so long as the withdrawal occurs prior to the acceptance of the plea by the court. In Mabry v. Johnson,[20] the Supreme Court appeared to agree that, when the prosecutor reneges on a deal prior to the plea hearing, the defendant is, at most, entitled to renegotiate a deal, not to specific performance of a withdrawn deal. The one constitutional limitation in this situation might be when the defendant can make out a claim of vindictiveness, but that type of claim can be overcome if the prosecution provides proof of a change in circumstances that warrants the withdrawal (see §8.5.3). In Mabry itself, the Court upheld a guilty plea to a harsher arrangement than had originally been proffered, based on an explanation from the prosecutor that the prosecutor making the original offer had made a mistake.

---

18 See United States v. Ammidown, 497 F.2d 615 (D.C. Cir. 1973).

19 Fed. R. Crim. P. 11(e).

20 467 U.S. 504 (1984).

Prosecutorial breaches of bargains *at* the plea hearing are impermissible, but proof of such a breach may be a pyrrhic victory for the defendant. In Santobello v. New York,[21] the prosecutor involved in the bargaining agreed not to recommend a sentence, but the prosecutor who was present at the plea hearing asked for the maximum one-year sentence, which the judge imposed. The Supreme Court held that when a guilty plea "rests in any significant degree on a promise or agreement of the prosecutor, so that it can be said to be part of the inducement or consideration, such promises must be fulfilled," even when, as alleged here, the breach was inadvertent. However, the Court was unclear whether the defendant in this situation is entitled to specific performance (in Santobello, that remedy presumably would have meant a new plea hearing, in front of a new judge, without the sentence recommendation). And in Mabry the Court subsequently suggested that renegotiation is "within the range of constitutionally appropriate remedies" after prosecutorial breach, which weakens the value of Santobello's holding; it is also asymmetrical, in the sense that defendants are not permitted to renege on a bargain after it has been accepted by the court, except under the narrow circumstances described above.

There can also be disputes over whether one side or the other has lived up to the bargain. In United States v. Benchimol,[22] the bargaining prosecutor agreed to recommend probation with restitution, but the government's presentence report failed to mention this promise, and at sentencing the prosecutor noted it had been made only after prompting from the defense attorney. While the lower appellate court overturned the resulting six-year sentence on the ground that the prosecutor's behavior had "left an impression of less-than-enthusiastic support for leniency," the Supreme Court reversed, holding that, unless the government agrees to support a particular recommendation "enthusiastically," or to give its reasons for a lenient recommendation, it need not do so. In interesting contrast is Ricketts v. Adamson,[23] where the defendant testified against his two co-defendants in return for a reduced charge of second degree murder. However, the defendant refused to testify again after the co-defendants' convictions had been overturned on appeal, at which point the prosecutor recharged the defendant with the original offense of first degree murder. Rather than allowing the defendant to challenge this interpretation of the

21 404 U.S. 257 (1971).

22 471 U.S. 453 (1985).

23 483 U.S. 1 (1987).

agreement and to make the choice of whether to testify if he lost, the Supreme Court upheld his subsequent conviction of first degree murder, based on its interpretation of language in the agreement that stated it was "null and void" if the defendant refused to testify. Defendants appear to be more at risk than prosecutors if they do not live up to the "spirit" of a bargaining agreement.

9.5 Permissible waivers during bargaining

The prosecution may want the defendant to reveal incriminating information before offering a deal, something the defendant is understandably reluctant to do. To promote the bargaining process, both the Federal Rules of Criminal Procedure and the Federal Rules of Evidence, as well as the rules of most states, prohibit use of statements "made in the course of plea discussions with an attorney for the government which do not result in a plea of guilty or which result in a plea of guilty later withdrawn."[24] Consistent with this rule, several jurisdictions permit "Queen for a Day" or "proffer" sessions at which defendants disclose to prosecutors what they know under a grant of immunity from prosecution based on their statements.

However, the Supreme Court has also held that the defendant can waive the protection of such rules as part of a plea bargain. In United States v. Mezzanatto,[25] the defendant agreed to waive his right to prevent prosecution use of his plea statements to impeach him if he later testified at trial. When negotiations failed and the defendant testified at trial, contradictory statements he made during the negotiations were used to impeach him. The Court held that, while rights that are "fundamental to the reliability of the fact-finding process" may be unwaivable, the right to prevent impeachment use of plea statements detracts from reliability, and thus can be waived. To the argument that such a conclusion will deter plea bargaining by defendants, the Court responded that the empirical evidence suggested otherwise, and that, without such a waiver provision, the prosecution might be unwilling to bargain. Left unclear by Mezzanatto is whether prosecutors can demand that defendants give up their protection against trial-use of plea statements even in the prosecution's case-in-chief.

---

24 Fed. R. Crim. P. 11(f).

25 513 U.S. 196 (1995).

Also unclear is which other rights might be waivable during bargaining. In federal jurisdictions, prosecutors often demand waiver of the Brady right to exculpatory evidence and the right to appeal and, until the practice was reversed in 2016 by the Department of Justice, the right to effective assistance of counsel. Yet these rights would seem to be "fundamental" to the reliability of the process. If these constitutional rights can be waived, presumably any evidentiary entitlements (such as, for instance, the prohibition on prosecution introduction of character evidence) could be as well.

9.6 Taking the plea

The plea hearing itself can often be pro forma, since the parties have already agreed upon the charges and possible sentences. However, as Boykin v. Alabama[26] held, guilty pleas must be intelligent and voluntary. The federal rules and the rules of most states require that the judge ascertain on the record that the defendant understands certain consequences of the plea and the nature of any bargain that forms the basis for the plea, and also that there is a factual basis for the plea.

9.6.1 Assuring understanding of the plea's consequences

Under Rule 11 of the Federal Rules of Criminal Procedure, the court may not accept a guilty plea until it has determined that the defendant understands: (1) the nature of the charge or charges to which the plea is offered; (2) the "consequences of the plea," including the possible sentence range under the relevant statute and sentencing guidelines and whether restitution to the victim may be required; and (3) the rights the defendant waives when pleading guilty (the rights to jury, trial counsel, confrontation of witnesses, and to remain silent). The rule also stipulates that any plea agreement must be disclosed at the time the plea is offered in court (unless the parties make a good cause showing why disclosure should be made in camera); this provision, which may be constitutionally required,[27] ensures that all parties are aware of the terms and facilitates later review of the bargain. Finally, the rule requires that defendants be informed that they may not back out of a plea if, after consideration of the presentence report and other submissions, the judge imposes a sentence higher than that anticipated under the

26 395 U.S. 238 (1969).

27 Blackledge v. Allison, 431 U.S. 63 (1977).

bargain.

In McCarthy v. United States,[28] the Supreme Court held that judges must strictly comply with these rules to ensure a truly informed plea and to minimize subsequent challenges to the plea. However, subsequent to McCarthy, the federal rules were amended to provide that "[a] variance from the requirements of this rule is harmless error if it does not affect substantial rights."[29] Some sense of the situations in which the Court thinks a "substantial right" is affected by a failure to inquire into the defendant's understanding of the plea can be derived from Henderson v. Morgan,[30] where the Court stated that the defendant must receive "adequate notice" of all "critical" elements of the offense (in Henderson's case, the difference between first and second degree murder), and Padilla v. Kentucky,[31] where the Court held that an attorney's failure to inform the defendant of the possibility of deportation constitutes ineffective assistance of counsel, over a dissent pointing out that deportation is a civil, not a criminal, penalty.

However, the Court has also held that the judge need not determine whether the defendant is aware of parole eligibility dates (at a time when federal law permitted parole),[32] and lower courts have held that inquiry into possible defenses available to the defendant would entail too much guesswork.[33] Moreover, the judge does not necessarily need to inquire directly about any of these matters. In Henderson, the Court held that "a representation [on the record] by defense counsel that the nature of the offense has been explained to the accused" can suffice. In the same vein is the Court's statement in Bradshaw v. Stumpf[34] that "[w]here defendant is represented by competent counsel, the court usually may rely on that counsel's assurance that the defendant has been properly informed of the nature and elements of the charge to which he is pleading guilty." Of course, as McCarthy suggested, the better practice is simply to follow the rules, and most judges do so.

28 394 U.S. 459 (1969).

29 Fed. R. Crim. P. 11(h).

30 426 U.S. 637 (1976).

31 559 U.S. 356 (2010).

32 Hill v. Lockhart, 474 U.S. 52 (1985).

33 See, e.g., Dismuke v. United States, 864 F.2d 106 (11th Cir. 1989).

34 545 U.S. 175 (2005).

9.6.2 Factual basis requirement

Federal Rule 11 requires the court to make "such inquiry as shall satisfy it that there is a factual basis for the plea," and the commentary to the rule states that the factual basis should be developed on the record, "for example, by having the accused describe the conduct that gave rise to the charge." The point, of course, is to ensure that the defendant's conduct falls within the scope of the charge that is the subject of the plea. In North Carolina v. Alford,[35] the Court appeared to give constitutional status to this requirement. However, the defendant need not explicitly admit guilt to meet it. In Alford the defendant pleaded guilty to a 30-year term but refused to admit he committed the crime. The Court held that, so long as the judge finds a factual basis for the plea, a defendant may plead guilty while insisting on innocence.

If the plea involves dispositional consequences, the factual basis requirement may be diluted. In Libretti v. United States,[36] the Court refused to overturn a plea despite the failure of the judge to inquire into the nexus between the defendant's crimes (involving drug, firearms and money-laundering laws) and property owned by the defendant that was subject to forfeiture under the plea agreement. Noting that the federal rules refer only to a "plea of guilty," the Court pointed out that forfeiture is an aspect of punishment, not the charge. At the same time, the Court indicated that the judge should engage in some inquiry into the underlying basis for a recommended sentence, or at least require a stipulation of relevant facts. Further, the sentencing guidelines require that the judge make certain findings before a sentence is imposed.[37]

Even when the judge takes the factual basis requirement seriously, the plea hearing falls far short of a trial. Witnesses are not called, and no tangible evidence need be presented. In many courts, the guilty plea hearing is carried out in a matter of minutes, at least for run-of-the-mill cases. The parties, not a judge or jury, are the real factfinders in such cases.

35 400 U.S. 25 (1970).

36 516 U.S. 29 (1995).

37 Fed. Sent. Guidelines Man. §6B2.1(b).

9.7 Preclusive effect of a plea

The voluntariness of a plea can be attacked on appeal, apparently even if the defendant agreed to a waiver of the right to appeal as part of the bargain.[38] However, other types of claims—claims alleging breaches of a bargain or allegations that the plea should be overturned due to defects in the investigation process (e.g., an illegal search or coerced confession)—are generally not reviewable on appeal. That is because appellate courts hear only challenges that can be assessed based on a trial court transcript or that are otherwise preserved on the record.

Challenges not reviewable on appeal may be challengeable through a habeas petition. But, as discussed in Chapter 12, habeas relief in federal court is difficult to obtain under any circumstances, and that is particularly so when conviction is based on a guilty plea. In Tollett v. Henderson,[39] the Court stated: "When a criminal defendant has solemnly admitted in open court that he is in fact guilty of the offense with which he is charged, he may not thereafter raise independent claims relating to the deprivation of constitutional rights that occurred prior to the entry of the guilty plea." On this reasoning, the Court has held that defendants who were convicted through a guilty plea may not use habeas to claim that their confession was coerced,[40] nor, as in Tollett itself, to challenge the racial composition of the grand jury that indicted them.

There are three exceptions to this rule. The first is when the failure to raise the claim about the pretrial defect was due to ineffective assistance of counsel (see §11.3.3). The second is when the alleged defect "goes to the very power of the State to bring the defendant into court to answer the charge brought against him."[41] Such claims include allegations that the charge is the result of prosecutorial vindictiveness,[42] is barred by the double jeopardy prohibition,[43] or is based on an unconstitutional statute.[44] The third exception arises when the state allows "conditional" pleas, which permit the

38 Garza v. Idaho, 139 S.Ct. 738 (2019).

39 411 U.S. 258 (1973).

40 McMann v. Richardson, 397 U.S. 759 (1970); Parker v. North Carolina, 397 U.S. 790 (1970).

41 Blackledge v. Perry, 417 U.S. 21 (1974).

42 Id.

43 Menna v. New York, 423 U.S. 61 (1975).

44 Class v. United States, 138 S.Ct.798 (2018).

defendant to reserve for appeal certain types of claims, such as those arising under the Fourth or Fifth Amendments. If such a claim is rejected on appeal, the Supreme Court has held that habeas review is available.[45]

45 Lefkowitz v. Newsome, 420 U.S. 283 (1975).

10 The right to a speedy, public jury trial

10.1 Overview

The idealized image of the American criminal process is a trial in which a group of laypeople decide whether the defendant is guilty beyond a reasonable doubt. As the last chapter made clear, however, trial occurs in less than 10 percent of all cases. Instead, the parties usually try to avoid trial, through negotiations that provide defendants with a lesser punishment than would be imposed upon conviction at trial and that allow the prosecution to save its resources for those cases that it cannot or will not resolve through plea bargaining.

When trial does occur, the Sixth Amendment states that the "accused shall enjoy the right to a speedy and public trial, by an impartial jury . . .; to be confronted with the witnesses against him; to have compulsory process for obtaining witnesses in his favor, and to have the assistance of counsel for his defense." The rights to speedy, public trial by an impartial jury are the subject of this chapter. The rights to confrontation, compulsory process, and counsel are the subject of the next.

10.2 Speedy trial

The Supreme Court first articulated the interests protected by the speedy trial right in United States v. Ewell,[1] which noted that a prompt trial prevents undue incarceration, reduces the anxiety accompanying public accusation, and minimizes impairment of the defendant's case due to delay. In Barker v. Wingo,[2] the Court elaborated that delay in adjudicating criminal charges disrupts the defendant's family life and employment, drains resources, and prolongs stigmatization; if the

1 383 U.S. 116 (1966).
2 407 U.S. 514 (1972).

defendant is detained, trial preparation can also be hindered. Barker also noted that postponing trial can harm society by weakening the prosecution's case, raising costs, and increasing the chances that arrested individuals will commit crime in the meantime. At the same time, Elwell emphasized, "the essential ingredient is orderly expedition and not mere speed." Adjudication that is too hasty can also harm defendants, as the history of "mass production" misdemeanor courts bears out.[3]

These various considerations all have some impact on the scope of the right to speedy trial. The Constitution sets the outer limits of the right, while every jurisdiction also has enacted a statute that more precisely prescribes when trial must occur.

10.2.1 The constitutional right

Given the language of the Sixth Amendment, the speedy trial right is only applicable to individuals "accused" of crime,[4] and only to pre-trial delay, not delay between conviction and sentence.[5] Pre-accusation delay is primarily the province of statutes of limitations, which for most crimes short of homicide require the state to bring charges within a certain time after commission of an offense as a means of ensuring that evidence does not go stale. In United States v. Lovasco,[6] the Court did hold that, even if the relevant limitations period has not expired, the Due Process Clause is violated if the delay "transgresses the community's sense of fair play and decency." However, that test will rarely be met. In Lovasco the Court emphasized that, given the benefits of thorough investigation, the government is not obligated to file formal charges as soon as it has probable cause or even when it has evidence sufficient to establish guilt. Rather delay will be unconstitutional only if it is intended "to gain tactical advantage over the accused," or is carried out "in reckless disregard of circumstances . . . suggesting that there existed an appreciable risk that delay would impair the ability to mount an effective defense."

Once a person has been formally accused, the speedy trial right is triggered. However, if charges are subsequently dropped and reinstated,

3 See Alexandra Natapoff, Misdemeanors, 85 S. Cal. L. Rev. 1313 (2012).

4 United States v. Marion, 404 U.S. 307 (1971).

5 Betterman v. Montana, 136 S.Ct. 1609 (2016).

6 431 U.S. 783 (1977).

the period during the dismissal is not counted in the analysis, on the ground that, during the dismissal, "any restraint on liberty, disruption of employment, strain on financial resources, and exposure to public obloquy, stress and anxiety is no greater than it is upon anyone openly subject to a criminal investigation." This was the holding in United States v. MacDonald,[7] which involved four years of delay between dismissal of the first charges and reindictment. In contrast, if charges are not dismissed, then the entire period until trial is relevant to speedy trial analysis, even if, as occurred in Doggett v. United States,[8] the defendant was out of the country and unaware of those charges during most of the period, and thus was not subject to prolonged pretrial stress or public obloquy.

In any event, the time lapse between accusation and trial is only one factor to consider in determining whether the Sixth Amendment is violated. As the Court stated in Barker, in addition to "(1) the length of delay," courts should consider:

> (2) the reasons for the delay (e.g., whether the defense or prosecution caused the delay and, if the latter, the degree of good faith effort expended to bring the case to trial as soon as possible); (3) whether and when the defendant asserted his right, and (4) whether any actual prejudice to the defendant resulted from the delay due to destruction or staleness of evidence, oppressive pretrial incarceration or the creation of excessive anxiety.

In Barker, the delay was 5½ years, and much of that delay had resulted from the illness of the state's key witness and the prosecution's repeated attempts to convict Barker's co-defendant (who otherwise would have been able to claim the privilege against self-incrimination when subpoenaed to testify against Barker). But the Court held that the right was not violated. Although it concluded that the four-year period necessary to convict Barker's co-defendants was not excusable, the Court noted that Barker had not asserted his right until the last of 16 continuances requested by the government, and suggested that such a failure "is not an uncommon defense tactic." It further found that neither the potential for witness memory loss during the 5½ years nor the ten months of incarceration during that period unduly prejudiced the defendant.

---

7 456 U.S. 1 (1982).

8 505 U.S. 647 (1992).

When a long delay is due to government negligence and, in contrast to Barker, the defendant does assert the right in a timely fashion, courts are more likely to find a violation of the speedy trial right. Indeed, in Doggett, the Court presumed prejudice, because the eight-year delay in that case was due to the government's failure to continue tracking the defendant after his arrest. According to the Court "[c]ondoning prolonged and unjustifiable delays in prosecution would both penalize many defendants for the state's fault and simply encourage the government to gamble with the interests of criminal suspects assigned a low prosecutorial priority." But Doggett involved a rare fact situation. More importantly, government-caused delay can often be characterized as non-negligent; for instance, time consumed pursuing government appeals is unlikely to lead to a finding that the right was violated (since, if the case proceeds to trial, presumably the appeals were meritorious). And prejudice is unlikely to be presumed in most situations. In fact, two years after Doggett the Court held that, in the usual case, "[a] showing of prejudice is required to establish a violation of the Sixth Amendment Speedy Trial Clause." While such a showing can be made (as in Dickey v. Florida,[9] where the Court found actual prejudice resulted from a seven-year delay during which two defense witnesses died and a third one became unavailable), it can be very difficult to meet this test.

One reason for the Court's relatively tough stance on the right to speedy trial is that the remedy for its violation is dismissal. In Strunk v. United States,[10] the Court concluded that, unlike other guarantees of the Sixth Amendment, violation of the speedy trial right cannot be cured by granting a new trial, given the prolonged "emotional stress" suffered while awaiting trial and the likely unavailability of trustworthy evidence. As illustrated by statutory approaches to the speedy trial right, discussed below, a more nuanced remedy is possible, and might be advisable in the constitutional context as well, given the dismissal remedy's impact on the scope of the right.

10.2.2 Federal speedy trial statute

Under the Federal Speedy Trial Act of 1974 (copied by well over two-thirds of the states), an indictment or information must be filed within 30 days of arrest, and trial should follow within 70 days, but no sooner

9 398 U.S. 30 (1970).

10 412 U.S. 434 (1973).

than 30 days from the first appearance in front of a judge.[11] Thus, under the statute, trial must generally take place within 100 days of arrest or receipt of summons, which is a much shorter timeframe than that demanded by the Sixth Amendment. However, various circumstances can lead to exemptions from or extensions to these time periods.

The most significant exemptions are delays caused by the defendant, such as hearings on competency to stand trial, pretrial motions, and interlocutory appeals, although in all of these situations delays are exempted only if the court makes case-specific findings that the ends of justice outweigh the benefits of a speedy trial to both the defendant and society. Also exempted are extensions contemplated by deferred prosecution agreements and, following MacDonald, periods during which charges are dismissed. Continuances granted by the court "to serve the ends of justice" are also exempted, including continuances granted because a case is so unusual or complex that more preparation time is needed.

If the statute is violated, judges have discretion to grant dismissal with or without prejudice, after considering the seriousness of the offense, the circumstances leading to dismissal (e.g., who is responsible for the delay), and the effect of reprosecution on the administration of justice, which includes consideration of prejudice to the defendant. In United States v. Taylor,[12] the Supreme Court concluded that a one-month delay beyond the statutory period, which the trial court found required dismissal with prejudice because the government was "lackadaisical" in going forward with the case, should instead result in dismissal without prejudice (meaning that the defendant could be reindicted). The Court found no evidence of prejudice to the defendant, and also noted that the government had been ready to proceed within the time limit, but had been unable to do so because the defendant had escaped from custody (although the one-month delay occurred after he had been reapprehended). Many lower courts appear to grant dismissal without prejudice for virtually any felony, while others have dismissed charges with prejudice even in the absence of bad faith and after relatively short delays, because, as one judge put it, "if dismissal without prejudice is permitted, then the defendant has achieved nothing but the privilege of being tried a second time."[13] At the least, however, a dismissal

---

11 18 U.S.C. §3161 et seq.

12 487 U.S. 326 (1988).

13 United States v. Mehrmanesh, 652 F.2d 766 (9th Cir. 1981 (Fletcher, J., dissenting).

without prejudice requires reindictment and negotiation of the pretrial process once again, which may deter some reprosecutions.

10.3 Right to jury

The right to jury trial has roots deep in the common law, going back to the Magna Carta, which provided that defendants should be tried by a "jury of peers." By the end of the seventeenth century, the jury had acquired its three essential elements: (1) a group of 12 lay citizens (2) whose unanimous verdict (3) is given exclusive effect. Along with the grand jury, the petit jury was seen by the colonists as "the palladium of free government."[14] In Duncan v. Louisiana,[15] which applied the jury trial right to the states, the Supreme Court emphasized that the jury not only provides "an inestimable safeguard against the corrupt or overzealous prosecutor and against the compliant, biased, or eccentric judge," but also reflects an "insistence upon community participation in the determination of guilt and innocence"; the Court also pointed to research finding that, while juries sometimes reach a different outcome than judges would in particular cases, "it is usually because they are serving some of the very purposes for which they were created and for which they are now employed." Article II, section 2 of the Constitution provides that "the trial of all crimes, except in cases of impeachment shall be by jury" and, as noted in the introduction to this chapter, the Sixth Amendment also guarantees "an impartial jury" in all criminal prosecutions. However, the Supreme Court has held that the scope of the jury trial right does not have to adhere to the common law in all respects, and the impartiality guarantee has turned out to be difficult to implement in practice.

10.3.1 Scope of the right

While Duncan was a strong affirmation of the jury trial right, it also indicated that the right does not apply in trials of "petty crimes or offenses." Weighing the benefits of a jury verdict against "speedy and inexpensive nonjury adjudication," the Court subsequently defined this exemption as any offense that can result in a punishment of six months or less.[16] The Court has also held that adding non-incarcerative

14 Francis Heller, The Sixth Amendment 25–6 (1951).

15 391 U.S. 145 (1968).

16 Baldwin v. New York, 399 U.S. 66 (1970).

penalties, such as fines or loss of license, to a six-month jail term does not trigger the jury trial right, at least as long as these added penalties are minor or short-term.[17]

Similarly, a trial on multiple counts, no one of which carries a punishment of more than six months, does not require a jury, even if the aggregate punishment would far exceed that amount.[18] The one exception to this aggregation rule is when a separate trial is held on multiple contempt-of-court charges, since before such a trial the penalty for a single contempt will not be known, and because the judge may be affected by personal bias in such cases[19] (although, as described in §10.4, another judge should usually preside over such proceedings). "Summary" contempt citations that occur during trial are not governed by this rule, despite a similar potential for judicial bias, given the "need to maintain order" in the courtroom.[20]

Engaging in the same balancing of interests, in the 1970s the Court held that the states need not abide by the federal model with respect to either the unanimity requirement or the requirement of a 12-member jury. In its two cases allowing non-unanimous verdicts,[21] it rejected arguments that allowing such verdicts might permit convictions when there is a reasonable doubt about the defendant's guilt or lead the minority to forego voicing their views because they see no point in doing so. Rather, the Court insisted that juries could be counted on to "weigh the evidence and reach a decision upon rational grounds," and pointed out that, even in federal court where unanimity is required, a lack of unanimity results in retrial, not in acquittal (which would be the appropriate verdict if a non-unanimous verdict in the defendant's favor meant reasonable doubt). However, a half-century later, in Ramos v. Louisiana,[22] the Court reversed itself and held that state as well as federal jury verdicts must be unanimous. The Court emphasized that, in the two states that still allowed non-unanimous verdicts in 2020, the rule had been adopted long ago in an attempt to disempower blacks, who had recently been given the right to serve on juries.

17 Blanton v. City of North Las Vegas, 489 U.S. 538 (1989).

18 Lewis v. United States, 518 U.S. 322 (1996).

19 Codispoti v. Pennsylvania, 418 U.S. 506 (1974).

20 Id.

21 Johnson v. Louisiana, 406 U.S. 356 (1972) (upholding 9-3 verdict); Apodaca v. Oregon, 406 U.S. 404 (1972) (upholding 11-1 and 10-2 verdicts).

22 140 S.Ct. 1390 (2020).

Another 1970s opinion contracting the right to jury trial, Williams v. Florida,[23] has yet to be overturned, although its reach has been circumscribed. There, the Court held that the 12-member jury is "a historical accident" and "unnecessary to effect the purposes of the jury system." Research subsequent to Williams indicated that, compared to 12-member juries, smaller groups are less likely to represent the community, foster deliberation, listen to the views of a (smaller) minority, and result in hung juries (which tend to favor defendants). Probably as a result, in Ballew v. Georgia,[24] decided eight years after Williams, the Court held that a five-member jury violated the Sixth Amendment. And in Burch v. Louisiana,[25] relying on the same considerations, the Court struck down a statute that allowed a non-unanimous verdict from a six-person jury.

While most of the Court's departures from the jury trial right announced in Duncan have allowed abridgement of the right, in one area its decisions have vastly expanded it. In Jones v. United States,[26] the defendant was sentenced to 25 years for the crime of carjacking. The normal sentence for that crime was 15 years, but the judge raised the sentence by another ten years under authority of a statute that permitted such an enhancement if the carjacking caused "serious bodily injury." The Supreme Court nullified the enhancement, reasoning that allowing the judge to unilaterally add ten years would "shrink" the jury's role "from the significance usually carried by determinations of guilt to the relative importance of low-level gatekeeping." A year later, in Apprendi v. New Jersey,[27] the Court more forcefully stated that a jury must determine, beyond a reasonable doubt, all factors other than prior convictions that lead to a sentence longer than the normal maximum sentence, because such factors are essentially elements of the defendant's offense. Thus, in Apprendi, the Court nullified an enhancement beyond the statutory maximum that was based on a judicial finding that the defendant's crime was motivated by racial hatred. Applying similar reasoning in other cases, the Court has held that the jury must find aggravating circumstances that justify a death sentence[28], as well as facts that lead

23 399 U.S. 78 (1970).

24 435 U.S. 223 (1978).

25 441 U.S. 130 (1979).

26 526 U.S. 227 (1999).

27 530 U.S. 466 (2000).

28 Ring v. Arizona, 536 U.S. 584 (2002).

to the imposition of fines above the maximum incarcerative sentence authorized by the jury's findings.[29]

Most importantly, the Court has held that the Sixth Amendment applies not only to enhancements that extend beyond the maximum statutory range for the offense tried to the jury, but also enhancements that extend beyond the maximum guidelines sentence for that offense. Until Blakely v. Washington[30] and United States v. Booker,[31] many states and the federal government required judges to sentence defendants within ranges, usually called "guidelines," that typically carried a lesser maximum than provided by statute, unless specific findings were made that justified departing from the guidelines. For instance, in the state of Washington, Blakely was charged with a class B felony that warranted a statutory sentence of up to ten years, but a guidelines range of only 49 to 53 months. The 90-month sentence imposed by the judge in that case was below the statutory maximum but considerably exceeded the guidelines maximum. The Court held that, because the above-guidelines enhancement was based on a finding of "deliberate cruelty" made by the judge, not the jury, it violated Apprendi. In Booker, which involved the federal sentencing guidelines, the Court avoided having to reach an analogous conclusion by construing the guidelines to be "voluntary" or "advisory," rather than mandatory, meaning that the only maximum term relevant for Sixth Amendment purposes is the statutory maximum. After Blakely and Booker, many states have likewise made their guidelines systems advisory, while others have either increased maximum guidelines sentences and permitted judges to reduce the sentence based on mitigating findings (such as the absence of racial motivation or deliberate cruelty), or have reverted to indeterminate sentencing, which eliminates guidelines entirely.

Despite the ease with which the decision's dictates can be avoided, the Court has stuck with Apprendi, even holding that facts relevant to a mandatory minimum sentence must also be found by a jury. That holding came in Alleyne v. United States,[32] where the defendant was sentenced to a five-year minimum for use of a gun during a crime, and sentenced to another two years for brandishing the gun during the crime. The jury made only the first finding, and thus, the Court held,

29 Southern Union Co. v. United States, 567 U.S. 343 (2012).

30 542 U.S. 296 (2004).

31 543 U.S. 220 (2005).

32 570 U.S. 99 (2013).

the judge's two-year enhancement based on the aggravating factor of brandishing violated the Sixth Amendment. As the Court summarized its Apprendi line of decisions, "a fact increasing either end of the range produces a new penalty and constitutes an ingredient of the offense" that must be decided by a jury.

10.3.2 Waiver

Defendants may waive the right to jury trial and often do. They may be worried that hostile community sentiment will be more influential with a jury than a judge. They may also be concerned that juries will be too easily influenced by prior crimes introduced for impeachment purposes or too easily confused by complex facts. In Patton v. United States,[33] the Supreme Court upheld not only the defendant's right to waive the jury, but also the right to be tried by a jury composed of the usual number of members (if, for instance, a juror becomes ill).

The waiver must be "express and intelligent," as well as voluntary, a requirement that can be violated if, as discussed in §9.3, state law mandates that a jury trial carries a heavier penalty than is available after a bench trial. More significantly, even a voluntary waiver can be overridden by the prosecution. In Singer v. United States,[34] the Court reasoned that "a defendant's only constitutional right concerning the method of trial is to an impartial trial by jury," meaning that a prosecutorial veto of a jury waiver subjects the defendant to "the very thing that the Constitution guarantees him." Only when "passion, prejudice [or] public feeling" produces a "compelling" reason to forgo the jury would such a veto be improper, and normally a change of venue is possible in such circumstances (see §10.6.1).

10.3.3 Selection of jury pool

The first stage in selecting a jury is creation of a jury pool or list, traditionally called the "master wheel." In most jurisdictions the names in this pool are randomly drawn from voter registration lists or telephone directories, although in the past "jury commissioners" or "key-men" often conducted a less random process (which, as described below, made the system more vulnerable to legal challenge). From this pool

---

33 281 U.S. 276 (1930).

34 380 U.S. 24 (1965).

a venire or panel is selected, again usually randomly, which is reduced further through statutory exclusions, typically focused on aliens, those unable to speak English, people under 18, persons charged with a felony or serving a felony sentence, and those suffering from mental or physical incapacity. Prospective jurors can also request an exemption if, for instance, they are engaged in a "critical" occupation (such as military or government jobs), have previously served as juror, or can show that jury duty would cause undue hardship.

Before the Sixth Amendment was applied to the states in Duncan, the principal means of challenging this process was the Equal Protection Clause; in several cases, the Court relied on the Clause in finding unconstitutional jury selection processes, occurring mostly in the South, that resulted in serious under-representation of blacks or Hispanics in the venire.[35] However, the primary ground for challenging the selection process is now the Sixth Amendment, which as early as 1942 the Court declared requires that the jury pool in federal cases represent a "cross-section of the community."[36] Shortly after Duncan applied the jury trial right to the states, the Court declared that this fair cross-section requirement is "fundamental to the jury trial."[37] As described in Duren v. Missouri,[38] a fair cross-section claim requires proof of three elements:

> (1) that the group alleged to be excluded is a "distinctive" group in the community; (2) that the representation of this group in venires from which juries are selected is not fair and reasonable in relation to the number of such persons in the community; and (3) that this underrepresentation is due to systematic exclusion of the group in the jury-selection process.

A Sixth Amendment challenge is easier to make out than an equal protection challenge, because it does not require purposeful discrimination and because it contemplates relief for exclusion of groups beyond the traditional "suspect classes" involving race and gender.

To meet Duren's first prong of distinctiveness, a group need not "act or tend to act as a class." However, it must be large, identifiable, and

35 See, e.g., Whitus v. Georgia, 385 U.S. 545 (1967); Castaneda v. Partida, 430 U.S. 482 (1977).
36 Glasser v. United States, 315 U.S. 60 (1942).
37 Taylor v. Louisiana, 419 U.S. 522 (1975).
38 439 U.S. 357 (1979).

help advance the objectives associated with the jury trial right. Those objectives, the Court outlined in Lockhart v. McCree,[39] are:

> (1) guard[ing] against arbitrary power, and ensuring that the commonsense judgment of the community will act as a hedge against the overzealous or mistaken prosecutor; (2) preserving public confidence in the fairness of the criminal justice system, and (3) implementing our belief that "sharing in the administration of justice is a phase of civic responsibility."

The courts have made clear that racial groups (blacks, Latinos, and Native Americans) as well as Jews and women are distinctive groups for Sixth Amendment purposes. In contrast, most courts have held that young people are not a distinctive group, in large part because identifying the relevant age range is difficult (although it can be noted that definitional problems arise with other groups as well—as one judge asked, "In what generation does a Mexican-American or Puerto Rican become simply a Texan or New Yorker and cease to be part of a cognizable group?"[40]). Even if a group is distinctive, valid state interests, such as those reflected in the exclusions described above, can justify keeping members of the group out of the jury pool. In Duren, for instance, the Court suggested that a statutory exclusion for any member of the family (man or woman) who is responsible for the care of children would not violate the Constitution, even if that practice predominately excused women.

The second, under-representation, component of Duren is usually met if the disparity between the group's presence in the general population and its proportion in the jury pool is more than 10 percent. But the Supreme Court has indicated that under-representation can also be calculated by dividing absolute disparity by the group's representation in the jury-eligible population rather than in the entire population, or by judging whether the actual representation is more than two or three standard deviations from the representation expected in the particular community.[41] And, again, even if a prima face case of disparity exists, the Sixth Amendment is not violated if a legitimate reason for the disparity exists.

If no such reason exists, then the third prong of Duren—systematic exclusion—may well be met, because intent to produce disparity is

39 476 U.S. 162 (1986).

40 Barber v. Ponte, 772 F.2d 982 (1st Cir. 1985).

41 See generally, Berghuis v. Smith, 559 U.S. 314 (2010).

not required (in contrast to equal protection analysis). In Taylor v. Louisiana,[42] the statute considered by the Court permitted any otherwise qualified woman to serve, and in Duren the statute required women to opt out of service rather than opt in to jury service; in neither case did the state takes steps to disqualify women. Yet the Court found that both statutes violated the Sixth Amendment because, even if no discriminatory intent was present, they systematically excluded women from the jury pool. However, in Berghuis v. Smith,[43] the Court concluded that it was not "unreasonable" to place the burden on the defendant to show that under-representation of a distinctive group in the jury pool resulted in systematic exclusion. It further held that Smith did not necessarily meet this burden simply by showing that the jurisdiction: routinely excused people on a bare allegation of hardship or failure to show up for jury service; failed to follow up on such failures or to enforce appearance orders; and used residential addresses at least 15 months old. It concluded that "hardship exemptions resembling those Smith assails might well survive a fair-cross-section challenge."

10.3.4 For cause challenges

The process of selecting the petit jury from the jury venire is called voir dire (literally, "to see what is said"). The goal here is no longer achieving a cross-section of the community (which is unlikely even with a 12-person jury, much less a smaller panel), but rather empaneling a jury that is partial to neither side. Toward that goal, in every jurisdiction both the defense and the prosecution are entitled to an unlimited number of "for cause" challenges that allow removal of prospective jurors (hereafter jurors) thought to be biased, as well as a limited number of "peremptory" challenges that, as explained in the next section, allow removal of jurors for any reason other than race or gender.

To help determine possible biases among the jurors, some degree of juror questioning occurs, conducted either by the judge (in federal court and many states) or by the attorneys. In jurisdictions where questioning is conducted by the judge, attorneys can submit questions for the judge to ask. Generally, the judge has discretion to accept or reject such suggestions. In death penalty cases, however, the Supreme Court has required that judges ask jurors whether they would either automatically impose the death penalty or automatically refuse to do so if

42 419 U.S. 522 (1975).

43 559 U.S. 314 (2010).

the defendant were convicted.[44] And in Ham v. South Carolina,[45] the Supreme Court held that, when racial issues are "inextricably bound up with the conduct of the trial," the defense is entitled to questions that go beyond the usual general inquiries, which normally ask something like: "Are you conscious of any bias or prejudice for or against the defendant?" In Ham, where the defendant was a well-known black civil rights activist whose marijuana charges, the defense alleged, resulted from a frame-up by South Carolina police, the Court required more specific questions aimed at discovering racial prejudice.

However, this questioning requirement is very limited. In Ristaino v. Ross,[46] where a black was charged with a violent crime against a white security guard, the Court found that racial issues did not sufficiently "permeate" the proceedings to warrant such questioning. And beyond situations involving capital punishment or race, the conduct of voir dire can be left to the judge even in cases likely to be highly charged. For instance, questions about political or religious beliefs need not be asked in obscenity cases,[47] and questions about the effects of pretrial publicity need not be asked even when such publicity has been substantial.[48]

Based either on such questioning or on information obtained outside the courtroom, attorneys can generally challenge for cause those jurors who: are related to one of the litigants; have a pecuniary interest in the outcome of the case; previously served on a jury that considered a similar crime; or are simply unable or unwilling to hear the case fairly and impartially. The Supreme Court has indicated that the latter finding must generally be based on explicit findings, rather than "implied bias." Thus, it has refused to find bias where there was an attempt to bribe a juror,[49] where a juror was seeking employment with the prosecutor's office during the trial,[50] and where some of the jurors worked for the federal government and were subject to discharge for disloyalty, in a case in which the defendant was being tried for failing to appear before the Committee on Un-American Activities.[51]

44 Morgan v. Illinois, 504 U.S. 719 (1992).

45 409 U.S. 524 (1973).

46 424 U.S. 589 (1976).

47 Hamling v. United States, 418 U.S. 87 (1974).

48 Mu'Min v. Virginia, 500 U.S. 415 (1991).

49 Remmer v. United States, 347 U.S. 227 (1954).

50 Smith v. Phillips, 455 U.S. 209 (1982).

51 Dennis v. United States, 339 U.S. 162 (1950).

The analysis has been more nuanced in the limited context of the death penalty. In Witherspoon v. Illinois,[52] the judge removed for cause all jurors who, during voir dire, "expressed scruples" against the death penalty. The Supreme Court held that the death sentence imposed on Witherspoon could not stand, since the jury empaneled by the judge was likely to be "uncommonly willing to condemn a man to die," and because those who do not harbor doubts about the wisdom of capital punishment are "a distinct and dwindling minority." However, the Court also indicated that the judge may exclude jurors who stated that they would never consider returning a verdict of death. And in later cases, the Court held that exclusion is permissible if a juror states that the prospect of the death penalty would "interfere" with the judgment on guilt or innocence,[53] indicates that imposing the death penalty is against his or her "principles,"[54] or would only impose that penalty in "severe" cases,[55] holdings that stand in interesting contrast to the Court's refusal to find that implied bias against the defendant in non-capital cases violates the Sixth Amendment.

Witherspoon only overturned the defendant's sentence, not his conviction. In Lockhart v. McCree,[56] the defendant argued, bolstered by a number of studies, that if all jurors with scruples against the death penalty are removed from a capital murder jury, then it is also "uncommonly willing" to convict a defendant of capital murder. But the Court concluded that, even if research shows that such juries tend to be "conviction-prone," in McCree's case all of the jurors had promised to abide by their oath of impartiality, and "exactly the same twelve individuals could have ended up on his jury through the 'luck of the draw,' without in any way violating the constitutional guarantee of impartiality." Further, the Court reasoned, the state has an interest in empaneling a single jury to adjudicate both guilt and sentence, given that the same or similar evidence is presented at both trial and sentencing proceedings in such cases (although, as the dissent pointed out, this interest could also be accommodated after conviction by replacing "automatic life sentence" jurors with jurors who have no such scruples).

---

52 391 U.S. 510 (1968).

53 Wainwright v. Witt, 469 U.S. 412 (1985).

54 Darden v. Wainwright, 477 U.S. 168 (1986).

55 Uttecht v. Brown, 551 U.S. 1 (2007).

56 476 U.S. 162 (1986).

The Court also rejected McCree's argument, based on Taylor, that exclusion of "death-qualified" jurors from trial violated the Sixth Amendment's fair cross-section requirement. The Court first noted that Taylor's cross-section analysis is focused on the jury pool, not the petit jury. But even ignoring that point, the Court reasoned, death-qualified jurors are not like women or people from ethnic groups who, if excused in violation of Taylor, are excluded based on an immutable characteristic and from all types of juries, not just capital juries. Perhaps mitigating the impact of McCree to some extent, six years after that case the Court decided Morgan v. Illinois,[57] which made clear that, just as prosecutors can exclude "automatic life sentence" jurors for cause, defendants can exclude "automatic death sentence" jurors from trial as well as at sentencing.

10.3.5 Peremptory challenges

Because they require no explanation, peremptory challenges are limited in number, from 3 to 20 or so, depending upon the jurisdiction, the size of the jury and the type of crime. As the name implies, they can be used to strike a juror simply because the attorney disliked "the look" of the juror or has an intuition about the person's proclivities. The Supreme Court has explained that the peremptory challenge "is often exercised upon the 'sudden impression and unaccountable prejudices we are apt to conceive upon the bare looks and gestures of another,' upon a juror's 'habits and associations,' or upon the feeling that 'bare questioning [of a juror's] indifference may sometimes provide a resentment.'"[58]

However, peremptories may not be used to exclude a juror because of his or her race. Borrowing from its equal protection jurisprudence in cases involving jury pools, in Batson v. Kentucky[59] the Supreme Court held that a defendant makes out a prima facie case that use of peremptory challenges has violated the Constitution if it can be shown that: (1) the defendant is a member of a cognizable racial group; (2) the prosecutor has exercised peremptories to remove members of the defendant's race; and (3) "these facts and any other relevant circumstances [such as a "pattern" of strikes and prosecutorial statements] raise an inference that the prosecutor used peremptories to exclude the veniremen from the petit jury on account of their race." Once this

57 504 U.S. 719 (1992).

58 Swain v. Alabama, 380 U.S. 202 (1965).

59 476 U.S. 79 (1986).

prima facie case is established, the prosecutor may rebut it by coming forward "with a neutral explanation for challenging black jurors," one that "need not rise to the level justifying exercise of a challenge for cause," but must go beyond merely stating that the juror might be partial to a defendant of the same race.

Batson has since been extended to the use of peremptories to exclude jurors on the basis of gender (female or male).[60] Further, the Court confirmed in Powers v. Ohio,[61] the defendant need not be of the same race or gender as the excluded jurors to raise the claim, as the right being protected is the juror's as much as the defendant's, in particular the juror's right to "participate in the democratic process," prevent "arbitrary use or abuse" of the judicial system, and develop civic mindedness; because the excluded juror is unlikely to have any meaningful means of protecting this right, the defendant must have standing to raise the claim. Finally, given the juror-oriented basis for the right, Batson applies to use of peremptories by the defense as well as the prosecution.[62]

The prima facie case required under Batson can be established by showing that all or most jurors within the selected group were excluded using peremptories. More difficult has been the implementation of the "neutral explanation," rebuttal component of Batson. In Hernandez v. New York,[63] the prosecutor explained his rejection of all three jurors with Hispanic names as well as another Latino by suggesting that two had relatives involved in criminal activity, and that the other two had looked away from him and had been hesitant when stating that they would accept the interpreter's version of testimony by Spanish-speaking witnesses rather than rely on their own translation. The Court found these latter explanations sufficient, because "[n]othing in the prosecutor's explanation showed that he chose to exclude jurors who hesitated in answering questions about following the interpreter because he wanted to prevent bilingual Latinos from serving on the jury." The Court put much emphasis on the prosecutor's sincere demeanor and his willingness to explain his exclusion before the defendant made out a prima facie case, his statement that he did not know that some of the jurors he excluded were Latino, and the

60 J.E.B. v. Alabama, 511 U.S. 127 (1994).

61 499 U.S. 400 (1991).

62 Georgia v. McCollum, 505 U.S. 42 (1992).

63 500 U.S. 352 (1991).

fact that many of the victims and prosecution witnesses were Latino (thus, suggesting that the prosecution would have preferred Latinos on the jury, all else being equal). In Purkett v. Elem,[64] however, the Court appeared to abandon this type of careful analysis. There it stated that any "genuine" reason for the strike, no matter how "silly or superstitious" or "implausible or fantastic," suffices to rebut the defendant's prima facie case, including, in Elem, the prosecutor's statement that he struck two blacks on the ground that one had long "unkempt curly hair, a mustache and a goatee type beard" and the other also had a mustache and goatee, which made them "look suspicious."

An explanation is less likely to be considered neutral if the prosecutor's explanation for exclusion would apply to other jurors who were not excluded. For instance, in Miller-El v. Dretke,[65] where a Batson violation was found, the Court made much of the fact that the prosecutor had explained his exclusion of one black because of the juror's belief that anyone could be rehabilitated, yet he had not excluded three non-black members who had made a similar comment. Likewise, the Court discounted as a valid reason for exclusion the fact that an excluded black had expressed ambivalence toward the death penalty, given the fact that several non-blacks who had not been excluded had evinced the same attitude. Another example of a Batson violation comes from J.E.B. v. Alabama,[66] which involved exclusion of women in a civil case; there, the Court found unacceptable the explanation that women might deliberate differently than men.

10.4 Right to impartial judge

Although the Sixth Amendment speaks only of juries, the Supreme Court has held that the Due Process Clause guarantees defendants an impartial judge as well. Thus, in one case the Court held that due process was violated when the judge, who was also the mayor, received the fees and costs he levied against violators,[67] and in another the Court came to the same conclusion where the fees collected by the mayor-judge did not go directly to him, but did provide a substantial portion

64 514 U.S. 765 (1995).
65 545 U.S. 231 (2005).
66 511 U.S. 127 (1994).
67 Tumey v. Ohio, 273 U.S. 510 (1927).

of the town's funds.[68] Due process may also require that when a separate contempt proceeding is held at the end of trial, a judge other than the trial judge preside, at least when the "sting of slanderous remarks" could influence the trial judge.[69]

Most importantly, the Court has strongly implied in a number of cases that the mere appearance of bias is sufficient to trigger removal of the judge; actual bias need not be shown.[70] Thus, in Williams v. Pennsylvania,[71] the Court held that due process was violated when a judge presided over a capital case which, in his earlier role as prosecutor, he had personally authorized be pursued, stating the test is "not whether a judge harbors an actual, subjective bias, but instead whether, as an objective matter, the average judge in his position is likely to be neutral, or whether there is an unconstitutional potential for bias."

Consistent with these rulings, in most jurisdictions a judge can be excluded not only for cause, but also peremptorily. If removal occurs, the trial is transferred to another judge (although this second judge can usually be removed only for cause). Additionally, ethical codes require recusal of a judge if: (1) "he has a personal bias or prejudice concerning a party, or personal knowledge of disputed evidentiary facts concerning the proceedings," (2) the judge or a former partner served as a lawyer or a material witness in the controversy; (3) the judge or a close relative has a financial or other "substantial interest in the outcome of the proceeding"; or (4) the judge is related, directly or by marriage, to one of the parties or lawyers.

10.5 Right to public proceedings

An important complement to the right to a trial heard by an impartial judge and jury is the right to a trial observed by the public. As the Supreme Court recognized in In re Oliver,[72] "[t]he knowledge that every criminal trial is subject to contemporaneous review in the forum of public opinion is an effective restraint on possible abuse of power . . . Without publicity, all other checks are insufficient; in comparison of

68 Ward v. Monroeville, 409 U.S. 57 (1972).

69 Mayberry v. Pennsylvania, 400 U.S. 455 (1971).

70 Rippo v. Baker, 137 S.Ct. 905 (2017).

71 136 S.Ct. 1899 (2016).

72 333 U.S. 257 (1948).

publicity, all other checks are of small account." The Court also noted that "the presence of interested spectators may keep [the accused's] triers keenly alive to a sense of their responsibility and to the importance of their functions." This type of reasoning has also led the Court to require that suppression hearings and voir dire proceedings be open to the public,[73] and probably applies to other pretrial and post-trial proceedings as well, other than the grand jury (see §8.7.2).

Any attempt by the government to close a presumptively public proceeding will need to overcome several hurdles. In Waller v. Georgia,[74] the Court stated that such closure is permitted only if: (1) the state proves that an overriding interest requires protection (such as the need to protect juror or witness privacy); (2) the closure is no broader than necessary to protect that interest; (3) reasonable alternatives are considered; and (4) findings adequate to support the closure are made. In Waller, where the judge closed a suppression hearing because the state wanted to play a tape that referred to a person not yet indicted, this test was not met, because the tape lasted less than 2½ hours, few of the conversations on the tape mentioned or involved parties not then before the court, and the state had failed to identify "whose privacy interests might be infringed, how they would be infringed, what portions of the tape might infringe them, and what portion of the evidence consisted of the tape." Similarly, in Globe Newspaper Co. v. Superior Court,[75] the Court found unconstitutional a state-requested closure of a trial under a statute that automatically denied access to the public in cases involving sex offenses against minors; instead, it required a "case-by-case" determination of whether closure is necessary, taking into account "the minor victim's age, psychological maturity and understanding, the nature of the crime, the desires of the victim, and the interests of parties and relatives."

Globe Newspaper was decided on First Amendment grounds, before Waller clarified the scope of the defendant's Sixth Amendment right to public proceedings, but it is consistent with that case. However, at times the public's right to know under the First Amendment can conflict with the Sixth Amendment interests of the defendant, as the next section illustrates.

---

73 Waller v. Georgia, 467 U.S. 39 (1984).

74 Id.

75 457 U.S. 596 (1982).

10.6 Fair proceedings and media access

While the press can expose government abuses and educate the public about the criminal process, it can also affect the fairness of the proceedings through publicity prior to or during trial that recounts inadmissible facts about the crime or prior offenses, or that disrupts the trial process by influencing the behavior of the participants. As a result, various mechanisms have developed for curtailing the impact of publicity or preventing it altogether.

10.6.1 Minimizing the effects of publicity

In theory, voir dire can weed out jurors who might be biased against the defendant because of pretrial publicity. And if voir dire cannot take care of the problem, a change of venue might. But, as noted in §10.3.4, the Supreme Court has not required that voir dire judges ask specific questions about the effects of such publicity. And even where voir dire produces evidence that jurors have heard and been affected by publicity, the Court's more recent cases indicate that, as long as the jurors state they can decide the case impartially, neither exclusion nor a change of venue need result.

That was not always the case. In Marshall v. United States,[76] the Warren Court overturned a verdict when it was shown that jurors had learned about the defendant's prior record from news sources and, in Irvin v. Dowd,[77] the Court discounted jurors' assertions they could be impartial in a murder trial, given extensive press coverage of the defendant's previous arson and forgery convictions, his violation of parole, his refusal to take a lie detector test, and his offer to plead guilty if he received a 99-year sentence. Similarly, in Rideau v. Louisiana,[78] the Warren Court held that the trial court, sitting in a small community, should have granted a change of venue when Rideau's confession was aired on television and three members of the jury admitted to seeing or hearing the interview.

More recent decisions evidence less concern about the effects of pre-trial publicity. In Murphy v. Florida,[79] the Court held that extensive

---

76 360 U.S. 310 (1959).

77 366 U.S. 717 (1961).

78 373 U.S. 723 (1963).

79 421 U.S. 794 (1975).

publicity about the defendant's prior crimes, including one murder, was offset by jurors' declarations of impartiality. And in Patton v. Yount,[80] where 126 out of 162 venire persons were excluded on the ground that they remembered the defendant's first conviction for a gruesome murder (later overturned on appeal) and 8 out of the 12 jurors and two alternatives admitted they had at one time formed an opinion as to the defendant's guilt, the Court held that the fact that the community might remember the first conviction was "essentially irrelevant" and that the four-year gap between the first conviction and Yount's second trial dissipated any prejudice.

A third tactic aimed at countering the negative effects of publicity, besides exclusion of tainted jurors and change of venue, is sequestration of the jury. Of course, this move only combats publicity during trial. Further, there is the danger the jury will resent whichever side it believes is responsible for its confinement (which will usually be the defense).

10.6.2 Preventing prejudicial publicity

Given the difficulty of alleviating the effects of publicity, another tactic is to prevent it from occurring, through gag orders on the media or the participants, or through closure of the proceedings. But the Supreme Court, cognizant of freedom of press concerns, has significantly restricted such steps. In Nebraska Press Ass'n v. Stuart,[81] for instance, the Court held that barring media coverage of an open hearing is an impermissible prior restraint and that prohibiting reporting information from other sources would be permissible only in extreme circumstances, after considering "(a) the nature and extent of pretrial coverage; (b) whether other measures [such as changes in venue, continuances, voir dire, and admonitions to the jury] would be likely to mitigate the effects of unrestrained pretrial publicity; and (c) how effectively a restraining order would operate to prevent the threatened danger." The Court also stressed the difficulty of "managing and enforcing pretrial restraining orders," a problem that social media has significantly exacerbated. In short, only a narrowly framed order aimed at preventing a "clear and present danger" (a phrase commonly found in First Amendment jurisprudence) of prejudicial reporting is likely to be constitutional.

80 467 U.S. 1025 (1984).

81 427 U.S. 539 (1976).

The Court has been somewhat more receptive toward gagging the sources of information. In Sheppard v. Maxwell[82] the Court suggested that, under appropriate circumstances, the trial judge has an obligation "to control the release of leads, information, and gossip to the press by police officers, witnesses, and the counsel for both sides." However, Sheppard was decided before Nebraska Press, and most lower courts have required that the claimant meet some version of the "clear and present danger" test before granting a gag order, a test that might only be met when highly incriminating yet potentially inadmissible evidence such as a confession could be disclosed.

In contrast, the American Bar Association's ethical rules counsel attorneys to avoid any "extrajudicial statement [that] will have a substantial likelihood of materially prejudicing an adjudicative proceeding,"[83] which has been interpreted broadly by most bar associations. In Gentile v. Nevada State Bar,[84] the Supreme Court sent mixed signals about a similar earlier version of this rule. Citing First Amendment concerns, it refused to uphold a reprimand of an attorney who had stated that his client was being framed by the police for the actions of one of it is officers, at the same time it indicated that statements short of those that present a clear and present danger could be the basis for discipline. Whatever the scope of Gentile's impact on attorneys, it clearly does not apply to witnesses or the defendant.

A final method of preventing information from getting to the press is to close the proceeding. In Gannett Co., Inc. v. DePasquale,[85] the Court indicated that the defendant who is worried about prejudicial impact can request that a hearing be closed. However, such a request will probably not be honored when a First Amendment right is asserted by the press or the public to keep the proceeding open. In Richmond Newspapers, Inc. v. Virginia,[86] the Court emphasized that "the right to attend criminal trials is implicit in the guarantees of the First Amendment; without the freedom to attend such trials, which people have exercised for centuries, important aspects of freedom of speech and of the press could be eviscerated." A later case added that the public access guaranteed by the First Amendment "serves to ensure

82 384 U.S. 333 (1966).

83 American Bar Association Model Rule 3.6(a)(b) and associated commentary.

84 501 U.S. 1030 (1991).

85 443 U.S. 368 (1979).

86 448 U.S. 555 (1980).

that the individual citizen can effectively participate in and contribute to the republican system of self-government," and also "fosters an appearance of fairness, thereby heightening public respect for the judicial process."[87]

While Richmond Newspapers stated that this First Amendment right can be subject to "reasonable restrictions" when there is an "overriding" interest in doing so, the only interest the Court mentioned was assuring "quiet and orderly" trials and preventing overcrowding in the courtroom. Thus, if public and media participation creates a "carnival atmosphere," as the Court found was the case in Sheppard, or, as the Court put it in Chandler v. Florida,[88] the presence of press coverage or television coverage "impairs the ability of the jurors to decide the case on only the evidence before them" or "adversely" affects the behavior of any of the participants in the trial, the First Amendment claim may not prevail. But, at least when the proceeding is a trial, these criteria are unlikely to be met. Sheppard involved egregious disruption of the trial process, and Chandler went on to hold Florida's rule permitting television broadcasts of trials should stand.

When the proceeding at issue occurs prior to trial, concerns about prejudicial publicity are heightened. Even here, however, the Court has held that the defendant must show a "substantial probability" of prejudice from the proceeding, and that voir dire and other alternatives will not alleviate the prejudice. In Press-Enterprise Co. v. Superior Court II,[89] where the Court announced this test, the Court held impermissible the closure of a 41-day preliminary hearing. The Court noted that such hearings have traditionally been open to the public, that they may be the last chance for the public to view the case given the number of charges resolved through guilty pleas, and that the absence of a jury meant that no other representatives of the public would be present. At the same time, the Court did not adopt the difficult-to-meet clear and present danger test in this setting. And Gannett indicated that, at least in some cases, providing the public with a transcript of the pretrial proceeding may be sufficient to meet First Amendment demands.

87 Globe Newspaper Co. v. Superior Court, 457 U.S. 596 (1982).

88 449 U.S. 560 (1981).

89 478 U.S. 1 (1986).

11 Adversarial rights

11.1 Overview

This chapter examines the conduct of trial and other proceedings through the prism of the right to counsel, the right of confrontation and the right to compulsory process—all rights guaranteed by the Sixth Amendment—as well as the due process right to testify. Each of these rights is aimed at assuring the defendant's side of the story is heard, and that the state's case is subjected to adversarial testing at trial. Some or all of these rights also apply at most other significant proceedings before and after trial. But each is also subject to restrictions aimed at promoting efficiency and avoiding obstacles to convicting the guilty.

11.2 Right to counsel

While the right to counsel at criminal trials is taken for granted today, it lacks the historical pedigree of the jury trial, the grand jury and the right of confrontation. In seventeenth century England, criminal defendants were allowed counsel only if they could afford one, and only when charged with misdemeanors or treason. Even by the time of the American Revolution—when attorneys, like the jury, were seen as a bulwark against tyranny—the right existed only for those who had enough money to hire counsel.[1] It was not until 1932, in Powell v. Alabama,[2] that the Supreme Court recognized a constitutional right to counsel for indigent defendants, and even then the right was guaranteed only on a case-by-case basis. While Powell held that the defendants in that case—nine black defendants charged with the rape of two white women—were entitled to counsel, it limited the right to "capital cases[s], where the defendant is unable to employ counsel, and

1 Francis Heller, The Sixth Amendment to the Constitution of the United States 10 (Kansas University Press, Lawrence, Kan. 1951).

2 287 U.S. 45 (1932).

is incapable adequately of making his own defense because of ignorance, feeble-mindedness, illiteracy or the like."

However, much of the language in Powell suggested that the right to counsel was much more fundamental. According to the Court,

> [t]he right to be heard would be, in many cases, of little avail if it did not comprehend the right to be heard by counsel. Even the intelligent and educated layman has small and sometimes no skill in the science of law. . . . Left without the aid of counsel he may be put on trial without a proper charge, and convicted upon incompetent evidence, or evidence irrelevant to the issue or otherwise inadmissible. He lacks both the skill and knowledge adequately to prepare his defense, even though he have a perfect one.

Six years after Powell, the Court recognized a right to counsel in all federal felony cases.[3] Still, however, for the next 25 years the Court refused to impose the right on the states except on a case-by-case basis. Finally, in Gideon v. Wainwright,[4] the Warren Court reversed these rulings, holding that "lawyers in criminal courts are necessities, not luxuries." The strongest indication of this "obvious truth" were the facts "[t]hat the government . . . hires lawyers to prosecute and defendants who have money hire lawyers to defend."

11.2.1 Scope of the right at trial

The right to counsel does not apply in every criminal case. Lower courts initially interpreted Gideon to be relevant only in felony cases, by analogy to the jury trial right, which does not apply to "petty crimes" resulting in imprisonment of six months or less (see §10.3.1). In Argersinger v. Hamlin[5] the Supreme Court extended the right to any misdemeanor case where imprisonment results, noting that it had no reason to believe that cases leading to imprisonment "even for a brief period[,] are any less complex than when a person can be sent off for six months or more." But in Scott v. Illinois,[6] the Court limited the right to cases where imprisonment actually results. A finding otherwise would only "create confusion and impose unpredictable, but necessarily substantial, costs on 50 quite diverse states," some of which criminalize

3 Johnson v. Zerbst, 304 U.S. 458 (1938).

4 372 U.S. 335 (1963).

5 407 U.S. 25 (1972).

6 440 U.S. 367 (1979).

traffic violations and other minor conduct. The Court ignored the Sixth Amendment's language applying its guarantees to "all" criminal prosecutions, and Powell and Gideon's language about the importance of counsel to ensuring reliable results. In Nichols v. United States[7] the Court followed the same logic in holding that uncounseled convictions can be used as a sentence enhancement. As the dissent pointed out, the effect of Nicols is that convictions for misdemeanors—verdicts that are often the result of very informal, hurried proceedings conducted in the absence of counsel—can lead to significantly longer sentences (in Nicols, a prior uncounseled driving-under-the influence conviction increased the defendant's sentence by over two years).

Scott and Nichols were undercut to some extent in Alabama v. Shelton,[8] where the Court held that a suspended sentence (often imposed as a way of providing leverage over defendants put on probation) may not be imposed on defendants who are denied counsel at the time the suspended sentence is imposed. Although the state argued that Nicols applied because such sentences are only served if a court subsequently makes a finding, at a hearing with counsel, that a condition of probation has been violated, the Court reasoned that, unlike in Nicols, such a sentence would be based on the underlying, uncounseled conviction, not on the new conduct. Shelton has had a major impact on misdemeanor justice since, at the time it was decided, as many as half the states did not provide counsel in cases involving suspended misdemeanor sentences.

11.2.2 Counsel at proceedings other than criminal trial

As recounted in other parts of this book, whether defendants who are guaranteed a Sixth Amendment right to counsel at trial are entitled to that right at other phases of the criminal process depends upon when "criminal prosecution" begins for Sixth Amendment purposes and whether the phase involves a "trial-like confrontation" involving an adversarial confrontation between the defendant and the state. The Supreme Court has held that criminal prosecution begins with formal charging in the form of an indictment or information or with the initial appearance in front of a judge (see §5.5), and that it ends with sentencing; this time frame means that the Sixth Amendment right to counsel does not apply to any pre-charge encounter with the police, nor does

7 511 U.S. 738 (1994).
8 535 U.S. 654 (2002).

it apply at appeal, collateral review, or probation or parole revocation proceedings.[9] And the requirement of an adversarial confrontation has meant that, even if charging has occurred, there is no Sixth Amendment right at the initial probable cause and bail determination by the judge, psychiatric interviews, photo arrays, fingerprinting, and the grand jury (see §§6.3; 8.2; 8.7.3). But there is a Sixth Amendment right to counsel at post-charging lineups and one-on-one confrontations, the preliminary hearing, suppression hearings, and sentencing (see §§6.3; 8.6; 12.2). Furthermore, as recounted in Chapter 5, the Fifth Amendment provides a right to counsel at all custodial interrogations, whether pre- or post-charge. Finally, the Due Process Clause and Equal Protection Clauses provide the basis for a right to counsel at some post-sentencing proceedings.

In the latter regard, the most important decision is Douglas v. California,[10] decided the same term as Gideon. There, the Supreme Court held that indigent defendants are entitled to counsel at appeals of right, primarily on the equal protection ground that "where the merits on the one and only appeal an indigent has as of right are decided without benefit of counsel, . . . an unconstitutional line has been drawn between rich and poor." This reasoning was suspect because, at the time the Court advanced it, even wealthy defendants did not have a right to counsel at appeals; technically, states could constitutionally bar lawyers from that proceeding. That problem was remedied in Evitts v. Lucey,[11] where the Court held that, as a matter of due process, every defendant is entitled to counsel at appeals of right; repeating what it had said in Douglas, the Court concluded that, otherwise, appeal would be a "meaningless ritual."

However, there is no right to counsel at discretionary appeals such as those granted on writs of certiorari, nor at collateral review (habeas) proceedings, both of which occur after appeals as of right. Employing equal protection analysis, in Ross v. Moffitt[12] the Court held that, because both indigent and non-indigent defendants receive the trial transcript, the brief filed in the lower appellate court and, if one is issued, the lower appellate court decision, failing to provide the indigent with counsel at discretionary appeals was not unfair. The same

9 Gagnon v. Scarpelli, 411 U.S. 778 (1973).

10 372 U.S. 353 (1963).

11 469 U.S. 387 (1985).

12 417 U.S. 600 (1974).

reasoning led, in Pennsylvania v. Finley,[13] to a finding that there is no right to counsel at habeas proceedings. In contrast, in Halbert v. Michigan,[14] the Court held that defendants who plead guilty are entitled to the assistance of state-paid counsel when they file a petition for leave to appeal their conviction (a petition required in many states, based on the assumption that a voluntary guilty plea is generally an admission that no appealable issues exist). Although this type of appeal is also discretionary, the majority noted that it differs from discretionary appeal after a trial and from habeas in at least two ways: it is likely to be the defendant's only chance to obtain review of the conviction and there are no appellate opinions or documents on which to base arguments.

If the proceeding is not criminal, the Court has usually refused to require counsel even when a deprivation of liberty may result. The one major exception is the juvenile delinquency proceeding, which in effect is criminal in nature.[15] But there is no right to counsel at civil commitment proceedings,[16] proceedings that result in transfer of prisoners to mental hospitals,[17] summary courts-martial,[18] and civil contempt proceedings,[19] at least where the opposing side is not represented by counsel. Nor is there an automatic right to counsel at parole hearings or probation or parole revocation proceedings, although in the latter two settings counsel may be required when "a disputed issue can fairly be represented only by a trained advocate."[20]

While the right to counsel is thus not constitutionally guaranteed in a wide range of situations, many states provide state-paid counsel in these and other settings by statute or as a matter of practice. For instance, in capital cases, every state provides post-conviction counsel. At the other end of the spectrum, virtually every state provides counsel at civil commitment proceedings. Most jurisdictions appear to recognize the essential insight of Gideon that counsel is a key component of fair legal proceedings.

---

13 481 U.S. 551 (1987).

14 545 U.S. 605 (2005).

15 In re Gault, 387 U.S. 1 (1967).

16 Parham v. J.R., 442 U.S. 584 (1979) (juveniles).

17 Vitek v. Jones, 445 U.S. 480 (1980).

18 Middendorf v. Henry, 425 U.S. 25 (1976).

19 Turner v. Rogers, 564 U.S. 431 (2011).

20 Gagnon v. Scarpelli, 411 U.S. 778 (1973); Morrissey v. Brewer, 408 U.S. 471 (1972).

11.2.3 Right to counsel of one's choice

Defendants who are indigent (over 75 percent of those charged with crime) are usually represented by a public defender, an attorney who is paid a salary by the state. When the jurisdiction does not have a public defender office, or that office has a conflict (because, for instance, it is representing a co-defendant), the court appoints an attorney from a list of private attorneys, many of whom primarily practice on the civil side of the docket. While the indigent defendant who is dissatisfied with the attorney may be able to obtain a replacement if there is "complete breakdown in communication" with counsel or some other "irreconcilable conflict," the Supreme Court has held that "a defendant may not insist on representation by an attorney he cannot afford."[21] Nor is the defendant entitled to a "meaningful relationship" with his or her attorney, but rather simply effective assistance.[22]

Wealthier defendants of course have more choice, and, in contrast to the situation with indigent defendants, that choice is constitutionally protected. In United States v. Gonzalez-Lopez,[23] the Court held that the Sixth Amendment not only guarantees effective counsel, but counsel of one's choice. Further, violation of this right is "structural error" that is not subject to harmless error analysis.

However, there are at least four exceptions to the non-indigent's right to choose his or her attorney. First, as discussed further in §11.3.2, the trial court may override the defendant's selection whenever it believes that, in light of that attorney's other clients, a serious potential for conflict of interest may develop. Second, the defendant's choice may be rejected if the attorney is not qualified to practice law under state or federal rules. Third, in some jurisdictions, a defendant is not permitted to discharge an already-chosen attorney to acquire another one. Finally, and most significantly, a defendant is not entitled to his or her counsel of choice when the resources that would pay for such an attorney are frozen by the provisions of a forfeiture statute of the type described in §4.10. In Caplin & Drysdale v. United States,[24] the Supreme Court held that the interest protected by such statutes (which include providing financial support for law enforcement efforts, preserving property

21 Wheat v. United States, 486 U.S. 153 (1988).

22 Morris v. Slappy, 461 U.S. 1 (1983).

23 548 U.S. 140 (2006).

24 491 U.S. 617 (1989).

for later reclamation, and reducing the economic power of organized crime) outweigh the defendant's right to counsel of choice, so long as there is probable cause the frozen property is ultimately forfeitable because of its nexus to crime. However, assets that are "untainted" by crime may not be encumbered, even if the government wants to do so to ensure the defendant will be able to pay fines or restitution if convicted.[25]

11.2.4 Right to expert assistance

Indigent defendants not only need counsel, they also often require investigative resources, a fact that every jurisdiction recognizes. For instance, federal law requires the trial court to provide for "investigative, expert, or other services upon a showing that the service is necessary for an adequate defense."[26] The Supreme Court has held that this type of language does not require a showing that the defense will prevail if the necessary expertise is provided, nor proof of "substantial need" for the service, but only that the service be "reasonably necessary" for adequate preparation.[27]

The Due Process Clause probably requires this type of rule. In Ake v. Oklahoma,[28] the Supreme Court held that defendants who can demonstrate that their sanity at the time of the offense or their dangerousness will be a "significant factor" in their case are entitled to the assistance of a mental health professional, state-paid if necessary. To the state's complaint that such a requirement is both expensive and unnecessary, the Court noted that most states already provide such assistance and that psychiatric experts usually play a "pivotal role" when an insanity defense is raised at trial or when dangerousness is an issue in capital sentencing.

The right announced in Ake is subject to significant limitations, however. First, as interpreted by the lower courts, the defense must show a "particularized need" for the assistance. While that need might be relatively easy to show in cases involving insanity, it may be more difficult with respect to other types of experts; for instance, a ballistics expert may not be provided to the defense if analysis by the state's

25 Luis v. United States, 136 S.Ct. 1083 (2016).

26 18 U.S.C. A. §3007(e)(1).

27 Ayestas v. Davis, 138 S.Ct. 1080 (2018).

28 470 U.S. 68 (1985).

ballistics expert is viewed to be sufficient. Second, Ake made clear that, as with the choice of counsel, the indigent defendant is not entitled to an expert of his or her choosing, and in fact may be required to consult with an expert who works at a state-funded hospital. Finally, consistent with this holding, the defendant is not entitled to an expert who will support the defense theory, but rather only an expert who can "assist" in preparation of the case. At the same time, this assistance must be concrete. In McWilliams v. Dunn,[29] the Court found that due process was violated when the state provided the defendant, charged with capital murder, a neuropsychologist, but did not pay for an expert who could interpret and explain the results of the neuropsychological test.

11.2.5 Waiver of counsel

Given the importance of an attorney, one could make the case that the right to counsel is unwaivable and that defendants should not be allowed to proceed pro se (i.e., represent themselves). But in Faretta v. California[30] the Court concluded that "[t]he language and spirit of the Sixth Amendment contemplate that counsel, like the other defense tools guaranteed by the Amendment, shall be an aid to a willing defendant—not an organ of the State interposed between an unwilling defendant and his right to defend himself personally." Acknowledging that its decision "seems to cut against the grain" of Gideon, the majority nonetheless insisted on the "inestimable worth of free choice," and opined that "[t]o force a lawyer on a defendant can only lead him to believe that the law contrives against him." To the dissent's argument that the decision would undermine society's interest in ensuring fair trials, the majority responded "[a]lthough [the defendant] may conduct his own defense ultimately to his own detriment, his choice must be honored out of 'that respect for the individual which is the lifeblood of the law.'"

While Faretta made clear that a defendant should be able to proceed pro se even if he or she is not well versed in legal technicalities such as the rules of evidence, in an earlier case a four-member plurality of the Court had indicated that a defendant who waives counsel must still understand "the nature of the charges, the statutory offenses included within them, the range of allowable punishments thereunder, possible defenses to the charges and circumstances in mitigation thereof, and

29 137 S.Ct. 1790 (2017).

30 422 U.S. 806 (1975).

all other facts essential to a broad undertaking of the whole matter."[31] At the least, this standard suggests that people with mental problems or sub-average intelligence will often be denied the right to proceed pro se. But that interpretation was challenged almost two decades after Faretta in Godinez v. Moran,[32] where the Supreme Court upheld the waiver of counsel and subsequent guilty plea of a defendant, charged with the three counts of capital murder, despite his depression and the fact that he was on several types of medication at the time of the waiver. The Court first noted that Moran had been found competent to stand trial by two mental health professionals and the trial judge, a finding which, as outlined further in §11.4.2, means that the defendant understands the charges and their consequences. It then concluded that, as long as a competent defendant "knowingly and voluntarily" waives the right to counsel—that is, "actually does understand the significance and consequences of a particular decision" and is not "coerced" into making it—the waiver should stand. The dissent protested that a finding that a defendant is competent to stand trial with counsel does not mean that the person will be competent to proceed without one. But the majority, citing Faretta, stated that "a criminal defendant's ability to represent himself has no bearing upon his competence to choose self-representation."

In Indiana v. Edwards,[33] the Court backed away from this language when, unlike in Moran, the defendant proceeds to trial rather than pleads guilty. In such cases, to ensure the fairness and dignity of the trial process, the trial court is entitled to ensure that a person with mental illness not only is competent to stand trial but is also able to carry out "basic trial tasks." Although the dissent argued that such a rule could make the defendant feel that the law "contrives against him" (in Edwards, for instance, the attorney who the trial court forced on the defendant argued lack-of-intent, overriding the defendant's desire to argue self-defense), the majority was convinced that its rule would be more protective of the defendant's dignity, as well as of society's interest in orderly trials.

Although Moran and Edwards appear to be in some tension, the Court may have felt that negotiating a guilty plea is easier than advocating at trial. Still, the necessity for the decision in Edwards is undercut to

31 Von Moltke v. Gillies, 332 U.S. 708 (1948).

32 509 U.S. 389 (1993).

33 554 U.S. 164 (2008).

some extent by the Court's holding, in McKaskle v. Wiggins,[34] that a defendant who has validly waived the right to counsel can nonetheless be required to work with "standby counsel," whose role is "to relieve the judge of the need to explain and enforce basic rules of courtroom protocol or to assist the defendant in overcoming routine obstacles that stand in the way of the defendant's achievement of his own clearly indicated goals." Faretta had held that the right to proceed pro se "is not a license . . . not to comply with relevant rules of procedural and substantive law." Further, as the dissent in Faretta pointed out, courts cannot let convictions stand when they are the result of completely inadequate self-representation. The standby counsel rule in Wiggins strikes an accommodation between the right to self-representation and the spectacle of pro se defendants attacking their own conduct as a means of obtaining retrial.

But the decision also requires a delicate balance. The majority in Wiggins concluded that Faretta is not violated by the active presence of standby counsel if the defendant retains actual control over the case and the factfinder has that perception. It rejected the dissent's preferred rule that standby counsel should be "seen and not heard" until the defendant expressly asks for assistance. The majority also stated that "[o]nce a pro se defendant invites or agrees to any substantial participation by counsel, subsequent appearances by counsel must be presumed to be with the defendant's acquiescence, at least until the defendant expressly and unambiguously renews his request that standby counsel be silent." Since there was no such request by Wiggins, his Faretta right was not violated, despite repeated "acrimonious" exchanges between the defendant and the standby attorney and the fact that the attorney made objections and motions without consulting the defendant.

11.3 Right to effective assistance of counsel

The right to counsel is empty unless counsel is adequate at representing the client. Not surprisingly, therefore, the Supreme Court has held that the Sixth Amendment guarantees the right to "effective" assistance of counsel, even when counsel is privately retained and thus is not a state actor.[35] But the right to effective assistance only applies when the

34 465 U.S. 168 (1984).

35 Cuyler v. Sullivan, 446 U.S. 335 (1980).

right to counsel attaches. Thus, in Wainwright v. Torna,[36] the Supreme Court held that failure to make a timely application for a discretionary appeal cannot constitute ineffective assistance, since there is no right to counsel at such proceedings. For the same reason, an ineffective assistance claim cannot be made in habeas cases.

Until 1984, the Supreme Court provided very little guidance on the content of the right to effective assistance of counsel. Lower courts had vacillated between a "farce and mockery" standard, which requires very little of the defense attorney, and a standard borrowed from the American Bar Association (ABA) Standards on the Defense Function, which imposed fairly specific investigative, counseling, and litigation duties on counsel, and equated their violation with a Sixth Amendment violation, regardless of the extent to which counsel's inadequacy affected the outcome of the adjudication. When the Supreme Court finally set out an explicit test in Strickland v. Washington,[37] it opted for an intermediate, two-prong test that looks at whether the defense attorney's performance was so "deficient ... that counsel was not functioning as the 'counsel' guaranteed by the Sixth Amendment" (the performance prong) and, if so, whether "counsel's errors were so serious as to deprive the defendant of a fair trial, a trial whose result is unreliable" (the prejudice prong).

Under the first, performance, prong, counsel must meet "prevailing professional norms," which the Court stated includes: (1) " a duty to avoid conflicts of interest"; (2) a duty "to advocate the defendant's cause," which encompasses the duties "to consult with the defendant on important decisions and to keep the defendant informed of important developments"; and (3) a duty "to bring to bear such skill and knowledge as will render the trial a reliable adversarial testing process." The latter includes a duty "to make reasonable investigations or to make a reasonable decision that makes particular investigations unnecessary." In a subsequent case, the Court made clear that a lawyer's adherence to obligations under the legal profession's ethical rules (e.g., threatening to withdraw if the defendant intends to commit perjury, a move permitted under the ethical codes) cannot be a deprivation of the right to effective assistance;[38] at the same time, in contrast to the ABA-based approach, it emphasized that a violation of

36 455 U.S. 586 (1982).

37 466 U.S. 668 (1984).

38 Nix v. Whiteside, 475 U.S. 157 (1986).

those rules does not automatically mean counsel is deficient. Strickland also stressed that "[j]udicial scrutiny of counsel's performance must be highly deferential" and that "counsel is strongly presumed to have rendered adequate assistance and made all significant decisions in the exercise of reasonable professional judgement."

In explaining why it did not provide more detailed guidelines akin to the bar's ethical rules in its performance prong, the Court candidly stated it wanted to avoid proliferation of ineffectiveness challenges, which it worried would lead to "second trials" on counsel's performance. It also suggested that stricter rules would "dampen the ardor and impair the independence of defense counsel, discourage the acceptance of assigned cases, and undermine the trust between attorney and client." This explanation echoed an earlier influential decision from the District Court of Appeals for the District of Columbia, which justified the adoption of a similar "judgmental" (as opposed to "categorical") approach on the grounds that it was less likely to inhibit defense tactics, occasion judicial or prosecutorial monitoring of counsel, and "reward" inept conduct designed to ensure a reversal.[39]

Strickland's prejudice prong is similarly narrow, requiring a showing that "there is a reasonable probability that, but for counsel's unprofessional errors, the result of the proceeding would have been different." A year later, the Court held that, when the defendant pleads guilty rather than convicted at trial, the second prong should instead inquire into whether "there is a reasonable probability that but for counsel's errors, [the defendant] would not have pleaded guilty and would have insisted on going to trial;"[40] as discussed in §11.3.4, the Court has developed similar formulations when counsel's error leads the defendant to reject a plea, or when counsel's error forecloses an appeal. Strickland explained that its focus on whether the error affects outcomes rather than on whether it seriously impaired counsel's performance was necessary, because "[t]he government is not responsible for, and hence not able to prevent, attorney errors that will result in reversal of conviction or sentence." Thus, an identical error may constitute ineffective assistance in some cases but not in others, depending on whether it affected the outcome of trial. Strickland also held that, if the defense is not able to demonstrate this type of prejudice, then a reviewing court need not even consider whether counsel's performance was defective.

39 United States v. Decoster, 624 F.2d 196 (D.C. Cir. 1976).

40 Hill v. Lockhart, 474 U.S. 52 (1985).

Strickland outlined three general categories of ineffective assistance of counsel claims. The first involves state interference with counsel's ability to represent the client, the second concerns conflicts of interest, and the third involves most attorney-produced errors, which is where Strickland's two-prong test is most relevant. Each of these areas is explored in turn.

11.3.1 State interference

Although Strickland adopted a deferential approach to attorney conduct, it made clear that when the state is responsible for poor representation, through "[a]ctual or constructive denial" of counsel or because of "interference with counsel's assistance," then prejudice is presumed. Here it cited as illustrative Powell v. Alabama, where counsel was appointed, but only on the day of trial, in a case involving nine defendants charged with rape. In Strickland's companion case of United States v. Cronic[41] it listed a number of other examples where it had found unconstitutional state interference with counsel: a state law that barred the defendant from having his testimony elicited by counsel through direct examination; a statute that restricted counsel's choice of when to put the defendant on the stand and allowed the judge to deny defense counsel a closing summation; and a judge's order directing a defendant not to consult with his attorney during an overnight recess between direct and cross-examination. These situations, the Court stated in Strickland, "are easy to identify . . . and easy for the prosecution to prevent," and not as likely to inhibit defense tactics or reward conduct designed to ensure reversal.

However, Strickland also stated that denial of counsel must be "complete," so that "counsel [is] either totally absent, or prevented from assisting the accused during a critical stage of the proceeding." In Cronic counsel was appointed only 25 days before trial of a case that took the government 4½ years to prepare. Nonetheless, the Court found that this period "is not so short that it even arguably justifies a presumption" of prejudice. Similarly, the Court has held that prejudice should not be presumed from prosecution failure to provide defense counsel with impeachment evidence,[42] nor from a judicial prohibition on counsel talking to his client during a 15-minute recess that occurred in the middle of direct testimony rather than after it had ended (as in

41 466 U.S. 648 (1984).

42 United States v. Bagley, 473 U.S. 667 (1985).

the above-mentioned case).[43] Even intrusion into the attorney-client relationship through an undercover agent does not amount to unconstitutional state interference if the agent does not testify or inform superiors about confidential communications and no prejudice from the intrusion is shown.[44]

11.3.2 Conflicts of interest

Conflicts can arise from an attorney's attempt to represent more than one co-defendant in the same trial, the attorney's prior representation of a prosecution witness, the fact that the attorney's fee is coming from a third party, and a host of other situations. Here too prejudice is assumed, because, as Strickland explained (summarizing its earlier opinion in Holloway v. Arkansas[45]), "the duty of loyalty [is] perhaps the most basic of counsel's duties," while the effect of failing to abide by that duty is difficult to measure. Perhaps most importantly, courts can "make early inquiry in certain situations likely to give rise to conflicts" and thus prevent them; when it fails to do so, in a sense the state is once again "interfering" with the defendant's right to counsel.

However, the presumption of prejudice is not triggered unless it is shown that the trial court should have detected the need for inquiry prior to trial. In cases of joint representation—as in Holloway, where the same attorney represented three defendants on the same matter and made a motion to withdraw from two of the clients—that need was evident. But if counsel does not notify the court of the conflict, the Court held in Cuyler v. Sullivan,[46] the court is not required to inquire on its own unless there is an "actual" conflict; further, a reversal of conviction is not required unless that conflict "adversely affected" the lawyer's performance. In Wood v. Georgia,[47] where the attorney's fees were paid by the defendant's employer (who had an interest in shifting liability to its employees), the Court remanded the case despite the absence of a motion from the attorney, strongly suggesting that an actual conflict existed that the trial court should have investigated, although not resolving whether the conflict adversely affected

43 Perry v. Leeke, 488 U.S. 272 (1989).

44 Weatherford v. Bursey, 429 U.S. 545 (1977); United States v. Morrison, 449 U.S. 361 (1981).

45 435 U.S. 475 (1978).

46 446 U.S. 335 (1980).

47 450 U.S. 261 (1981).

counsel's performance. But in Mickens v. Taylor,[48] where counsel had represented the victim of the murder at the time of his death—a fact that the trial judge likely knew—the Court held that no inquiry was mandated, even in a case, such as this, where the attorney might be reticent about pointing out a conflict exists. Further, at least in cases of successive representation, such as Mickens, the Court stated that, even when the attorney brings the conflict to the attention of the judge, the question is "open" as to whether a judicial failure to inquire triggers the presumption of prejudice in the absence of actual conflict that adversely affects the defense.

This latter standard supposedly focuses solely on the attorney's performance, not on whether it affects the outcome of the proceeding (as with Strickland's prejudice inquiry), but as implemented it comes close to prejudice analysis. In Burger v. Kemp,[49] lawyers from the same firm represented both Burger and his co-defendant, both charged with capital murder. Burger argued that his representation was adversely affected by this joint representation because the attorneys did not make a "lesser culpability" argument in his favor, despite his relative youth and evidence that he had originally resisted his co-defendant's plan to commit murder. But the Court concluded that there may not have been even an actual conflict, given the fact that it was Burger who committed the murder. Even had there been an actual conflict, the Court stated, his attorneys' performance was not adversely affected, because they argued throughout Burger's trial that the co-defendant was the architect of the crime. As the dissent pointed out, however, the lesser culpability argument was not made during plea negotiations involving the two defendants, when it was more likely to have had an impact than at Burger's trial, which was severed from his co-defendant's and thus prevented direct comparison of the two individuals.

Occasionally, defendants will want to waive a conflict, especially when they think they might benefit from a joint defense that prevents the prosecution from pursuing a "divide and conquer" strategy by offering one defendant a deal in return for testimony against the other. In Wheat v. United States,[50] the Supreme Court held that such waivers are permissible, but also held that the trial judge has wide discretion to override the defendant's choice of counsel whenever it finds an "actual"

48 535 U.S. 162 (2002).

49 483 U.S. 776 (1987).

50 486 U.S. 153 (1988).

conflict or a "serious potential" for conflict. In Wheat, three defendants all indicated they wanted to be represented by the same attorney, but the trial judge forced them to accept separate attorneys. On its face, that decision was reasonable; as Burger illustrates, while joint representation can prevent the divide-and-conquer strategy, it may also harm the defendant with the better case. But looking closely at the specific facts in Wheat, the dissent pointed out that, at the time the judge rejected Wheat's waiver, the judge knew that one co-defendant would plead guilty, and that a second would not be able to testify against Wheat because he had never met him and could not identify him; thus, in the dissent's opinion, the potential for actual conflict was minimal.

11.3.3 Attorney errors

Far more common than state interference and conflicts cases are assertions that defense counsel was inadequate because of a failure to investigate or make certain arguments. The Supreme Court's cases reveal three factors that should be considered in determining whether deficient representation has occurred (a determination then followed by an assessment of whether the deficiency prejudiced the defendant).

The first factor is the specificity with which error is alleged. In Cronic, the Court strongly suggested that ineffective assistance claims based on the "overall performance" or character of the defense attorney will rarely succeed. Thus, lower courts have refused to find ineffective assistance simply because of an attorney's lack of experience, youth, or intoxication, and the Supreme Court has held that a "poor" attorney-client relationship is not likely to lead to reversal either.[51]

If an alleged error is specified, the second factor courts look at in analyzing the attorney's performance is whether there is a "reasonable" explanation for the error. In Kimmelman v. Morrison,[52] for instance, the Supreme Court found that the performance prong of Strickland was violated by counsel's "total failure" to conduct pretrial discovery, so that he did not find out about a warrantless search of his client's apartment until trial, when it was too late to file a suppression motion; counsel could only offer "implausible" non-strategic explanations for the lack of preparation (to wit, he thought the state was obligated to

51 Morris v. Slappy, 461 U.S. 1 (1983).

52 477 U.S. 365 (1986).

provide the defense with all inculpatory information). The Court has also found unreasonable counsel's explanation for error in a number of death penalty cases. For instance, in Rompilla v. Beard,[53] counsel failed to look at a case file of a prior crime that the prosecution had indicated would be a central part of the case in aggravation. The dissent pointed out that Rompilla's two defense counsel had interviewed five family members and retained three mental health experts, but the majority stated "we . . . cannot think of any situation in which defense counsel should not make some effort to learn the information in the possession of the prosecution and law enforcement authorities."

This type of categorical pronouncement contrasts with the Court's usual case-by-case analysis, which looks carefully at the reasons why counsel took or did not take certain steps. Indeed, in Strickland, the Court came up with its own explanation for why, despite significant evidence of mental dysfunction in the defendant, counsel failed to obtain a psychiatric examination and develop and present character evidence at the defendant's capital sentencing proceeding. The Court speculated that, given the strength of the case against the defendant, counsel could "reasonably surmise" that such evidence would have been "of little help." Further, the defendant's testimony during the adjudication phase had already revealed to the factfinder considerable information about his emotional problems, which if presented at sentencing would have opened the door to contrary psychological evidence and criminal history that counsel had successfully moved to exclude. Similarly, in Burger v. Kemp,[54] the failure to discover and introduce evidence of the defendant's personality and unhappy childhood was not ineffective assistance when based on a conclusion that such evidence may have suggested potential dangerousness and harmed the defendant as much as helped him.

When the attorney failure to raise constitutional challenges occurs in a case where the defendant pleaded guilty, the Court has been even more reluctant to find attorney deficiency, influenced in part, perhaps, by the fact that the defendant has admitted to committing the crime. For instance, in McMann v. Richardson,[55] the defendants argued that their guilty pleas had been motivated by coerced confessions that counsel had not challenged. The Court denied the claim, stating "[t]hat this

53 545 U.S. 374 (2005).
54 483 U.S. 776 (1987).
55 397 U.S. 759 (1970).

Court might hold a defendant's confession inadmissible in evidence, possibly by a divided vote, hardly justifies a conclusion that the defendant's attorney was incompetent or ineffective when he thought the admissibility of the confession sufficiently probable to advise a plea of guilty."

A third consideration in analyzing the performance prong of ineffective assistance of counsel claims is the defendant's role in causing the alleged error. For instance, in Schriro v. Landrigan,[56] the Court excused counsel's failure to fully investigate mitigating evidence because the defendant had told him he did not want any such evidence introduced.

Not clear from Landrigan is whether the Court would have held that counsel was ineffective had he acted against his client's instructions by presenting mitigating evidence, or by refusing to present such evidence had Landrigan told him to do so. In Jones v. Barnes,[57] the Supreme Court quoted approvingly from the ABA Model Rules of Professional Conduct to the effect that the client should hold ultimate authority to make certain "fundamental" (as opposed to "tactical") decisions, such as whether to plead guilty, waive the right to jury trial, testify, and forgo an appeal. But the decision at issue in Landrigan involving whether to present particular evidence might well be considered tactical. For instance, Jones held that a defendant cannot compel his attorney to argue particular claims on appeal, even claims that are concededly non-frivolous, when the attorney has decided, in the exercise of professional judgment, not to present them. The dissent argued that Faretta required that the defendant be allowed to decide such issues after receiving advice from the attorney. But the majority stated that such an approach would undermine the attorney's ability to make effective arguments, and that the attorney's decision in Jones to override the defendant's wishes, "far from being evidence of incompetence, is the hallmark of effective appellate advocacy."

In contrast, when the decision should clearly be the domain of the defendant, as with filing an appeal of right, counsel's failure to abide by the defendant's decision violates both Strickland's performance prong and its prejudice prong.[58] However, the defendant must make his or her wishes explicit. When those wishes are not clear, the Supreme

56 550 U.S. 465 (2007).

57 463 U.S. 745 (1983).

58 Garza v. Idaho, 139 S.Ct. 738 (2019).

Court has indicated that the prejudice inquiry should still take place; for instance, in the failure-to-appeal situation, a defendant who did not specifically tell counsel to file the appeal must demonstrate that "but for counsel's deficient failure to consult about an appeal, he would have timely appealed."[59] Also illustrative of this point is Florida v. Nixon,[60] where counsel, without obtaining the defendant's explicit consent to do so, conceded guilt at trial in the hopes that, in light of the state's overwhelming evidence of guilt, such a concession would have a mitigating impact on the jury at sentencing. A unanimous Court refused to find ineffective assistance, reasoning that this "strategic choice is not impeded by a blanket rule demanding the defendant's explicit consent." However, in McCoy v. Louisiana,[61] the Court held that if the client specifically forbids counsel to concede guilt, counsel's conduct is not only deficient but automatically results in reversible error, with no showing of prejudice required.

11.3.4 Prejudice

If a court finds state interference with counsel, an actual conflict that adversely affects counsel's representation, or that counsel has ignored the defendant's express wishes on a decision that is ultimately the defendant's, then prejudice is presumed. But in all other cases, an ineffective assistance of counsel claim will be successful only if prejudice is also found. Indeed, the Supreme Court has held that, outside of presumptively prejudicial situations, the prejudice inquiry must be undertaken even when the attorney's error is "structural" and normally would not be subject to harmless error analysis (a topic discussed in §12.3.2).[62]

In cases like Rompilla, the Court was willing to find prejudice on the ground that there was a reasonable probability that at least one juror would have resisted a death sentence had the attorney error (involving a failure to investigate) not occurred; a similar prejudice test applies when there is inadequate performance at trial. When the defendant pleads guilty based on erroneous advice, in contrast, the question is whether the defendant would have pleaded guilty and instead have gone to trial if the error had not occurred. In Hill v. Lockhart,[63] the

59 Roe v. Flores Ortega, 528 U.S. 470 (2000).

60 543 U.S. 175 (2004).

61 138 S.Ct. 1500 (2018).

62 Weaver v. Massachusetts, 137 S.Ct. 1899 (2017).

63 474 U.S. 52 (1985).

case that announced this rule, the Court stated, by way of example, that if the claimed error is that counsel failed to advise the defendant of an affirmative defense, the defendant must show that "the affirmative defense would likely have succeeded at trial." However, in the subsequent case of Lee v. United States,[64] the Court appeared to back off from this position. In Lee, the state acknowledged that counsel had mistakenly told Lee that pleading guilty would not lead to deportation, but pointed out that the likelihood of deportation was extremely high even had Lee gone to trial, and thus a reasonable defendant would have pleaded guilty regardless of counsel's advice. But, in contrast to the example it gave in Hill, the Court stated that the focus is "on a defendant's decision-making, which may not turn solely on the likelihood of conviction after trial," nor on whether most defendants in a similar situation would have gone to trial. Since in Lee both the defendant and his attorney stated that avoiding deportation was the "determinative issue" in Lee's calculus, a finding of prejudice was required.

A somewhat different inquiry occurs when the error leads the defendant to reject a plea offer and go to trial. In Lafler v. Cooper,[65] Lafler rejected a plea based on erroneous information from the attorney about state assault law, and received a mandatory minimum sentence several years longer than the plea offer he rejected. In the companion case of Frye v. Missouri,[66] counsel never communicated a plea offer that was over two years shorter than the sentence Frye received after conviction at trial. In these types of situations, the defendant:

> must show that but for the ineffective advice there is a reasonable probability that the plea offer would have been presented to the court (i.e. that the defendant would have accepted the plea and the prosecution would not have withdrawn it in light of intervening circumstances), that the court would have accepted its terms, and that the conviction or sentence, or both, under the offer's terms would have been less severe than under the judgment and sentence that in fact were imposed.

The dissent argued that no prejudice occurred in these cases because the defendant received a fair trial. But the majority refused to accept the notion that a fair trial "wipes clean any deficient performance by defense counsel during plea bargaining."

64 137 S.Ct. 1958 (2017).

65 566 U.S. 156 (2012).

66 566 U.S. 134 (2012).

At the same time, defendants who prevail in such cases are not necessarily entitled to the original plea offer. In Lafler, for instance, the Court held that, while the state had to reoffer the original plea, the trial judge still had the options of rejecting the bargain, letting the trial sentence stand, or even imposing some other disposition.

11.4 Right to confront accusers

The right to confront one's accusers consists of several components. The right would be meaningless if the defendant is not present in the courtroom to confront the accuser. Further, physical presence alone is not enough; the defendant must be mentally present as well, so that he or she can help the attorney challenge the prosecution's case. Of course, the accuser must also be in the courtroom if confrontation is to occur, which means that the Sixth Amendment prohibits at least some uses of hearsay by the prosecution. Finally, limitations on counsel's ability to challenge witnesses can violate the right of confrontation.

11.4.1 Right to be present

In Illinois v. Allen,[67] the Supreme Court stated that the "accused's right to be present in the courtroom [exists] at every stage of his trial," a statement that the Court later clarified entitles the defendant to be present at all post-charging proceedings at which the defendant's presence "would contribute to the fairness of the prosecution."[68] As construed, this language means that the defendant has a right to be present at suppression hearings, the preliminary hearing, and sentencing, but no right to be present during the first appearance, bail hearing, or grand jury proceeding, for much the same reason there is no right to counsel at these proceedings (see §11.2.2).

If the right exists, it may not be undermined by state actions that could prejudice the defendant. In an effort to avoid biasing the factfinder, the Supreme Court has held that the state may not compel a defendant to wear jail garb,[69] or be forced to appear in visible shackles (unless security demands it), either at trial or at capital sentencing proceedings.[70]

67 397 U.S. 337 (1970).

68 Kentucky v. Stincer, 482 U.S. 730 (1987).

69 Estelle v. Williams, 425 U.S. 501 (1976).

70 Deck v. Missouri, 544 U.S. 622 (2005).

For the same reason, and to protect the Fifth Amendment right to silence, the Court has held that if the defendant decides to forgo testifying—an option exercised by upwards of half of all defendants who go to trial—the prosecutor may not comment on that fact. As the Court noted in Griffin v. California,[71] a suggestion by the prosecutor that an innocent defendant would have taken the stand "solemnizes the silence of the accused into evidence against him," even though a decision not to testify could in fact be due to "timidity . . . nervousness" or fear that the introduction of prior crimes, ostensibly for impeachment, will prejudice the jury. The Court has also held that the defendant is entitled to an instruction that the jury may not draw adverse inferences from a failure to testify.[72]

Like most other rights, the right to be present can be waived, if the waiver is knowing and voluntary. It can also be forfeited if the defendant fails to appear at trial once it has started, or absconds before trial.[73] Further, Allen held that a defendant who acts "in a manner so disorderly, disruptive, and disrespectful of the court that his trial cannot be carried on with him in the courtroom" can also forfeit the right to be present. Generally in this situation, however, there are alternatives, such as binding and gagging the defendant, a contempt citation, or—with due regard to the defendant's right to confront accusers (see §11.4.4)—the use of technology that allows remote observation of the proceedings and access to counsel.

11.4.2 Competence to proceed

Defendants have a right to be mentally, as well as physically, present. In Dusky v. United States,[74] the Supreme Court held that a defendant may not be tried unless "he has sufficient present ability to consult with his lawyer with a reasonable degree of rational understanding—and . . . a rational as well as factual understanding of the proceedings against him." Without the ability to communicate with the attorney about facts pertinent to the case, based on an understanding of the proceedings and the various rights that apply, the defendant can neither help the attorney confront witnesses nor make rational decisions about whether to waive the jury or testify. As applied, only about 30

71 380 U.S. 609 (1965).

72 Carter v. Kentucky, 450 U.S. 288 (1981).

73 Taylor v. United States, 414 U.S. 17 (1973); Tacon v. Arizona, 410 U.S. 351 (1973).

74 362 U.S. 402 (1960).

percent of those whose competency is questionable enough to trigger an evaluation motion are found incompetent; thus, in the absence of very serious mental disability, the competency test is usually met, whether the defendant pleads guilty or goes to trial. However, as discussed in §11.2.5, if a defendant with mental problems is nonetheless found competent and goes to trial after waiving the right to counsel, additional requirements must be met.

Because the state as well as the defendant have an interest in ensuring a reliable proceeding, the judge and the prosecutor may raise the competence issue if the defendant does not, at any time prior to or during trial.[75] If the issue is raised, a psychiatric evaluation usually takes place. The defendant is not entitled to counsel at this evaluation under either the Fifth or Sixth Amendments, but the results may only be used on the competence issue unless the defendant relies on them for some other purpose, a rule meant to protect the defendant's Fifth Amendment interest.[76] (Analogously, if the insanity defense is raised, the state is entitled to its own evaluator, but the results of that evaluation may only be used to address insanity, not in the prosecution's case-in-chief to prove guilt.)

The party asserting incompetence bears the burden of proving it.[77] If the defendant is found incompetent, hospitalization is the usual result, during which the state may administer treatment to restore competency, over the defendant's objection if necessary, at least when the crime is serious and the treatment does not cause significant side effects and is the less restrictive way of effectively rendering the individual competent.[78] However, in Jackson v. Indiana,[79] the Supreme Court held that, if treatment does not restore competence within a reasonable period of time, the state must either release or civilly commit the defendant, because such individuals have not been, and cannot be, convicted of crime.

75 Drope v. Missouri, 420 U.S. 162 (1975).

76 Estelle v. Smith, 451 U.S. 454 (1981); Kansas v. Cheever, 571 U.S. 87 (2013).

77 Medina v. California, 505 U.S. 437 (1992).

78 Sell v. United States, 539 U.S. 166 (2003).

79 406 U.S. 715 (1972).

11.4.3 Right to in-court testimony

The defendant's right "to confront the witnesses against him" could be construed as a requirement that the defendant be able to cross-examine at trial every individual who provides the prosecution with evidence, which would mean that the prosecution could not introduce hearsay (typically defined as out-of-court declarations offered for the truth of the matter asserted). The Supreme Court has never adopted that stance, however. For some time, it tried to develop rules that, analogous to traditional evidentiary rules governing the admissibility of hearsay, focused on whether the out-of-court statement was sufficiently reliable.[80] Then, in a line of cases beginning with Crawford v. Washington,[81] the Supreme Court ruled that the only hearsay subject to exclusion is that which is "testimonial," and that even testimonial evidence may be admissible under various circumstances.

Crawford linked the Confrontation Clause's protection to "testimonial" statements based on both its interpretation of the Clause's language, which speaks of "witnesses," and its understanding of the Clause's genesis, which reflected a distrust among eighteenth century English jurists and the Framers of out-of-court statements sought by the government for the specific purpose of obtaining evidence for trial. Thus, Crawford indicated, statements that trigger the Clause definitely include "formalized testimonial materials, such as affidavits, depositions, prior testimony, or confessions" made to government officials. Further, the Court subsequently made clear, out-of-court statements by government officials or agents, made in preparation for prosecution, are testimonial, even if they meet a traditional hearsay exception. In Melendez-Diaz v. Massachusetts,[82] for instance, the Court held that a notarized forensic laboratory report certifying that a substance was cocaine was inadmissible because its author was not proffered by the prosecution, and in Bullcoming v. New Mexico,[83] the Court held that the Confrontation Clause was violated because the forensic expert who testified about blood test results had not conducted the test himself, even though both reports probably met the "business record" hearsay exception found in most evidentiary rules.

---

80 Ohio v. Roberts, 448 U.S. 56 (1980).

81 541 U.S. 36 (2004).

82 557 U.S. 305 (2009).

83 564 U.S. 647 (2011).

In contrast, when its "primary purpose" is something other than providing or accumulating evidence for trial, a statement is not likely to be testimonial. In practice, that test has meant that most statements made to individuals who are not government officials or their agents, such as doctors,[84] relatives,[85] or co-conspirators,[86] are not testimonial. Nor are statements made to government officials, if the official's goal is something other than investigating crime. The Court has held to be non-testimonial statements that are made during a 911 call describing violent events as they were happening;[87] statements made in response to police questioning of an apparent shooting victim aimed at assessing "the situation, the threat to their own safety, and possible danger to the potential victim and to the public";[88] and statements by a three-year-old to school teachers who, although required by law to report abuse, asked the child questions in the context of an "ongoing emergency . . . aimed at identifying and ending a threat" involving abuse.[89]

If evidence is not testimonial as defined in these cases, the Confrontation Clause does not bar its admission (although hearsay rules might still require exclusion). As Crawford stated of the testimonial/non-testimonial distinction, "a limitation so clearly reflected in the text of the constitutional provision must fairly be said to mark out not merely its core, but its perimeter." Further, even when evidence is testimonial, it can be introduced if one of four exceptions is met.

Not surprisingly, two of these exceptions are triggered by the unavailability of the declarant, which can occur not only when the declarant is deceased, but also when he or she is permanently out of the country, is unable to be located through diligent effort, has suffered a memory loss, or has validly asserted the Fifth Amendment. The most important such exception also requires that the declarant was subject to cross-examination at the time the statement was made. Thus, the typical declaration against interest made to police by an unavailable co-defendant, even though admissible under the hearsay rules in many jurisdictions, is not subject to cross-examination at the time it is made, and so is not admissible under Crawford.[90] The same should

84 White v. Illinois, 502 U.S. 346 (1992).

85 Id.

86 Bourjaily v. United States, 479 U.S. 881 (1986).

87 Davis v. Washington, 547 U.S. 813 (2006).

88 Michigan v. Bryant, 562 U.S. 344 (2011).

89 Ohio v. Clark, 576 U.S. 237 (2015).

90 Lilly v. Virginia, 527 U.S. 116 (1999).

be true of a declaration made on the verge of death despite the "dying declaration" exception to the hearsay rule (although Crawford stated that this practice may need to be continued "on historical grounds"). At the same time, only an "opportunity" to cross-examine must exist at the time of the statement; how that opportunity is exercised is irrelevant. In California v. Green,[91] for instance, the Court held that the defense attorney at Green's preliminary hearing had an opportunity to examine the witness even though the witness was called by the defense rather than the prosecution and cross-examination was not particularly aggressive.

A special situation arises when the declarant is a co-defendant whose confession implicates the defendant as well, and who asserts the Fifth Amendment privilege at their joint trial. Like the typical against-interest and dying declaration, here the declarant is unavailable and the defendant did not have an opportunity to cross-examine at the time of the statement. Consistent with the foregoing, in Bruton v. United States,[92] the Court held that such a confession cannot be introduced verbatim, because the defendant is unable to confront the co-defendant. However, the Court has also held that a co-defendant confession may still be introduced if references to the defendant's existence are removed and an instruction is given to the jury to disregard its possible inferences about the defendant, over a dissent arguing that such a procedure is unlikely to fool the jury.[93] Further, even an unredacted co-defendant confession may be introduced if the co-defendant takes the stand.[94]

A second exception to the usual rule that testimonial evidence is inadmissible arises when a declarant's unavailability is due to the defendant's misconduct, which usually involves killing the declarant. In Giles v. California,[95] the Court explained that this "forfeiture" exception applies only when the killing was provably motivated by a desire to prevent the victim from testifying against the defendant.

A third exception occurs when the declarant is available at trial (which some lower courts have indicated can be the case not only when the state could call the witness, but also when the defendant

---

91 399 U.S. 149 (1970).

92 391 U.S. 123 (1968).

93 Richardson v. Marsh, 481 U.S. 200 (1987).

94 Nelson v. O'Neil, 402 U.S. 622 (1971).

95 554 U.S. 353 (2008).

could do so through compulsory process[96]), and thus is subject to cross-examination. This exception applies even if the declarant is no longer able, or purports to be unable, to remember the event in question, and the earlier, out-of-court statement was not subject to cross-examination. In United States v. Owens,[97] the Supreme Court concluded that "confrontation" can still take place in such a situation, because the attorney can still expose memory gaps and why they might have occurred.

Finally, if the testimonial evidence is used for a non-hearsay purpose, it is admissible. In Tennessee v. Street,[98] the prosecution introduced an accomplice's testimony solely to contradict the defendant's assertion that his own confession was a coerced imitation of his accomplice's, not to prove the truth of the accomplice's confession.

11.4.4 Right to challenge witnesses

In lay terms, confrontation does not take place unless the defendant can challenge the witness in open court. Consistent with this notion, in Coy v. Iowa,[99] the Supreme Court held that "the Confrontation Clause guarantees the defendant a face-to-face meeting with witnesses appearing before the trier of fact." However, in Maryland v. Craig,[100] the Court held that under very limited circumstances—specifically when face-to-face testimony "will result in [a] child suffering serious emotional distress such that the child cannot reasonably communicate"—such a meeting is not required. In Craig the relevant statute required an individualized determination that a face-to-face encounter would cause serious trauma to the witness, and then required that the witness, the prosecutor, and defense counsel withdraw to a separate room, while the judge, jury, and defendant remained in the courtroom, able to observe direct and cross-examination over a video hookup, and with the defendant able to communicate electronically with counsel. The majority found this procedure acceptable because it "does not impinge upon the truth-seeking nor symbolic purposes of the Confrontation Clause," at the same time it furthers the state's interest in protecting

---

96 See, e.g., State v. Campbell, 719 N.W.2d 374 (N.Dak. 2006): cf. United States v. Inadi, 475 U.S. 387 (1986).

97 484 U.S. 554 (1988).

98 471 U.S. 409 (1985).

99 487 U.S. 1012 (1988).

100 497 U.S. 836 (1990).

children. The dissent objected: "[F]ace-to-face presence may, unfortunately, upset the truthful rape victim or abused child; but by the same token it may confound and undo the false accuser, or reveal the child coached by a malevolent adult."

In keeping with its relatively strict face-to-face confrontation requirement, the Supreme Court has also been reluctant to limit the defense's ability to cross-examine the prosecution's witnesses who appear in court (although, of course, to the extent "witnesses" testify via hearsay, there is no chance to cross-examine them). The Court has reversed convictions when the key prosecution witness was allowed to conceal his identity,[101] and when the judge, applying the state's "voucher" rule that only permits a party to conduct direct examination of witnesses it has called, prevented defense counsel from cross-examining a witness called by the defense who had confessed to the defendant's crime.[102] However, as detailed in §8.4.2, the Court has been much more reluctant to provide the defense with broad-ranging discovery that could enable it to do a better job cross-examining the state's witnesses.

11.5 Right to present evidence

The defense's ability to present its own case, as distinct from its ability to challenge the prosecution's case, is also relatively unfettered. The Supreme Court summed up its approach in this area by stating that "competent, reliable evidence . . . central to the defendant's claim of innocence" should be admitted because, "[w]hether rooted directly in the Due Process Clause . . . in the Compulsory Process or Confrontation Clause . . . the Constitution guarantees criminal defendants a 'meaningful opportunity to present a complete defense.'"[103] This right to present a defense has played out in cases involving the defendant's rights: (1) to testify; (2) to introduce his or her own out-of-court statements; (3) to subpoena witnesses; and (4) to present witnesses.

Although they often decline to testify for reasons outlined in §11.4.1, defendants have a constitutional right to tell their story on the stand. That was the holding of Rock v. Arkansas,[104] which reasoned that this

101 390 U.S. 129 (1968).

102 Chambers v. Mississippi, 410 U.S. 284 (1973).

103 Crane v. Kentucky, 476 U.S. 683 (1986).

104 479 U.S. 1079 (1987).

right derives from the Due Process Clause's guarantee of fairness, the Compulsory Process Clause's guarantee that the defendant can "obtain[] witnesses in his favor," and the Fifth Amendment's protection of silence unless the defendant "chooses to speak in the unfettered exercise of his own will." Of course, if the defendant decides to testify, he or she cannot avoid cross-examination by the prosecution, at least when the prosecution's questioning stays within the scope of direct examination.[105] Further, if the defendant waits until all other evidence is presented before testifying (which, as noted earlier, is a constitutional entitlement), the prosecution may not only ask specific questions designed to expose how a defendant might have tailored testimony to fit the evidence, but also may make a more general statement during closing argument to the effect that the defendant testified last for that purpose.[106]

Defense presentation of the defendant's out-of-court statements is treated in a similarly nuanced fashion. In Rock, after establishing the right to testify, the Court struck down a state rule that categorically barred post-hypnosis testimony. Although conceding that such testimony might be fabricated or distorted, the Court stated that its admissibility must be determined on a case-by-case basis, unless the state can show "that hypnotically enhanced testimony is always so untrustworthy and so immune to the traditional means of evaluating credibility that it should disable a defendant from presenting her version of the events for which she is on trial." But in United States v. Scheffer,[107] the Court upheld a trial court's ruling rejecting introduction of expert testimony describing the results of a polygraph test indicating the defendant had not been lying to investigators when he denied drug use, on the ground that "[t]here is simply no consensus that polygraph evidence is reliable." Also important to the Court was the distinction that, in Rock, the statute precluded the defendant from telling her side of the story, whereas in Scheffer the defendant was not prevented from presenting "factual evidence" relevant to the charge, but "was barred merely from introducing expert opinion testimony to bolster his own credibility," which is normally the preserve of the jury, not experts.

The defendant also has the right, under the Compulsory Process Clause, to subpoena witnesses, documents, and objects to support the defense.

105 Brown v. United States, 356 U.S. 148 (1958).

106 Portuondo v. Agard, 529 U.S. 61 (2000).

107 523 U.S. 303 (1998).

A Warren Court opinion, Roviaro v. United States,[108] held that the defendant is entitled even to the identity of a confidential informant, at least when that informant is the only witness to the criminal act other than the perpetrator. But in United States v. Valenzuela-Bernal,[109] the Court rejected a rule that the defendant is entitled to any witness or tangible evidence that has a "conceivable benefit" to the defense, instead requiring the defendant to provide "some explanation of how [a proposed witness] would have been favorable and material." Thus, in Valenzuela-Bernal the Court refused to find the Compulsory Process Clause violated by the government's deportation of one of three aliens found in the defendant's car, noting that the other two aliens were still available at trial. Many lower courts, influenced by Valenzuela-Bernal, have resisted the full implications of Roviaro, although others continue to adhere to it.[110]

Finally, the Court has made clear that when the defense calls a witness, the state is rarely permitted to limit the substance of non-prejudicial testimony, even if that means a state evidentiary rule will be violated. In Scheffer, as described above, the Court refused to allow polygraph evidence it considered unreliable and highly prejudicial, given its probable effect on the jury, and in United States v. Salerno[111] it signaled that it would not permit the defense to present hearsay from an unavailable witness who had not been subject to cross-examination. But in Chambers v. Mississippi,[112] the Court held that the Due Process Clause was violated when the trial judge excluded the testimony of three individuals who had heard another person confess to Chambers' alleged crime, even though the testimony was hearsay and the jurisdiction did not recognize the declaration-against-interest exception to the hearsay rule. In other cases, the Court held that either the Compulsory Process Clause or Due Process Clause is violated by rules or trial court pronouncements that prevent one co-defendant from testifying on behalf of another,[113] that "effectively [drive] the witness off the stand" by lengthy admonitions not to lie,[114] and that prevent the jury from hearing evidence about the voluntariness of a confession

108 353 U.S. 53 (1957).

109 458 U.S. 858 (1982).

110 Compare United States v. Saa, 859 F.2d 1067 (2d. Cir. 1988) to United States v. Rutherford, 175 F.3d 899 (11th Cir. 1999).

111 505 U.S. 317 (1992).

112 410 U.S. 284 (1973).

113 Washington v. Texas, 388 U.S. 14 (1967).

114 Webb v. Texas, 409 U.S. 95 (1972).

after a judge has found the confession voluntary.[115] And in Holmes v. South Carolina,[116] the Court struck down a South Carolina rule that prohibited introduction of evidence suggesting a third party committed the crime when strong forensic evidence of the defendant's guilt exists. The Court explained that the law was deficient because it was not premised on flaws in the defense's evidence, which might have been a permissible ground for exclusion, but rather on the strength of the prosecution's case.

115 Crane v. Kentucky, 476 U.S. 683 (1986).
116 547 U.S. 319 (2006).

12 Post-adjudication proceedings

12.1 Overview

Several stages of the criminal process follow an adjudication of guilt. Sentencing usually occurs soon after conviction, although in some cases preparation of the presentence report or docket pressures can delay the dispositional phase. Defendants who want to appeal their conviction or sentence must do so within a limited period of time, except in capital cases, when appeal is usually automatic. Defendants who are dissatisfied with the outcome of appeal may, under limited circumstances, "collaterally attack" the conviction or sentence through writs of coram nobis or habeas corpus, or through analogous proceedings created by state rule or statute.

This chapter covers these three stages of the criminal process. The chapter also discusses the meaning of the Fifth Amendment's guarantee that no person shall be "subject for the same offence to be twice put in jeopardy of life and limb." Although the Double Jeopardy Clause, when it applies, prohibits trial or punishment, it usually has the effect of preventing a second trial on charges on which the defendant has already been convicted or acquitted, and so comfortably fits in this chapter about post-adjudication proceedings.

12.2 Sentencing

Notwithstanding the fact that it determines whether, and for how long, offenders will be incarcerated, the sentencing process can be remarkably informal. While sentencing is considered a critical stage for purposes of the right to counsel, other Sixth Amendment rights either do not apply at all, or only minimally so. There is no federal constitutional right to a jury at sentencing except in capital cases;[1] while a trial jury

1 Ring v. Arizona, 536 U.S. 584 (2002).

must find beyond a reasonable doubt the facts required to justify a sentence beyond the statutory or mandatory guidelines maximum (see §10.3.1), other sentencing facts can be found by a judge, need not be proven by more than a preponderance of the evidence, and can even consist of conduct that led to acquittal.[2] Defendants are entitled to be present during sentencing, and have a right to remain silent during it.[3] But they do not have a right to testify in the normal sense, only a right to "allocution" (a statement by the defendant that can be restricted to a plea for mercy).[4] Nor is there a right to confront accusers or to compulsory process at sentencing; thus, in non-capital cases hearsay is admissible and "sentencing decisions may be based upon unsworn written assertions by probation officers, prosecutors, police, victims and others in presentence reports, sentencing worksheets, or other documents that are never made public and that the defendant and his counsel never see."[5]

The historical explanation for this state of affairs is that, in the eighteenth and early nineteenth centuries, the range of sentences was very narrow (with death the penalty for most felonies), so that little discretion was exercised on the issue of punishment. Today, however, judges (or juries in the handful of states that permit jury sentencing) often have significantly greater sentencing discretion. Thus, the case for more formality at sentencing is much stronger.

At least in capital cases, the Supreme Court has recognized that more process is due during sentencing. In Gardner v. Florida,[6] the defendant argued that, before his sentence was imposed, he had a right to discover and rebut the contents of his presentence report. The government objected to this claim on a number of grounds: such discovery, it claimed, would make sources reluctant to provide information, would delay the process, might disrupt rehabilitation if psychologically damaging information is in the report, and is not necessary given the expertise of judges. But the Supreme Court rejected all of these arguments, stating: "Our belief that debate between adversaries is often essential to the truth-seeking function of trials requires us also to rec-

2 Watts v. United States, 519 U.S. 148 (1997).

3 Mitchell v. United States, 526 U.S. 314 (1999).

4 McGautha v. California, 402 U.S. 183 (1971).

5 Nancy King, Procedure at Sentencing, in Oxford Handbook of Sentencing and Corrections 317, 319 (Oxford University Press, New York, N.Y. 2011).

6 430 U.S. 349 (1977).

ognize the importance of giving counsel an opportunity to comment on facts which may influence the sentencing decision in a capital case." This language could easily support more robust procedural rights in non-capital sentencing proceedings as well, but to date the Court has refused to move in that direction.

12.3 Appeal

Although the Supreme Court has held that, because a right to appeal was not recognized at common law, there is no constitutional right to appeal, almost every state permits felony defendants to file an appeal "as of right" to an intermediate appellate court and, if unsuccessful there, at least one opportunity to seek "discretionary review" to a higher court. In the federal system, for instance, defendants have an appeal as of right to a circuit court of appeal, with further appeal to the U.S. Supreme Court usually dependent on whether the Court grants a writ of certiorari. A state defendant is usually afforded the same appellate opportunities within the state system. Further, a state defendant can take a direct appeal to the U.S. Supreme Court in cases where the highest available state court has invalidated a federal statute or upheld a state statute on constitutional grounds, and can seek a discretionary writ of certiorari to the U.S. Supreme Court where the state court "draw[s] the validity" of a federal or state statute into question, or where a claim based on the federal constitution, treaties, or federal statutes involved.[7]

12.3.1 Rights during appeal

As discussed in §11.2.2, the right to counsel and the right to effective assistance of counsel attaches at appeals as of right, but not at discretionary appeals. Thus, while counsel's failure to meet a filing deadline for an appeal as of right requires reinstatement of the appeal (on ineffective assistance grounds), a similar failure in connection with discretionary review does not.[8] There is also no right to proceed pro se at any stage of the appellate process; in Martinez v. Court of Appeal,[9] the Supreme Court stated that it was "entirely unpersuaded that the risk of disloyalty by a court-appointed attorney, or the suspicion of

7 28 U.S.C. §§1254; 1257.

8 Wainwright v. Torna, 455 U.S. 586 (1982).

9 528 U.S. 152 (2000).

such disloyalty, that underlines the constitutional right of self-representation at trial is a sufficient concern to conclude that such a right is a necessary component of a fair appellate proceeding."

For similar reasons, although defendants control the decision whether to appeal, they do not control the content of arguments made on appeal (see §11.3.3). Indeed, after an appeal is filed at the defendant's behest, counsel can even decide that there are no substantial appellate claims to be argued. In such cases, the Supreme Court held in Anders v. California,[10] counsel must file a brief "referring to anything in the record that might arguably support the appeal," to which the defendant is entitled to add arguments; the point of this "Anders brief" is to force counsel to think carefully about the decision to forgo appellate claims and confirm that they are "wholly frivolous." However, the Court has also held that an Anders brief that merely provides a summary of the case's procedural and factual history is sufficient, at least as long as counsel stands ready to provide analysis of any points the appellate court subsequently wants addressed.[11]

Analogous to the right to avoid vindictive charging by the prosecution after a plea deal falls through (see §8.5.3), a presumption of vindictiveness arises when a sentence is increased after a successful appeal, whether the increase results directly from a judge's decision, or indirectly from a prosecutor's decision to "up the ante" on the charge after the appeal; otherwise, the Supreme Court reasoned in North Carolina v. Pearce,[12] the right to appeal might be inhibited by fear of retaliation. The presumption of vindictiveness can be overcome, however, if the trial judge or prosecutor can provide a reasonable explanation for the increase, one that is based on "identifiable conduct occurring after the time of the original sentencing proceeding." Thus, in Texas v. McCullough,[13] the judge's post-appeal sentence increase of 30 years was permissible, since the pre-appeal sentence was imposed by a jury, and the second sentence came after a trial that the judge herself had concluded was necessary because of misconduct by the prosecutor during the first trial. According to the Supreme Court, "unlike the judge who has been reversed, the trial judge here had no motivation to engage in self-vindication." Further, new evidence about the

10 386 U.S. 738 (1967).

11 Smith v. Robbins, 528 U.S. 259 (2000).

12 395 U.S. 711 (1969).

13 475 U.S. 134 (1986).

defendant's personality and criminal history came to light during the second trial. Similarly, in Alabama v. Smith,[14] the Court held that the presumptive of vindictiveness is not triggered when the first sentence results from plea bargaining and the second sentence is handed down after a trial, because "relevant sentencing information available to the judge after the plea will usually be considerably less than that available at trial," and because "the facts that may have indicated leniency as consideration for the guilty plea [such as the defendant's willingness to forgo trial] are no longer present."

Finally, as with other rights, the right to appeal can be relinquished, in at least three ways. First, it can be waived; such waivers have been found voluntary even when the waiver is demanded by the prosecutor as a condition of obtaining a favorable plea deal.[15] Second, the defendant can forfeit the right by becoming a "fugitive from justice" during the pendency of the appeal.[16] Finally, the defendant can forfeit the ability to appeal a particular issue if counsel does not object to the appealed error in a timely fashion (usually during trial or sentencing). The major exception to this type of forfeiture is called the "plain error" rule, which involves a claimed error "that affect[s] substantial rights [and that] seriously affects the fairness, integrity or public reputation of judicial proceedings."[17] The issue of when a claim involves plain error that need not be raised at trial to be appealable is closely associated with the issue of when an error can be deemed "harmless."

12.3.2 Harmless error

A finding of error by an appellate court does not always require reversal. In every American jurisdiction, if an error is considered "harmless," conviction may still be affirmed. This is so even for most errors of constitutional magnitude.

However, if the constitutional error is considered "structural," reversal is required. Various Supreme Court opinions have indicated that infringement of the right to trial counsel, the right to give summation at the end of trial, the right to an impartial judge, the right to speedy trial, the guarantee against double jeopardy, the right to a representative

14 490 U.S. 794 (1989).

15 See Garza v. Idaho, 139 S.Ct. 738 (2019).

16 Ortega-Rodriguez v. United States, 507 U.S. 234 (1993).

17 Johnson v. United States, 520 U.S. 461 (1997); see Fed. R. Crim. P. 52(b).

jury and grand jury, and the right to an Anders brief should never be deemed harmless. As the Court explained in Arizona v. Fulminante[18]—in the course of noting these decisions and holding that admission of a coerced confession can be considered harmless—structural error such as "total deprivation of the right to counsel at trial" and the right to an impartial judge infect the entire trial and thus "defy analysis by harmless error standards." If instead, as with admission of a coerced confession, the error occurs "during the presentation of the case to the jury, and . . . may therefore be quantitatively assessed in the context of other evidence presented," harmless error analysis is appropriate.

The language of the Court's tests for determining when error is harmless implies that such a finding should be rare. In Chapman v. California,[19] the Supreme Court held that when the error is constitutional, the prosecution must prove "beyond a reasonable doubt that the error complained of did not contribute to the verdict obtained." Even if the error is not of constitutional import, the Court has stated, in language akin to the plain error rule, that if "one cannot say, with fair assurance, after pondering all that happened without stripping the erroneous action from the whole that the judgment was not substantially swayed by the error, it is impossible to conclude that substantial rights were not affected."

In theory, both of these tests focus solely on whether the error could have affected the jury, not on whether the remaining error-free evidence was sufficient to support conviction. However, many of the Court's decisions appear to adopt what has been called the "overwhelming evidence" test, which looks at whether the left-over, properly admitted evidence was sufficient to convict. An example of the first, effect-on-the-factfinder test is Chapman itself, where the prosecutor repeatedly referred to the defendant's failure to take the stand during closing argument and the judge instructed the jury it could draw an adverse inference from that failure, in clear violation of Griffin v. California (see §11.4.1). The Warren Court found reversal necessary, stating that "though the case in which this occurred presented a reasonably strong 'circumstantial web of evidence' against petitioners, it was also a case in which, absent the constitutionally forbidden comments, honest fair-minded jurors might very well have brought in not-guilty verdicts." The Court found it "completely impossible" to say beyond a reasonable

18 499 U.S. 279 (1991).

19 386 U.S. 18 (1967).

doubt that the error did not affect the jury. However, in United States v. Hasting,[20] involving the same type of error, the post-Warren Court focused on the strength of the prosecution's evidence and subtly rearranged Chapman's inquiry by stating "[t]he question a reviewing court must ask is this: absent the prosecutor's allusion to the failure to the defense to proffer evidence to rebut the testimony of the victims, is it clear beyond a reasonable doubt that the jury would have returned a verdict of guilty?" This question focuses on whether, in the absence of the error, enough evidence remains to convict the defendant beyond a reasonable doubt. Similarly, in Schneble v. Florida,[21] the Court held harmless a violation of Bruton v. United States (see §11.4.3), because "the independent evidence of guilt [was] overwhelming" and the improperly admitted evidence was "insignificant in comparison."

Note that even under the overwhelming evidence test, some types of errors require automatic reversal because they can occur only if the error affected the outcome of the case. For instance, denial of effective assistance of counsel cannot be found unless the attorney's incompetence is shown to have "deprive[d] the defendant of a fair trial" (see §11.3.4), and a similar finding must be made for a Brady violation (see §8.4.2). Further, when the error does not involve the admission of evidence, but rather instructions to the jury about elements of the crime, the Court is much more likely to reverse, because, like structural error, the effect on the jury is difficult to assess regardless of the strength of the prosecution's evidence.[22]

12.3.3 Final judgment rule

The parties sometimes want to appeal a judicial ruling before the trial verdict or sentence, because of the nature of the claim. To avoid piecemeal, time-consuming, and possibly duplicative litigation, these "interlocutory appeals" are permitted only if the challenged judgment is "final," the claim would "be lost, probably irreparably" if review is delayed until the verdict, and the issue is not an aspect of the merits that would require the appellate court to prejudge the case before it is decided. Given their tangential relationship to the issue of whether the

---

20 461 U.S. 499 (1983).

21 405 U.S. 427 (1972).

22 Compare Connecticut v. Johnson, 460 U.S. 73 (1983) and Yates v. Evatt, 500 U.S. 391 (1991) with Neder v. United States, 527 U.S. 1 (1999).

defendant deserves punishment, decisions regarding bail,[23] whether a prosecution is barred by double jeopardy,[24] and whether a defendant may be subject to forcible medication to restore competence[25] may be subject to interlocutory appeal. But decisions refusing to exclude evidence under the Fourth or Fifth Amendments[26] or to dismiss a case on speedy trial grounds are not.[27] Illegally seized evidence is usually crucial at trial, so such orders are not "independent" of the ongoing case against the defendant, and speedy trial analysis requires, in part, an assessment of whether delay prejudiced the defendant, which is best undertaken after trial has taken place.

Less obviously, the Court has held that a refusal to grant relief on a claim of prosecutorial vindictiveness (§§8.5.3; 12.3.1) cannot be appealed on an interlocutory basis, even though, like a double jeopardy claim, it would prevent trial on particular charges. In United States v. Hollywood Motor Car Co.,[28] the Supreme Court explained that pretrial vindication of a vindictiveness claim would merely delay trial, rather than prevent it entirely, because the prosecutor can still file a (lower) charge against the defendant.

In contrast to the rules governing the defense, in many jurisdictions the prosecution is able to appeal suppression hearing decisions and various other types of pretrial decisions prior to trial. The rationale is that an erroneous finding in such cases would "irreparably" harm the prosecution: if the evidence is excluded and acquittal results, the Double Jeopardy Clause would prevent reprosecution. Although such appeals can undermine the speedy trial right, the relevant federal statute exempts such delays from the speedy trial calculation and the Supreme Court appears to have upheld this practice.[29]

12.3.4 Retroactivity

If, in the course of correcting error, an appellate court announces a rule of general applicability, the question arises as to whether other defendants whose cases involved similar errors should benefit from it,

23 Stack v. Boyle, 342 U.S. 1 (1951).

24 Abney v. United States, 431 U.S. 651 (1977).

25 Sell v. United States, 539 U.S. 166 (2003).

26 DiBella v. United States, 369 U.S. 121 (1962).

27 United States v. McDonal, 435 U.S. 850 (1978).

28 458 U.S. 263 (1982).

29 See United States v. Loud Hawk, 474 U.S. 302 (1986).

which triggers "retroactivity" analysis. Full retroactivity would impose enormous costs on the criminal justice system, and perhaps also make appellate courts reluctant to announce new rules. Thus, for some time prior to the 1960s, the Supreme Court only granted relief to the parties before it.

The Warren Court, which announced a large number of new constitutional rules, was more generous. While it continued to deny relief in cases for which all review was complete or for which the relevant event—e.g., an illegal police search or a trial error—took place before the Court's ruling, it was willing to contemplate applying its new rulings to all cases on direct appeal and on habeas review. At the same time, in Linkletter v. Walker,[30] the Court concluded that only certain of its rules should be given this retroactive effect, based on an assessment of: (1) the extent to which the new rule affected the truth-finding process; (2) the extent to which law enforcement relied on the old standard; and (3) the impact retroactive application would have on resources. Thus, in Linkletter, the Court did not apply Mapp v. Ohio's holding on the Fourth Amendment exclusionary rule retroactively because that ruling did not directly affect the truth-finding function, state officials had justifiably relied on state court rulings that did not require exclusion, and a contrary ruling would have flooded the courts with litigation. Other rulings not given retroactive effect include the right to counsel at lineups,[31] the redefinition of "search" in Katz v. United States,[32] and Taylor v. Louisiana's holding that women may not be systematically excluded from juries.[33] In contrast, the Warren Court declared retroactive its holdings that defendants are entitled to counsel in misdemeanor cases[34] and that non-unanimous six-member juries violate the Sixth Amendment.[35]

Over time several justices expressed concern that Linkletter's multi-factor approach to retroactivity was unfair to defendants on direct appeal whose case was not the vehicle for a non-retroactive Supreme Court ruling. While the defendant in front of the Supreme Court received the benefit of the rule announced by the Court, no other

30 381 U.S. 618 (1965).

31 Stovall v. Denno, 388 U.S. 293 (1967).

32 Desist v. United States, 394 U.S. 244 (1969).

33 Daniel v. Louisiana, 420 U.S. 31 (1975).

34 Berry v. Cincinnati, 414 U.S. 29 (1973).

35 Brown v. Louisiana, 447 U.S. 323 (1980).

defendant on direct review in state or federal court did, unless the rule was considered retroactive under the Linkletter test or the slightly different test that replaced it in 1982 (which denied retroactive application to rules that were "clear breaks" with previous rulings, on the ground that officials could have reasonably relied on the old rule[36]). To avoid this disparate result, in Griffith v. Kentucky,[37] the Court concluded that all defendants on direct appeal should benefit from a rule announced on direct review, regardless of how it fared under Linkletter's test or whether it was a clear break. A more complicated analysis occurs when a defendant who has completed direct review and is seeking habeas relief asks for retroactive application of a new ruling; that analysis is taken up below.

12.4 Habeas corpus

The writ of habeas corpus has a long history. The writ appears to have originated in thirteenth century England as a means of ensuring that a party would appear before the court; literally, "habeas corpus" means "you shall have the body." But it was not until the seventeenth century that the "Great Writ," as Blackstone called it, became a vehicle for challenging arbitrary confinements by the Crown. In the United States most colonies recognized the writ, and Article I, section 9 of the Constitution specifically provides that the "privilege of the Writ of Habeas Corpus shall not be suspended, unless when in cases of Rebellion or Invasion public safety may require it" (language which the courts have dubbed the Suspension Clause).

Congress has also passed a series of statutes that recognize the scope of the writ at the federal level. Since 1867, Congress has provided that the writ is available to "any prisoner" (which originally referred only to federal prisoners but today means any federal or state prisoner) who is "in custody in violation of the Constitution or laws or treaties of the United States."[38] While this language suggests a broad scope to the writ, it has been subject to both judicial and statutory limits. Most importantly, in 1996, Congress passed the Antiterrorism and Effective Death Penalty Act of 1996 (AEDPA),[39] which significantly changed

36 United States v. Johnson, 457 U.S. 537 (1982).

37 479 U.S. 314 (1987).

38 28 U.S.C. §2241(c)(3).

39 Amending 28 U.S.C. §§2244 and 2253–5.

the statutory contours of the writ. The focus of this discussion will be on these developments in federal habeas, although it is important to recognize that each state also provides a process for collateral review of convictions.

Today's complicated statutory and case law regarding the writ in federal court reflects two competing goals. On the one hand, the view of the Warren Court, which significantly expanded the scope of the writ, was that "[c]onventional notions of finality of litigation have no place where life or liberty is at stake and infringement of constitutional rights is alleged."[40] The Court expressed particular concern that popularly elected state court judges might not be as attentive to constitutional rights as federal judges with lifetime tenure, and it probably was also worried that its "revolution" in criminal procedure would be stymied as a practical matter unless there was federal overview of state court decisions.[41] The post-Warren Court, in contrast, is much more focused on assuring finality, because the "[p]assage of time, erosion of memory, and dispersion of witnesses may render retrial difficult, even impossible," and because of the workload habeas writs impose on the federal courts.[42] Noting that few state court decisions are overturned by the federal courts, the post-Warren Court also manifests greater faith in the capabilities of state court judges, and a greater willingness to promote "comity" between the federal and state systems by affording deference to the state courts. This tension between the desire for federal overview on the one hand, and finality and comity goals on the other, is reflected in the law governing the types of substantive claims that may be heard on habeas, the procedural hurdles that prisoners must clear to gain access to federal court, and the extent to which factual findings by state courts are given deference by federal courts.

12.4.1 Substantive scope

Brown v. Allen,[43] decided in 1953, represented the pinnacle of federal court jurisdiction over habeas claims (hereafter, habeas review). Until Brown, federal habeas courts usually only heard claims from state prisoners in cases in which the state's "corrective process" was inadequate. In contrast, in Brown, which governed habeas review for the next two

40 Sanders v. United States, 373 U.S. 1 (1963) (Brennan, J.).

41 Kaufman v. United States, 394 U.S. 217 (1969) (Brennan, J.).

42 Engle v. Isaac, 456 U.S. 107 (1982).

43 344 U.S. 443 (1953).

decades, the Supreme Court held that federal habeas courts could hear any properly raised federal constitutional claim brought by state (as well as federal) prisoners.

Beginning in the 1970s, however, the Supreme Court began whittling away at the scope of the writ. This trend culminated in the AEDPA, which provides that habeas review is available to state prisoners only when the challenged state court determination: (1) "resulted in a decision that was contrary to, or involved an unreasonable application of, clearly established Federal law, as determined by the Supreme Court of the United States"; or (2) is based on "an unreasonable determination of facts."[44]

The first ground for habeas relief grew out of the Supreme Court's 1989 decision in Teague v. Lane,[45] which dealt with the seemingly unrelated issue of when new constitutional rulings apply to cases on habeas review. Recall from §12.3.4 that, to ensure equity among litigants, all new rules announced on direct appeal apply to any case that is also on direct appeal. In Teague, the Court opted for the opposite retroactivity rule for litigants who have completed direct review and are seeking habeas relief. Positing that the principal purpose of federal habeas review is to deter state courts from misapplying federal law prevailing at the time of trial and appeal, the Court reasoned that, since a "new" constitutional ruling—which the Court defined as a ruling not "dictated by precedent"—was obviously not the prevailing law at the time of the state decision, it should not be given any retroactive effect to other cases on habeas. And, to ensure equity among litigants, even the petitioner who seeks the new rule should not be able to benefit from it. The practical result of that conclusion is that, when federal courts receive a habeas petition, they must first determine whether the claim asks for a new rule, that is, a rule not dictated by precedent; if so, they are not to consider its merits.

In Williams v. Taylor,[46] the Court interpreted the first prong of the AEDPA language quoted above to provide even less relief than Teague, pointing out that the statute only permits habeas review of state court holdings that are directly "contrary to" (i.e., not distinguishable from on its facts) a clear holding of the U.S. Supreme Court (not just a

44 28 U.S.C. §2254(d).

45 489 U.S. 288 (1989).

46 529 U.S. 362 (2000).

holding of a lower federal court). Thus, all other state court decisions challenged on habeas call for "new" rulings that should not be heard in federal court. Taylor's interpretation of AEDPA results in a very broad definition of "new" rule; for instance, in Chaidez v. United States,[47] the Court concluded that its holding in Padilla v. Kentucky that a defendant must be informed about a guilty plea's effect on deportation, while based on earlier decisions requiring counsel to inform defendants of the consequences of a plea, was an "unanticipated" extension of those decisions, and thus could not provide a basis for habeas relief;[48] as the Court said in another case, habeas relief will not be granted if it "would effectively create a new rule by extending . . . precedent to a novel context."[49]

Furthermore, even if a state court ruling is clearly "contrary to" a U.S. Supreme Court ruling and therefore can be heard on habeas, the AEDPA stipulates that it may not be reversed by a federal court unless it is "unreasonable," which Taylor defined as a determination that the state ruling is "objectively unreasonable," not simply incorrect. In a later decision, the Court stressed that, because this test is objective, a state court's determination can be reasonable even if that court provides no reasons for its opinion, as long as "fair-minded jurists" could reach the same result.[50] The result of this approach is a number of Supreme Court decisions that, because they involve habeas petitions, do not indicate whether the Constitution was violated but rather merely conclude that the state court was not "unreasonable" in its determination that no constitutional violation occurred; for instance, in Bell v. Cone,[51] the lower federal court found that counsel's failure to present mitigating evidence and make a closing argument in a Virginia capital sentencing proceeding was ineffective, but the Supreme Court held that the Virginia Supreme Court was reasonable in holding otherwise, stressing that "an unreasonable application is different from an incorrect one." Meanwhile, until these types of issues are resolved on a direct appeal to the Court, lower federal and state courts are left to wonder about the Court's view, and might well simply adopt the "not unreasonable" position in the meantime.

47 568 U.S. 342 (2013).

48 Although, contrary to Teague's holding, Padilla himself did benefit from the rule.

49 Stringer v. Black, 503 U.S. 222 (1992).

50 Harrington v. Richter, 562 U.S. 86 (2011).

51 535 U.S. 685 (2002).

Clearly, the finality and comity goals heavily influenced both the AEDPA and the post-Warren Court's jurisprudence. Teague did recognize two exceptions to its ban on habeas petitions for new rules, however. The first is when the claim goes to the substantive ability of the courts to hear the case, such as a double jeopardy claim or a claim that the statute that is the basis for conviction is unconstitutional. The second exception is when the claim implicates procedures or rules "central to an accurate determination of innocence or guilt." As Teague recognized, this second exception will rarely apply, since at this point in history few such issues remain unresolved (although in 2016 the Court held that its decision barring mandatory life without parole sentences for juveniles was such a "watershed rule"[52]).

The AEDPA's second basis for habeas jurisdiction for state prisoners, focusing on whether the state court determination is based on "an unreasonable determination of facts," applies whether or not the petition asks for a new rule. But this basis is also construed narrowly. Its language resonates with another post-Warren Court opinion limiting habeas review, Stone v. Powell,[53] decided 12 years before the AEDPA was passed, which held that habeas review for Fourth Amendment claims is precluded unless the petitioner did not receive a "full and fair hearing" in state court. While the AEDPA extends that exception to all claims, not just those based on the Fourth Amendment, state court determinations of facts are likely to be considered reasonable unless the factfinding process was non-existent or deeply flawed (on this point, see §12.4.3).

When the petitioner is a federal rather than state prisoner, neither the AEDPA's unreasonable interpretation rule nor its full and fair hearing limitation—both of which are based on a reluctance to overturn state court decisions—are applicable. Furthermore, in Boumediene v. Bush,[54] the Supreme Court held that even those federal prisoners who are foreign nationals thought to be terrorists have access to federal district courts via a writ of habeas corpus, at least if they are in custody in the United States or Guantanamo, as opposed to overseas. Thus, legislative efforts to bar habeas relief for such petitioners are constitutional only if Congress suspends the writ during wartime or "rebellion," pursuant to the Suspension Clause.

---

52 Montgomery v. Louisiana, 136 S.Ct. 718 (2016).

53 428 U.S. 465 (1976).

54 553 U.S. 723 (2008).

A final substantive requirement of federal habeas jurisdiction, for both state and federal prisoners, is that the claim must involve federal constitutional or federal statutory law. Although this requirement may seem obvious, its impact was brought home in dramatic fashion in Herrera v. Collins,[55] where the Supreme Court held that a claim of factual innocence—at least one that is not "truly persuasive"—is not justiciable on habeas unless it is associated with an error of federal law; according to the Court, in the absence of a federal claim, clemency "is the historic remedy for preventing miscarriages of justice where judicial process has been exhausted." Further, if the error is based on a federal statute rather than the Constitution, only those claims that involve "a complete miscarriage of justice" or a "fundamental defect" can be heard on habeas.[56] Thus, for instance, a failure to follow Federal Rule of Criminal Procedure 11 during a guilty plea hearing (see §9.6) is not a basis for habeas relief.[57]

12.4.2 Procedural requirements

Separate from rules limiting the types of substantive claims that can be heard in federal court are rules barring claims on procedural grounds. The Warren Court tried to remove most of these barriers, but the post-Warren Court and the AEDPA have reinforced them. These barriers arise when: (1) there is procedural default based on an "adequate and independent ground" (usually, a state or federal rule providing that failure to raise a claim in a timely fashion bars relief on the claim); (2) the claimant has not exhausted all other judicial remedies; (3) the claim has been addressed in a previous petition and thus is "successive" or, alternatively, the claim was not included in a previous petition; (4) the petitioner was not "in custody" at the time the petition was filed; or (5) a filing deadline is missed.

In Fay v. Noia,[58] the Warren Court overturned previous precedent that barred habeas relief on claims not raised in state court, instead holding that state procedural default rules prevented such relief only when the defendant "deliberately bypassed" the opportunity to assert the claim, and thus made a "considered choice" to do so; the Court stated that even "a choice made by counsel not participated in by

55 506 U.S. 390 (1993).

56 Hill v. United States, 368 U.S. 424 (1962).

57 United States v. Timmreck, 441 U.S. 780 (1979).

58 372 U.S. 391 (1963).

the petitioner does not automatically bar relief." However, within 15 years, the post-Warren Court had reversed Noia, instead permitting habeas review only when the defense could show both "cause" as to why the claim was not raised at the state-level trial, and "prejudice" resulting from the failure to hear it on habeas. As the Court explained in Wainright v. Sykes,[59] procedural default rules ensure both that claims will be considered when recollections "are freshest," and that state trials will remain a "decisive and portentous event" rather than a proceeding subject to second-guessing by a federal court on a claim the trial court had no chance to consider. The Court also stated that such rules deter "sandbagging" by counsel who want to avoid an adverse state court ruling and instead hope to pursue the claim only in (a more receptive) federal court, although that concern is presumably alleviated by Noia's deliberate bypass standard as well. The Court subsequently applied the cause and prejudice standard to procedural defaults on appeal, even though the first two reasons Sykes gave for honoring such rules do not apply as strongly to procedural default on appeal.[60]

In Murray v. Carrier,[61] the Court indicated that "cause" for a procedural default can arise in three situations: (1) when the factual or legal basis of the claim was not reasonably available at the time the claim should have been made (i.e., the claim is based on newly discovered facts or a legal rationale that is "novel"); (2) when state officials interfered with counsel's ability to avoid default (as when the prosecution conceals information from the defense); and (3) when default is the result of attorney error rising to the level of ineffective assistance of counsel (which only applies where there is a right to counsel, and thus cannot constitute cause for failing to raise a claim on state post-conviction relief[62]). Note with respect to (1), however, that if the "legal basis" of the claim was not "reasonably available" or "novel" at the time of the state proceeding, then it is probably a new rule barred from consideration on habeas by Teague. Further, even if one of these three grounds for cause is shown, the petitioner is entitled to habeas review only upon a showing of prejudice, which appears to be defined in terms of whether there is a "reasonable probability" that the error affected the

59 433 U.S. 72 (1977).

60 Coleman v. Thompson, 501 U.S. 722 (1991). But see §11.3.3.

61 477 U.S. 478 (1986).

62 Davila v. Davis, 137 S.Ct. 2058 (2017) (involving failure of state post-conviction counsel to raise a claim on ineffective appellate counsel).

"outcome of the proceeding," the same standard used in ineffective assistance of counsel cases.[63]

Petitioners who cannot show cause and prejudice may still obtain relief in two situations. The first is when the state procedural default rule is not "adequate and independent." A rule is not "adequate" if it is not "consistently or regularly applied"[64] or its application is "exorbitant" (as when the rule is applied because counsel objected orally rather than in writing).[65] The rule lacks "independence" when, despite the procedural default, a state appellate court considers the claim and thus signals the default is not the real reason for denial of the claim;[66] however, the Supreme Court has indicated that any doubt as to whether the state court's rejection of the petitioner's claim is based on procedural default should be resolved in favor of preclusion.[67]

The second situation in which a petitioner who fails to show cause and prejudice can obtain federal relief is when the claim is one of "actual innocence," which requires proof that "it is more likely than not that no reasonable juror would have convicted [the petitioner]" or, in the case of convictions by plea, proof by a preponderance of the evidence that the petitioner is not factually guilty.[68] The Court has also held, in Sawyer v. Whitley,[69] that a death sentence can be challenged on federal habeas despite procedural default, if the petitioner can show by clear and convincing evidence that "no reasonable juror would have found [the petitioner] eligible for the death penalty."

A second procedural barrier to habeas review, perhaps even more common than the cause and prejudice limitation, is the exhaustion requirement, which under the AEDPA prevents habeas review "unless it appears that the applicant has exhausted the remedies available in the courts of the State . . ."[70] The exhaustion rule can create serious inefficiencies, because the additional petitions to state courts it requires after a loss on direct appeal are unlikely to overturn that decision. Nonetheless, the Supreme Court views exhaustion as an important

63 Strickler v. Greene, 527 U.S. 263 (1999).

64 Cf. Dugger v. Adams, 489 U.S. 401 (1989) (four members of the Court only).

65 Lee v. Kemna, 534 U.S. 362 (2002).

66 County Court of Ulster County v. Allen, 442 U.S. 140 (1979).

67 Coleman v. Thompson, 501 U.S. 722 (1991).

68 Schlup v. Delo, 513 U.S. 298 (1995).

69 505 U.S. 333 (1992).

70 Id. §2254(b).

way of achieving the comity goal, because it "serves to minimize friction between our federal and state systems of justice" by preventing disruption of state proceedings and giving state courts an opportunity to correct federal violations before a federal court does.[71]

In practice, exhaustion of "available" remedies requires that the petitioner has sought both direct and discretionary review at the highest level of state court (which, ironically, could undermine comity by creating an incentive to pursue discretionary appeals that most states want to discourage).[72] Further, the petitioner must give the state courts a "fair opportunity" to consider the claims presented in the habeas petition, which means that the petitioner must make the precise federal claim in state court that is later raised at the federal level.[73] When the petitioner submits a "mixed petition" to a federal habeas court—that is, one that contains both exhausted and non-exhausted claims—the Court has required that it be dismissed, with leave to amend the petition to include only exhausted claims, or that it be held in abeyance for a "reasonable time" while the petitioner seeks relief in state court on the non-exhausted claims (with this second option available only when the latter claims are not "plainly meritless," and there is "good cause" for the failure to exhaust those claims).[74]

A third procedural barrier arises when the petitioner raises the same claim in successive petitions or failed to raise the claim in a previous petition. The Warren Court tended to take a lenient approach in both situations, when "the ends of justice" would be served and there was no evidence of "abuse of the writ."[75] However, the AEDPA provides that "a claim presented in a second or successive habeas corpus application . . . that was presented in a prior application shall be dismissed," and that a claim raised for the first time in a second petition must be dismissed unless it seeks a new rule considered retroactive under Teague's limited exceptions or is based on newly discovered facts that "establish by clear and convincing evidence that, but for constitutional error, no reasonable factfinder would have found the applicant guilty of the underlying offense."[76] Mitigating the impact of the first provision to

71 Duckworth v. Serrano, 454 U.S. 1 (1981).

72 O'Sullivan v. Boerckel, 526 U.S. 838 (1999).

73 Picard v. Connor, 404 U.S. 270 (1971).

74 Rose v. Lundy, 455 U.S. 509 (1982).

75 Sanders v. United States, 373 U.S. 1 (1963).

76 28 U.S.C. §2244(b)(1) and (2).

some extent, the Supreme Court has held that a second petition that includes exhausted claims that were dismissed because they were in a mixed petition, or that were dismissed without addressing the merits, are not "second or successive" under the statute.[77]

A fourth procedural barrier to federal habeas is the requirement, long a fundamental aspect of habeas law, that the petitioner be in "custody" at the time the petition is brought. The Court has concluded or suggested that "custody" includes non-prison encumbrances such as parole, restrictions on entering the country, various "civil disabilities" (such as prohibitions on voting or serving as a juror), and even release on one's own recognizance (at least when no state remedies are available), because in all of these situations the petitioner is subject to "restraints not shared by the public generally."[78] However, if a person has completed a sentence, he or she is no longer in custody, even if that sentence can be used to enhance a subsequent sentence,[79] unless the completed sentence was ordered to run consecutively with the challenged sentence.[80]

A final procedural barrier arises when the petitioner fails to file the petition in a timely fashion, which under the AEDPA is defined as within one year from the date on which the judgment being challenged becomes final.[81] Consistent with the foregoing procedural barriers, exceptions to the deadline include situations where the state does not have a competent post-conviction bar, the state otherwise impedes timely filing, or the claim is based on a ruling, made after the deadline, that is retroactive or on newly discovered evidence that could not have been discovered with due diligence.[82] The Supreme Court has also recognized an actual innocence exception to the deadline,[83] and granted habeas courts discretion to toll the one-year period when "extraordinary circumstances,"[84] such as gross attorney incompetence that the petitioner tried to rectify, can be shown.

77 Stewart v. Martinez-Villareal, 523 U.S. 637 (1998); Slack v. McDaniel, 529 U.S. 473 (2000).

78 Hensley v. Municipal Court, 411 U.S. 345 (1973).

79 Lackawanna Cty. Dis. Atty. v. Coss, 532 U.S. 394 (2001).

80 Garlotte v. Fordice, 515 U.S. 39 (1995).

81 28 U.S.C. §2264.

82 See generally, Clay v. United States, 537 U.S. 522 (2003).

83 McQuiggin v. Perkins, 569 U.S. 383 (2013).

84 Holland v. Florida, 560 U.S. 631 (2010).

12.4.3 Independent factfinding

While Brown expanded the ability of federal courts to review state court legal conclusions, it was more reticent about allowing federal courts to reassess their factual findings in the absence of a "vital flaw" in the proceedings below, given the possibility that witnesses or other evidence were no longer available by the time of a habeas hearing. In contrast, the subsequent Warren Court decision in Townsend v. Sain[85] was more willing to authorize not only federal court reconsideration of the facts, but also federal court hearings to redetermine the facts, when "for any reason it appears that the state trier of fact did not afford the habeas applicant a full and fair hearing"; indeed, the Court indicated that the only situation in which a hearing was clearly not called for was when counsel "deliberately bypassed" an opportunity to develop facts in state court. Even the early post-Warren Court was unwilling to grant deference to state court determination of issues that involved mixed questions of law and fact, such as a determination of whether a confession is voluntary in the "totality of the circumstances,"[86] although it also held that federal courts should not hold a new hearing on factual or mixed law and fact issues unless the cause and prejudice standard discussed in §12.4.2 was met.[87]

The AEDPA has since reduced even further the ability of federal courts either to reassess state court determinations of fact or to hold another hearing at the federal level. First, it "overruled" Townsend, simply stating that "a determination of a factual issue by a State court shall be presumed to be correct," with the burden on the petitioner to show otherwise.[88] Additionally, as already noted, it provides that federal habeas courts can only reverse a state court ruling on factual grounds when there has been an "unreasonable determination of the facts." Finally, it provides that if the failure to develop relevant facts in the court below is the defense's fault (rather than the result of state malfeasance), then a hearing is permitted only when the claim involves the by-now familiar triad: either a new rule that is retroactive under Teague or facts that could not have been discovered with due diligence, and "clear and convincing evidence that but for constitutional

85 372 U.S. 293 (1963).

86 Miller v. Fenton, 474 U.S. 104 (1985).

87 Keeney v. Tamayo-Reyes, 504 U.S. 1 (1992).

88 28 U.S.C. §2254(d).

error, no reasonable factfinder would have found the applicant guilty of the underlying offense."[89]

12.5 Double jeopardy

The Fifth Amendment's prohibition on subjecting a person "to be twice put in jeopardy of life or limb" for the "same offense" has been interpreted to protect against four types of post-jeopardy events that involve the same offense: reprosecution after acquittal; reprosecution after conviction; separate punishments; and, in some circumstances, reprosecution after an aborted trial. As conceptualized by the Warren Court, the "underlying idea" of the double jeopardy prohibition

> is that the State with all of its resources and power should not be allowed to make repeated attempts to convict an individual for an alleged offense, thereby subjecting him to embarrassment, expense and ordeal and compelling him to live in a continuing state of anxiety and insecurity, as well as enhancing the possibility that even though innocent he may be found guilty.[90]

More recent Supreme Court decisions have minimized this avoidance-of-repeated-prosecutions rationale and focused instead on whether the defendant has been previously subject to a determination of criminal guilt. These competing views play out differently in: (1) defining when "jeopardy" attaches; (2) deciding when a person has been "convicted," "acquitted," or deprived of a chance at acquittal by the prosecution; (3) defining "same offense"; and (4) determining the scope of the doctrine that permits double jeopardy for the same offense when the second prosecution is brought by a different "sovereign."

12.5.1 When jeopardy attaches

An individual is not put in "jeopardy" at arrest or charging, but only once a jury has been empaneled and sworn (when trial is by jury), when the first witness is sworn (in a bench trial), or when the judge accepts a plea (in guilty plea cases).[91] While there were suggestions to the contrary in some Warren Court opinions, the Court has since made clear

89 Id. §2254(e)(2).

90 Green v. United States, 355 U.S. 184 (1957).

91 Crist v. Bretz, 437 U.S. 28 (1978); Ohio v. Johnson, 467 U.S. 493 (1984).

that if a judge "acquits" a defendant before any of these events (for instance, by dismissing charges), reprosecution is not barred, because the accused has not been "subjected to the risk of conviction."[92] For the same reason, the Double Jeopardy Clause does not bar prosecution for conduct that was previously used to enhance a sentence but was never the subject of prosecution.[93]

Nor is the person who has been convicted or acquitted of an offense subjected to double jeopardy by a second proceeding when the second proceeding is not considered "criminal" in nature. In making this determination, the Supreme Court concluded in Hudson v. United States,[94] the legislature's characterization of the proceeding as "civil" is dispositive, unless there is "clear proof" to the contrary on the "face" of the authorizing statute. Relevant to such proof is whether the potential sanction "has historically been regarded as a punishment," whether its primary focus is retribution and deterrence rather than remedial, whether it requires proof of "scienter" (or intent), and whether it is "excessive in relation to the alternative purpose assigned."

Applying this test, the Court has held that a juvenile delinquency proceeding is criminal,[95] but that post-sentence commitment under a sexually violent predator statute, where the primary goal is incapacitation and treatment, is not, despite the potential for extremely long confinement.[96] The Clause bars a civil proceeding that occurs subsequent to conviction on fraud charges when it imposes a "civil" fine amounting to roughly eight times the damages suffered by the fraud victim and to over 200 times the money gained through the fraud.[97] But it does not bar civil forfeiture proceedings based on a criminal conviction that deprives an individual of property with a nexus to the crime because, the Court explained, such proceedings are aimed not at punishment, but at preventing illegal use of property, ensuring criminals do not profit from crime, and compensating the government.[98] For similar reasons, the Clause is not implicated by a civil penalty of $100,000

92 Serfass v. United States, 420 U.S. 377 (1975).

93 Witte v. United States, 515 U.S. 389 (1995). However, as discussed in §10.3.1, the Sixth Amendment is violated if the enhancement goes beyond statutory or mandatory guidelines maxima.

94 522 U.S. 93 (1997).

95 Breed v. Jones, 421 U.S. 519 (1975).

96 Kansas v. Hendricks, 521 U.S. 346 (1997).

97 United States v. Halper, 490 U.S. 435 (1989); see also Montana v. Kurth Ranch, 511 U.S. 767 (1994).

98 United States v. Ursery, 518 U.S. 267 (1996).

and "debarment" from further employment in the banking industry imposed by a federal banking agency rather than by the Department of Justice.[99]

12.5.2 When two prosecutions are permitted

Even if a proceeding is a second criminal prosecution for the same offense, it is not barred by the Double Jeopardy Clause if it occurs: (1) after a successful appeal by the defendant; (2) after a dismissal that does not amount to an acquittal; or (3) after a mistrial required to avoid "manifest injustice," so long as the mistrial is not manufactured by the prosecution to obtain a new trial.

A defendant who is convicted and does not appeal the conviction, or appeals and loses, cannot be tried for the same offense. But if the defendant appeals and wins reversal of the conviction, a retrial is permissible, on the ground that jeopardy is "continuing"; additionally, as the Supreme Court explained in Green v. United States,[100] "it would be a high price indeed for society to pay were every accused granted immunity from punishment because of any defect sufficient to constitute reversible error." Further, "it is at least doubtful that appellate courts would be as zealous as they now are in protecting against the effects of improprieties at the trial or pretrial stage if they knew that reversal of a conviction would put the accused irrevocably beyond the reach of further prosecution."

One exception to this rule, announced in Burks v. United States,[101] occurs when the appellate court rules that the prosecution failed to prove its case, because that finding is the equivalent of an acquittal (to be distinguished from a ruling that a conviction was "against the weight of the evidence," which is not the functional equivalent of an acquittal[102]). Furthermore, if the jury at the defendant's first trial convicts on a lesser charge than the prosecution seeks (as in Green, where the jury convicted for second degree murder rather than first degree murder), the jury verdict is considered an "implied acquittal" of the greater charge and the defendant can only be retried on the lesser offense. If, however, the defendant pleaded guilty to the lesser offense

99 Hudson v. United States, 522 U.S. 93 (1997).

100 355 U.S. 184 (1957).

101 437 U.S. 1 (1978).

102 Tibbs v. Florida, 457 U.S. 31 (1982).

and successfully appeals, the same result is not required, because the plea judge does not have the opportunity to convict on the greater offense[103] (although, as discussed in §8.5.3, a greater charge might be barred by the due process prohibition on prosecutorial vindictiveness).

A defendant can also be "acquitted" of a capital sentence. In Bullington v. Missouri,[104] the Supreme Court held that a defendant who is sentenced to life, appeals, and then is reconvicted and sentenced, cannot be given the death penalty after the second proceeding, on the theory that the first sentence was an implied acquittal of the latter penalty. However, the Court has refused to apply the same reasoning in non-capital cases, in part because determining the reason for the lower sentence at the first proceeding is often more difficult to discern in the less structured non-capital setting.[105]

A judge might also abort a trial before a verdict is reached, either through dismissal of charges or a mistrial declaration. With respect to dismissals, if the court's decision is not the equivalent of an acquittal, then reprosecution is always permissible. Prior to United States v. Scott,[106] the Supreme Court had suggested that the double jeopardy protection is triggered by any trial court decision that truncated trial in a way that would require further proceedings against the defendant. But in Scott, where the defendant obtained dismissal on the ground of prejudicial pretrial delay, the Court concluded that the prosecution was entitled to appeal the dismissal, because the defendant chose "to seek termination of the proceedings against him on a basis unrelated to factual guilt or innocence of the offense," and thus was in the same position as a defendant who successfully appealed a conviction on grounds other than evidentiary insufficiency. The Court also asserted that prosecution appeal of such a dismissal and any subsequent retrial is a "far cry" from "an all-powerful state relentlessly pursuing a defendant who had either been found guilty or who had at least insisted on having the issue of guilt submitted to the first trier of fact."

In contrast, retrial is barred by an explicit post-jeopardy, pre-verdict finding by the trial court that is the equivalent of an acquittal, which includes findings that the prosecution is trying the defendant on an

103 Ohio v. Johnson, 467 U.S. 493 (1984).

104 451 U.S. 430 (1981).

105 Monge v. California, 524 U.S. 721 (1998).

106 437 U.S. 82 (1978).

offense not in the indictment,[107] or has failed to prove an element of the offense.[108] Further, retrial is barred "even if the legal rulings underlying the acquittal were erroneous."[109] Given these decisions, the trial judge is probably well advised to wait to dismiss charges until after a jury conviction; when that route is taken, prosecution appeal is permitted because, if the prosecution wins, the jury verdict can be reinstated and no further proceeding against the defendant is required.[110] This type of reasoning was also the basis of United States v. DiFrancesco,[111] which permitted prosecution appeal of a sentence, assuming statutory authority to do so, because such an appeal, if successful, does not subject the defendant to the ordeal of new trial-like proceedings.

Closely related to a trial court dismissal is a trial court declaration of a mistrial, which always permits retrial if it is declared out of "manifest necessity."[112] One of the most common reasons for a mistrial declaration is a hung jury. Some justices have argued that a hung jury is equivalent to a finding that the prosecution has failed to prove its case and thus should trigger Burks, and have also pointed out that granting a new trial after a hung jury can allow the prosecutor to profit from its mistakes. But the Supreme Court has consistently permitted retrial in such cases, in recognition of "society's interest in giving the prosecution one complete opportunity to convict those who have violated its laws."[113]

Generally, any mistrial declaration that results from defense misconduct will also permit retrial; thus in Arizona v. Washington,[114] where defense counsel improperly mentioned during opening argument the prosecution's failure to provide exculpatory evidence in a previous proceeding, the Court allowed retrial. When the mistrial is a result of improper behavior by the judge or the prosecution, retrial is more likely to be barred, but even here the Court has held that this result is required only if the prosecutor "intended to goad" the defense attorney into asking for a mistrial. In the case that announced this rule,

107 Sanabria v. United States, 437 U.S. 54 (1978).

108 Michigan v. Evans, 568 U.S. 313 (2013); Smalis v. Pennsylvania, 476 U.S. 140 (1986).

109 Sanabria v. United States, 437 U.S. 54 (1978).

110 See United States v. Wilson, 420 U.S. 332 (1975).

111 449 U.S. 117 (1980).

112 United States v. Perez, 22 U.S. 579 (1824).

113 Richardson v. United States, 468 U.S. 317 (1984).

114 434 U.S. 497 (1978).

Oregon v. Kennedy,[115] defense counsel's cross-examination of the state's expert established that the witness had filed a complaint against the defendant; on redirect the prosecution asked the witness, over defense counsel's objection, "Is that because he is a crook?" The Court held that the subsequent mistrial declaration did not prevent retrial because the prosecutor's purpose had not been to abort the case, over a dissent that argued "[i]t is almost inconceivable that a defendant could prove that the prosecutor's deliberate misconduct was motivated by an intent to provoke a mistrial instead of an intent simply to prejudice the defendant."

12.5.3 Definition of same offense

If the defendant has been acquitted or convicted of an offense, reprosecution is barred on the "same offense." The Court has not interpreted this phrase literally, but neither has it interpreted this language broadly. It is also important to note that, even if two charges are considered the same offense, the prosecution is not barred from prosecuting both. Rather, as explained in §8.5.4, the prosecution simply must try them in the same proceeding.

To encourage the latter practice and avoid repeated prosecutions, one might define "same offense" to include all offenses committed during the same "transaction" (e.g., a theft of a weapon later used to commit a burglary and assault a person inside a home). But in 1932, the Supreme Court settled on a different definition. In Blockburger v. United States,[116] reaffirmed 60 years later in United States v. Dixon[117] (after a few feints toward other tests), the Court stated that "[w]here the same act or transaction constitutes a violation of two distinct statutory provisions, the test to be applied to determine whether there are two offenses or only one, is whether each provision requires proof of an additional fact which the other does not." Under this test, an offense and its lesser included counterparts (e.g., murder and manslaughter/assault) are the same offense. But a single criminal act involving three victims constitutes three offenses. Likewise, overlapping statutes that require different elements (e.g., burglary, which involves entering a dwelling but not theft, and larceny, which requires theft but not entering a dwelling), or a single transaction that involves discrete crimes, as

115 456 U.S. 667 (1982).

116 284 U.S. 299 (1932).

117 509 U.S. 688 (1993).

in the theft-burglary-assault example given above, are considered different offenses and may be tried separately. Thus, although the Court has held that joyriding and theft of a car are the same offense,[118] and that robbery and felony murder based on the robbery are as well,[119] it has also held that a person can be tried separately for conspiring to sell drugs and selling the drugs (because conspiracy requires an agreement, and selling drugs requires a sale),[120] and for violating a protective order and the crime of assault that was the predicate for the violation (because the first offense involves a court order and the second involves an assault).[121]

Perhaps more importantly to most defendants, if two offenses are not the same for double jeopardy purposes, and conviction results from both, the sentences can be imposed consecutively. The definition of same offense in this situation depends entirely on legislative intent. Thus, in Missouri v. Hunter,[122] even though the two offenses in question—armed robbery and "armed criminal action"—were the same offense under Blockburger, the Missouri legislature had made "crystal clear" that it intended the penalty for armed criminal action to be added to the penalty for related crimes. In such a situation, "a court's task of statutory construction is at an end" and cumulative punishment is permissible. However, if the legislature has not indicated how punishments are to be imposed, the Blockburger test is applicable.

Even if two offenses are the same for double jeopardy purposes, two adjudications are permissible in four situations: (1) when a fact key to the prosecution in the first trial changes (e.g., the victim of an assault, on which the defendant is convicted, subsequently dies, at which point trial on homicide charges is permitted);[123] (2) when the defendant seeks severance—for instance, to avoid trial with co-defendants—in a situation where joinder would not severely prejudice the defendant's Sixth Amendment right to a fair trial;[124] (3) when the lesser charge is tried to

---

118 Brown v. Ohio, 432 U.S. 161 (1977).

119 Harris v. Oklahoma, 433 U.S. 682 (1977). Note that, technically, since felony murder can be based on any felony, and robbery does not require a death, the Blockburger test made these separate offenses.

120 United States v. Felix, 503 U.S. 378 (1992).

121 United States v. Dixon, 509 U.S. 688 (1993).

122 459 U.S. 359 (1983).

123 Diaz v. United States, 223 U.S. 442 (1912).

124 Jeffers v. United States, 432 U.S. 137 (1977).

an inferior court with no jurisdiction over the greater charge;[125] and (4) when a judge overrides a prosecutor's objection to the defendant's plea on lesser charges, and the prosecutor wishes to reinstate greater charges originally sought by the prosecution. In this last, unusual, situation, the Court explained in Ohio v. Johnson,[126] the defendant "ha[s] not been exposed to conviction on the charges to which he pleaded not guilty, nor has the state had the opportunity to marshal its evidence and resources more than once or to hone its presentation of its case through a trial."

A final legal doctrine that is related to the same offense prohibition under the Double Jeopardy Clause is collateral estoppel, which was given constitutional status by the Supreme Court in Ashe v. Swenson.[127] There, after being acquitted of a holdup of one of six men, Ashe was tried for holding up a second member of the group and convicted. Although the offenses involved were not the same under the Blockburger test (since the victims were different), the Court held the second trial unconstitutional, stating that "when an issue of ultimate fact has once been determined by a valid and final judgment [here, that Ashe did not commit the holdup], that issue cannot again be litigated between the same parties in any future lawsuit." The Double Jeopardy Clause, the Court explained, "surely protects a man who has been acquitted from having to 'run the gauntlet' a second time."

However, for Ashe to apply, there must be clear evidence that the issue sought to be precluded in the second proceeding was resolved in favor of the defendant in the first proceeding. Thus, in Schiro v. Farley,[128] the Supreme Court found that the jury's choice of felony murder (a strict liability offense) from among ten verdict options, including "knowingly" killing, did not preclude the state from arguing in the subsequent death sentence hearing that the homicide was "intentional" and thus aggravated; according to the Court, the first verdict did not definitively indicate that the jury found intent was lacking. Furthermore, a finding, even if "ultimate" in a criminal trial, does not have preclusive effect either in a civil proceeding, where the lower of standard of proof can be met by evidence that could not overcome reasonable doubt in the criminal trial, or in another criminal proceeding brought by a separate sovereign, which was not a party to the first proceeding.

125 Waller v. Florida, 397 U.S. 387 (1970).

126 467 U.S. 493 (1984).

127 397 U.S. 436 (1970).

128 510 U.S. 222 (1994).

12.5.4 Separate sovereign doctrine

Even when a defendant is subject to prosecution after conviction or acquittal on the identical offense, the Double Jeopardy Clause is inapplicable when the second trial is brought by a "separate sovereign." As the Supreme Court explained in the 1922 decision of United States v. Lanza,[129] "an act denounced as a crime by both national and state sovereignties is an offense against the peace and dignity of both and may be punished by each," a rationale the Court affirmed almost 100 years later in Gamble v. United States,[130] which also reasoned that an "offense" is "defined by law, and each law is defined by a sovereign." These reasons trumped the goal, most evident in Warren Court decisions, of avoiding subjecting defendants to multiple prosecutions for the same conduct.

The Court has held that the separate sovereign doctrine permits trial for the same offense not only in state and federal court,[131] but also trials in two different states,[132] as well as in tribal court[133] (assuming, of course, each sovereign has jurisdiction over the offense because of where it occurred). However, municipalities are not considered separate sovereigns, because they are "subordinate governmental instrumentalities created by the State to assist in the carrying out of state government functions."[134]

129 260 U.S. 377 (1922).

130 139 S.Ct. 1960 (2019).

131 Bartkus v. Illinois, 359 U.S. 121 (1959).

132 Heath v. Alabama, 474 U.S. 82 (1985).

133 United States v. Wheeler, 435 U.S. 313 (1978).

134 Waller v. Florida, 397 U.S. 387 (1970).

13 Conclusion

This book has focused on the Supreme Court's jurisprudence because it is the primary source of the rules that regulate the criminal process. The courts are not institutionally equipped to solve many of the most pressing problems of American criminal justice, such as mass incarceration, racial disparities in policing, overzealous prosecutors, and inadequate defense counsel; legislatures, not courts, are primarily responsible for overly harsh sentencing policies and inadequate resources, and policing and prosecutorial agencies are ultimately responsible for how the law is enforced. Nonetheless, as this book has demonstrated, the courts' construal of the Bill of Rights, and of related statutes and rules, can significantly influence the police, prosecutors, defense attorneys, and judges in ways that affect all of these areas.

Recall from Chapter 1 the most commonly advanced goals of American criminal procedure: reliably determining whether the criminal law has been violated; cabining government power; providing a process that appears fair; and ensuring lay participation in decision-making. That the criminal justice system only imperfectly achieves all of these goals is, to some extent, inevitable, since they often directly conflict. Most obviously, sanctions meant to penalize government misconduct—whether they involve exclusion of probative evidence obtained in violation of the Fourth or Fifth Amendments or dismissal of a case on the ground that the prosecutor or judge is responsible for structural error—can prevent conviction of clearly guilty people. The requirements that the government prove its case beyond a reasonable doubt, without any help from a defendant who wants to remain silent, are further examples of the tension inherent between these goals, particularly the first two.

In recent years, the Supreme Court has tended to favor the reliability goal over the other three goals. It has chipped away at the exclusionary rule, the warrant and probable cause requirements, and Miranda—three central pillars of the Warren Court revolution that, if implemented as intended by that Court, make conviction of the guilty more difficult to achieve. Because of a desire to achieve efficiency and finality in cases that it assumes prosecutors and states courts normally resolve accurately, the modern Court has also allowed the expansion of plea bargaining and aggressive charging practices, and the diminishment of independent review by grand juries and federal courts. For many rights—in particular, the rights to effective assistance, to exculpatory evidence, and to habeas relief in the absence of adequate state remedies—the Court is willing to allow vindication only if the defense can show that the error would have affected the outcome of the case.

At the same time, the Court has for the most part staunchly defended the right to counsel, protected the public's right to observe proceedings, bolstered the right to jury trial, and assured that people cannot be removed from juries simply on the basis of race or gender. While decisions in this vein could improve reliability—and the right to counsel is probably crucial to that goal—the last three legal stances are more closely associated with limiting government power, enhancing perceived fairness, and increasing lay participation. Another example of this tendency is the Court's willingness to exclude out-of-court declarations obtained with the aim of gaining evidence against the defendant, regardless of how reliable that evidence might be. These types of cases are significantly outnumbered, however, by those that give the reliability goal priority.

In addition to favoring that goal, the Court has tended to opt for rules, consciously or not, that expand state power. In its opinions affecting matters such as stop and frisk, pretextual police actions, pretrial detention, prosecutorial charging, and double jeopardy doctrine, the modern Supreme Court has seemed almost oblivious to the possibility that its rulings facilitate racial discrimination, overincarceration and overcharging by the government. Tempering any criticism of the Court along these lines, however, must be the recognition that it is required to adhere to constitutional and statutory language, and cannot easily ignore budgetary constraints and the strong societal interest in bringing criminals to account.

For those enmeshed in the system as defendants, the procedures adopted and followed in the criminal justice system can be just as consequential as the substantive rules defining crimes and sentencing. And procedural rules are probably even more important than substantive ones for victims of or witnesses to crime, and for those affected more indirectly by crime or the government's efforts to fight it (which, as a practical matter is probably everyone). A firm understanding of criminal procedure doctrine and its various rationales is crucial not only for policy-makers but for those who want to be informed about the society in which they live.

Further reading

For those readers interested in a more in-depth treatment of the subjects discussed in this book, one resource is Criminal Procedure: An Analysis of Cases and Concepts (7th ed., Foundation Press, St. Paul, Minn. 2020), by Charles H. Whitebread and Christopher Slobogin. A much deeper dive into the material is provided by the seven-volume treatise Criminal Procedure (4th ed., West Academic Publishing, St. Paul, Minn. 2020), authored by Wayne LaFave, Jerold Israel, Nancy King, and Orin Kerr.

Index